FOREIGN DIRECT INVESTMENT AND THE REGIONAL ECONOMY

Foreign Direct Investment and the Regional Economy

JONATHAN JONES and COLIN WREN
University of Newcastle upon Tyne, UK

ASHGATE

Published by
Ashgate Publishing Limited
Gower House
Croft Road
Aldershot
Hampshire GU11 3HR
England

Ashgate Publishing Company
Suite 420
101 Cherry Street
Burlington, VT 05401-4405
USA

Ashgate website: http://www.ashgate.com

British Library Cataloguing in Publication Data
Jones, Jonathan
    Foreign direct investment and the regional economy
    1. Investments, Foreign 2. Regional economics
    I. Title II. Wren, Colin
    332.6'73

Library of Congress Cataloging-in-Publication Data
Jones, Jonathan.
    Foreign direct investment and the regional economy / by Jonathan Jones and Colin Wren.
          p. cm.
    Includes bibliographical references and index.
    ISBN 0-7546-4522-3
    1. Investments, Foreign. 2. Investments, Foreign--Great Britain. 3. Economic development. 4. Great Britain--Economic policy. I. Wren, Colin. II. Title.

    HG4538.J66 2006
    332.67'3--dc22

2005034901

ISBN 0 7546 4522 3

Printed and bound by Athenaeum Press Ltd,
Gateshead, Tyne & Wear.

Contents

Part 2 Inward Investment in a Regional Economy

List of Figures

List of Tables

Preface

This book is the product of many years' work, and represents the development of a study originally undertaken by Jonathan Jones. It also reflects the long-standing interest of Colin Wren in economic development, and in particular the regeneration of lagging regions in developed countries, of which foreign direct investment has been an important element over recent decades. The book has been possible with the support of a number of people, which is gratefully acknowledged. Thanks go to Dr John Bridge, the former Chairman of the Regional Development Agency, *One NorthEast* (and before that, the *Northern Development Company*), who kindly made available the project-based records on foreign direct investment. This is the foundation on which the empirical part of the book is built. Thanks also go to Ms Lesley Boughton, the Investor Development Manager of *One NorthEast*, for help in accessing and in interpreting the data. The contribution of Prof Jim Taylor and Dr Roxana Radulescu is gratefully acknowledged, as are the comments of the many participants at conferences, seminars and workshops where the results of the book have been presented. Some of the research on which the book is based has been published, of which details can be found in the bibliography.

Finally, we express our appreciation to many individuals who gave their time to assist with the research, including the construction of the dataset. These (and their employment status at the time) include Ms Diane Robertson of *UK Trade and Investment*, Mr Mark Lea of the Department of Trade and Industry in London, and the following in the North-East region: Mr Graham Adams, Business Development Manager of Northumberland County Council; Mr Gordon Ramsey, Chief Executive of the Tyne and Wear Development Company; Mr John Elliott and Ms Joanne Newton, respectively the Business Development Executive and Marketing Assistant of the County Durham Development Company; and Mr David Wood, the Inward Investment Manager of the Tees Valley Development Company. We also thank Ms Joan Davison of the Tyne and Wear Research and Information Unit at Newcastle, and local authority officers at Darlington, Hartlepool, Middlesbrough, Redcar and Stockton. Overall, our hope is that the book will provide a sounder understanding of the nature and contribution of foreign direct investment at the regional level, and that this in turn will help to improve economic development policy in relation to these foreign-owned plants.

Jonathan Jones
Colin Wren
December 2005

Introduction

Foreign direct investment (FDI) is of interest to students of the regional economy. FDI began to emerge on a significant scale in the immediate post-war period, but it was not until the 1960s that it began to spread-out from the South East of England and locate in other UK regions.[1] This was no doubt prompted partly by the availability of loans and grants for regional development from that time.[2] Most of this investment was from the United States, and it was given fresh impetus and created new interest in the 1980s and 1990s: first by the arrival of investment from the Far East; but then from western Europe in the run-up and completion of the Single European Market; and finally by the mergers and acquisitions 'boom' of the late 1990s. This period is unparalleled in the history of international capital flows. In 1970 the world FDI stood flows at $13 billion, but by the year 2000 they are believed to have been $1,500 billion. Virtually all the FDI has involved flows out of the developed world, and to a substantial degree it has also flowed into these areas, of which the United Kingdom (UK) is a major beneficiary over the 1990s.[3] While FDI has fallen-back recently, there can be no doubt about the central role that FDI plays in the phenomenon of 'globalisation', and the central importance of multinational enterprises to modern economic activity.

So what does all this mean for the regional economy? This book explores the implications of foreign direct investment for regional development, and it has a number of purposes. First, it examines the recent trends in FDI, occurring both internationally and at the UK national and regional levels. The purpose of this is to explore the underlying reason for the upsurge in FDI in recent decades, in terms of its underlying nature and motivations for foreign direct investment that have been advanced in the academic literature. As we see, these go hand-in-hand, so that the changing nature of FDI over time has promoted new theories. Importantly, FDI should not be seen as a homogeneous entity, either over time or at moment of time, although its heterogeneous nature has frequently been overlooked in the literature.[4]

---

[1] Scotland was a major beneficiary of start-up investment from the United States in the 1950s, but by the 1960s the South East and East Anglia together had more than two-thirds of the UK manufacturing employment in foreign ownership.

[2] At 1971, the North of England, Scotland and Wales had virtually all of the employment in foreign ownership located in the designated Assisted Areas, but partly reflecting the way the areas were selected for financial assistance.

[3] Relative to GDP, since the 1970s the UK has consistently received inflows above average world levels, and the highest of any nation over the 1990s.

[4] For example, the fact that FDI can occur by 'greenfield' start-up or merger and acquisition is often not recognised in the empirical literature, perhaps owing to data limitations.

The second purpose of the book is to review the accumulating literature on FDI, of which two aspects are relevant. One, is the research studies that seek to establish the factors determining FDI location, and the other is the studies that examine the benefits of FDI to the host economy. As we see, the latter have concentrated on the efficiency effects, i.e. productivity 'spillovers', even though FDI has been subsidised to locate in the Assisted Areas primarily for distributional reasons, i.e. job creation. The empirical and applied literature reviewed is mainly econometrics-based, although the discussion includes material from disciplines as diverse as economic geography, industrial organisation and regional economics. The final purpose of the book is to provide an in-depth study of foreign direct investment in an English region that has been a long-term recipient of FDI and regional policy. This is the North-East England over the period from the middle of the 1980s until the turn of the century, which covers the fresh wave of FDI.

The contribution of the book is that it provides, perhaps for the first time, a detailed project- and plant-based analysis of FDI in an English assisted region over a substantial period of time, and relates this to the burgeoning literature on FDI, arising out of a number of disciplines. The data that are analysed are the project-based data that are collected for each region and collated for the UK as a whole by the main national inward investment agency, *UK Trade and Investment*, and its predecessors. These are the data used to report FDI for the UK as a whole and by region. There are issues with the data, not least that they are prospective, so that not all of the investment may have arrived nor have been implemented at the proposed scale.[5] However, substantial efforts are made to check, refine and add to the data in order to form the Inward Investment Dataset, which is the basis for the study, and which organises the project data onto a plant basis. As such, it offers insights on the nature of the *UK Trade and Investment* data more broadly. Overall, it is believed that all of the projects went ahead in some form, so that they provide a comprehensive account of 'significant' investments carried out by foreign-owned plants in the North-East of England over the period 1985-98.[6] This includes FDI by start-up, merger and acquisition, joint venture or by re-investment. In total, the data identify 550 projects carried out by 337 plants. These projects promised £8.7 billion in investment (1995 prices) and in excess of 80,000 jobs.

The book is divided into two parts. The first part on the *Theory and Pattern of FDI* provides the description of FDI trends and reviews the literature on theory and empirical evidence. The second part, which is titled, *Inward Investment in a Regional Economy*, provides the detailed analysis of FDI in North-East England. Much of the populated part of the region has been subject to UK regional policy since this policy commenced in the early 1960s. The Assisted Areas in the region

---

[5] The data have major advantages. They enable us to identify discrete investment projects, while they give a much better account of FDI in the round compared to production census-type data. We find that three-quarters of foreign-owned start-ups have less than 100 employees on entry, while the UK production 'census' may include as little as 1 in 5 firms with less than 100 employees (Griffith, 1999).

[6] As we see, an analysis of project jobs indicates that at the median the project scales are achieved, but that the larger plants are less able to fully implement their investments.

are defined in terms of socio-economic indicators, largely based on unemployment, but more recently per capita GDP levels under European Union regional policy. However, over the period of interest, the grants for FDI are provided by UK central Government under the Regional Selective Assistance scheme.[7] Essentially, this supports job creation projects in the Assisted Areas that would not otherwise have been undertaken. The Inward Investment Dataset is described in the Appendix to this book, and frequent reference is made to the Appendix in the second part of the book. In particular, it describes out nature of the data, and defines what is a meant by 'plant'.[8] It sets out the nature of the variables and labels, providing many useful descriptive tables on these variables, so that reference should be made to it when considering the empirical findings in the body of the text.

Both parts to the book contain four chapters, and the detailed structure of the book can be found in the Contents. Briefly, the structure is as follows. The first part has chapters titled, *Background, Theory, Location* and *Regional Development*. The first of these considers the definition of FDI, and the vessel for this in the form of the multinational enterprise. It gives a brief history of international operations, but focusing on the Twentieth Century, and especially the fresh wave of FDI from the 1980s, including cross-border mergers and acquisitions. It considers what is meant by 'globalisation' and the characteristics of foreign direct investment arising from different sources. The principal theories of FDI are discussed in Chapter 2, providing a critical review of the competing 'ownership' and 'internalisation' schools, as well as explanations based on the strategic actions of firms. Chapter 3 examines the locational determinants of FDI, and has several strands. It includes the econometric studies that have sought to distinguish between the classical and agglomeration motivations for FDI, and reviews various studies that have explored FDI at the UK regional level. It also explores the regional distribution of FDI in the post-war period, and shows that most projects are now in activities other than manufacturing and tending to occur in the South-East region. As a result of this it shows that in regions such as North-East England, FDI has trended downwards over the last decade or so. Finally, Chapter 4 looks at the implications of FDI for regional development. The benefits are mainly couched in terms of the potential productivity gains of FDI for domestic industry, while the costs are expressed in terms of the potentially poor-quality of the investment and jobs, and the 'footloose' nature of FDI. The arguments are explored based on recent evidence.

The second part of the book contains on the analysis for North-East England, and has chapters titled, *Investment, Projects Jobs, Plant Employment* and *Survival*. The investment is known for only about two-thirds of projects, so that a major task is to explore the representativeness of this, using the job data, which is known in virtually every case. On this basis it is estimated that FDI in the region has run at about £1 billion per annum. The chapter explores the concentration of investment, and also undertakes an analysis at the plant level. Chapter 6 undertakes the analysis of project jobs. As well as examining the pattern of these jobs, the chapter carries

---

[7] In England, it has recently been replaced by the Selective Finance for Investment scheme, but which essentially has the same eligibility criteria.

[8] This is essential for putting the projects onto a plant basis.

out an analysis of variance and covariance to determine the characteristics of the projects that promise relatively more jobs. These two chapters are primarily at the project level, but Chapters 7 and 8 are at the plant level. The first of these looks at the pattern of plant employment in the foreign-owned plants at around the turn of the century. It distinguishes between the plants arriving prior to the mid-1980s and subsequently, and in the case of the latter focuses on start-up plants. A concern is whether these plants deliver their job targets. Finally, Chapter 8 investigates issues to do with plant survival. It examines the survival time durations of plants, both small and large on entry. Further, it examines the probability and time duration to plant re-investment, and explores whether this induces significantly longer survival time durations, thereby 'embedding' the plants. Conclusions then follow.

Part 1

Theory and Pattern of FDI

Chapter 1

Background

Foreign direct investment (FDI) is the name given to the process where a firm from a country provides capital to an existing or newly-created firm in another country. For example, a foreign firm may decide to set-up production in the UK and by so doing will be engaging in the process known as FDI. Firms locating production in more than one country are often referred to as multinational enterprises (MNEs). Over the last four decades, the number of MNEs and the level of FDI in the global economy have risen spectacularly, with world FDI inflows rising by one-hundred-and-twenty-fold, from $13 billion in 1970 to $1,492 billion by the year 2000.[1] Not only is this a huge increase in absolute terms, but it indicates the importance of FDI to the world economy; FDI flows in the year 2000 made up nearly $50 for every $1,000 of GDP compared with less than $1 in 1970. A major beneficiary of this increased flow of FDI has been the United Kingdom (UK), with levels of inflows per $1,000 of GDP consistently above average world levels since the 1970s and the highest of any nation over the 1990s.

The purpose of this chapter is to provide a brief introduction to foreign direct investment and to review the overall pattern of FDI in the world economy and UK. This encompasses a discussion of formal definitions, the evolution of FDI and a review of its contemporary setting. The chapter begins by defining FDI, before examining the role that MNEs play in international production. The chapter then proceeds to look at the history of international investment, from its origins in the Fourteenth Century through to its modern form, highlighting the important role that FDI played in the Twentieth Century, especially in the latter-half of this century. The reasons why an upsurge in FDI occurred are then considered, of which a main component seems to be the rise in merger and acquisition activity. Attention then turns to the UK, which has traditionally been the main recipient of FDI outside of the US. An examination is undertaken of the countries that have been the main providers of inward investment to the UK. This analysis allows the current main sources of FDI to be placed in an historical context, and gives a comprehensive review of the factors generating inward investment to the UK.

---

[1] Since the year 2000 there has been a large fall in FDI flows, with FDI in 2003 standing below $600 billion, under half the amount of year 2000 levels. However, this downward trend has begun to reverse itself. FDI flows increased to over $600 billion in the year 2004 and there are predictions that this upward pattern will continue throughout the rest of the decade (United Nations, 2004).

Definition of Foreign Direct Investment

The standard definition of foreign direct investment is given by the Organisation for Economic Cooperation and Development (OECD, 1996). A key aspect of this is that it represents the notion of one enterprise in a particular country having a degree of control over another enterprise in a different country, as opposed to just the provision of financial capital. It is classed as, "investment that adds to, deducts from or acquires a lasting interest in an enterprise operating in an economy" arising from outside the country in order to "have an effective voice in the management of the enterprise" (OECD, 1996, p. 7). In the event that a foreign investor does not have an effective voice in the management of the company, then the investment is classified as 'portfolio investment'.

A natural question to ask of this definition is what constitutes an "effective voice" in a company? Continuing the OECD benchmark definition, it is when "a firm in one country has a foreign investor controlling 10 per cent or more of the equity capital or voting power in the firm" (OECD, 1996, p. 8). An exception to this is when the 10 per cent is insufficient for the investor to have control in the management of the firm, or conversely when the investor has management control in the firm even though it owns less than 10 per cent of the equity capital. The United Kingdom, as with almost all other countries, uses the OECD benchmark definition of FDI, although up until 1999 the UK used a 20 per cent instead of 10 per cent lower bound level of equity capital.[2] Even though the threshold level of equity capital was 10 percentage points higher in the UK, Walker (1983) notes that in practice the amount of investment between 10 and 20 per cent is very small in volume, so it makes virtually no difference to the official figures.

The OECD recommended procedure for calculating FDI flows is given in Table 1.1. It is calculated as the sum of four components: retained earnings, equity capital, intra-company loans and intra-company borrowing. Retained earnings are profits generated and kept by the overseas enterprise. These are classified as FDI, despite there is no cross-border transfer of capital, as the investor has the choice of either taking the retained earnings made by the overseas enterprise to their home country or by reinvesting them back into the enterprise.[3] The remaining rows of Table 1.1 show the other flows of capital that occur between the direct investor and the overseas enterprise and that are treated as FDI. For example, the transfer of shares or loans between the investor and the enterprise will result in a flow of capital into the overseas enterprise and therefore an increase in FDI. The final row of Table 1.1 shows the outflows that may occur from the overseas enterprise, for

---

[2] Canada, France and Japan are notable exceptions to the 10 per cent level of equity capital due to their own system of accounting, although the OECD recommends that the aggregate value of transactions above the 10 per cent level is identified in order to facilitate international comparisons of FDI.

[3] The retained earnings of the overseas enterprise are classed as reinvested earnings since the earnings are being reinvested back into the overseas enterprise.

Table 1.1 OECD Benchmark Definition of FDI

Foreign Direct Investment

equals   Retained earnings (i.e. direct investors share of earnings / losses)

plus   Direct investors purchase *less* sales of enterprises' shares

plus   Net increase in long and short term loans, credit and other amounts given by the direct investor to the overseas enterprise

minus   Overseas enterprise borrowing of money from host country or from their own resources in order to give to the direct investor in home country

---

Sources: Walker, J. (1983) and Office for National Statistics (1996).
Note: This is the benchmark condition for the calculation of FDI.

example, when the overseas enterprise is borrowing money from the host country to supply to the direct investor. Any outflows are deducted from the inward FDI flow into the host country, and are a disinvestment. If the overseas enterprise lends a greater amount of money to the direct investor than the amount it receives from the overseas enterprise then a negative inflow of FDI occurs.[4]

The above definition of FDI provides a benchmark calculation that allows a degree of transparency in comparing international direct investment flows. In practice though, the calculation of FDI is difficult. This is because of different laws and regulations that exist between countries on how to record and measure components of FDI. Examples include the measurement of intra-company loans, the recorded date of the realisation of project investments, the implementation of internationally-agreed guidelines for measuring balance of payments and the lack of data for many developing countries (Stocker, 2000). An as alternative way of measuring the scale of FDI in a country, data can be examined on the employment or sales of overseas enterprises. FDI is increasingly concentrated in the hands of a number of large enterprises known as multinational enterprises (MNEs).

The Multinational Enterprise

The presence and significance of multinational enterprises in the global economy is growing. UNCTAD (2004) estimate that there are at present over 60,000 MNEs in the world with production occurring in over 900,000 foreign affiliates. In total,

---

[4] Again there are international disparities. Japan, Canada and most European countries, except the UK and Germany, do not include retained earnings in FDI due to their accounting practices and therefore understate inward investment.

multinational enterprises account for around one-tenth of world GDP and one-third of world exports. These figures are increasing, demonstrating the growing levels of international production by multinational enterprises in the world economy. However, it is only a relatively small number of MNEs, originating in a handful of countries that exert a dominant influence on international production. The top 100 multinational enterprises in 2002 (as calculated by UNCTAD) made up just 0.2 per cent of the overall number of MNEs in the world, yet accounted for 14 per cent of total MNE sales.[5] A heavy concentration of these enterprises by source country is evident, as over 80 of the top 100 MNEs have headquarters in either the United States or the European Union. Indeed, 71 of the top 100 MNEs have headquarters in just 4 countries: the United States, the United Kingdom, France and Germany.

Definitions of MNEs were not formed until the 1960s, so that research on multinational enterprise is relatively new. Prior to 1960 a firm that operated in more than one country was known either as a 'multi-territorial firm' or as a 'firm engaged in FDI' (Dunning, 1996). Even in the 1970s a universal definition was not in use, with Tugendhat (1981) classifying firms that produce and sell goods in different countries as 'international firms', leaving the term MNE to apply only to larger international companies, although a formal definition was not given. Moosa (2002) provides a distinction between three terms – *international, multinational* and *transnational corporations* – which are, or have been, commonly used to define the international operations of firms. An international corporation is a company that is concerned solely with importing and exporting goods between countries. The term multinational applies when the international operations of a firm begins to involve actual production in another country. The term transnational company is used when the firm becomes globally active to such an extent that its identity becomes detached and independent from its home or any other particular country.[6] In practice, the terms multinational and transnational corporations are often used synonymously (see below).

Formal definitions of multinational enterprise are given by the Organisation of Economic Cooperation and Development and by UNCTAD in its *World Investment Report*. The OECD classifies MNEs as "companies or other entities established in more than one country, and so linked that they may co-ordinate their

---

[5] UNCTAD use a 'transnationality index' to rank the top 100 transnational corporations. The index is calculated as an average of foreign to total sales, foreign to total assets and foreign to total employment for each transnational corporation. Details can be found in UNCTAD's *World Investment Report*.

[6] This is the view of Ohmae (1990), who believes that the number of linkages between firms in different parts of the world has become so large that the national identities of firms is becoming more difficult to define. However, other authors, such as Porter (1990), challenge the idea that firms become truly transnational, as they believe that the firm will always have an identity with their home country as it is the place where they developed their specific advantage. Evidence for this viewpoint is provided by Pauly and Reich (1997).

operations in various ways" (OECD, 2000, p. 17).[7] The term 'entities' covers the parent and other related entities of the company, although the former will be the main source of influence. A similar definition is issued by UNCTAD, although its definition refers to transnational corporations rather than multinational enterprises. A transnational corporation is "an enterprise whether of public, private or mixed ownership, comprising entities in two or more countries, regardless of the legal form and fields of activity of these entities" (UNCTAD, 2003, p.66). The corporation has a 'common strategy' through one or more decision-making centres, but where one or more of these centres exercises a significant influence over the activities of the others. A key role of the corporation is "to share knowledge, resources and responsibilities with the others" (UNCTAD, 2003, p.66). As with the OECD definition, the corporation refers to the enterprise as a whole, and so includes all its various entities.[8]

Many authors treat foreign direct investment and multinational enterprises as one and the same thing, with John *et al* (1997) suggesting that the terms FDI and MNE are treated synonymously with each other.[9] Dunning and Pearce (1995) state that since MNEs finance overseas subsidiaries from their funds through capital markets or reinvested earnings, then these overseas affiliates are the same as foreign direct investment. However, Hennart (2001) points out that FDI will not give a perfect measure of MNE activity as foreign plants can raise capital by borrowing from the host country, thus understating MNE growth. Wilkins (2001) also points out that FDI is just one of many activities that a MNE carries out, as follows, "A multinational enterprise provides intra-firm connections ... it is not merely a channel for one-time transactions but a basis for different sorts of internal and external organisational relationships" (p. 6). For studies of MNEs these issues

---

[7] The entity in the home country is the 'parent enterprise' and the entity in the host country is the 'foreign affiliate'. A foreign affiliate can be classified into subsidiaries, associates and branches. Subsidiaries and associates refer to incorporated enterprises, where the former is when more than 50 per cent of equity is held by the foreign entity and the latter is when more than 10 per cent but less than 50 per cent of equity is held by the investor. A branch refers to an unincorporated enterprise.

[8] Overall, it can be seen that the key aspects of a multinational (or transnational) enterprise are as follows: first, it must be present in two or more countries; second, it can be of private, public or mixed ownership; third, it consists of several entities within its structure, although only one of the entities will be the main source of influence over the others; and fourth, it will co-ordinate its resources and operations between the various entities.

[9] Dunning (1996) believes that MNEs are now beginning to encompass a broader role than just undertaking FDI, thereby making a precise definition of the MNE more difficult and eroding the link with FDI. For example, MNEs are now engaging in 'co-operative alliances' with foreign firms. These alliances appeal to firms engaged in complementary, although dissimilar activities, as it lowers the transaction costs of organising dissimilar activities while not diluting control. Dunning suggests that this form of alliance could lead to a blurring of the boundaries between firms, and make the classification of what constitutes a MNE more difficult. For more on multinational alliances see Chapter 2.

are of interest, but for the study of FDI the point is that multinational enterprise can be seen as the vessel for FDI. The evolution of MNEs and the history of FDI are now charted from their early conception through to their current form.

The History of International Investment

Early Investment

There have been international organisations engaged in trading activities as far back in time as 2500BC, with banks and churches also having formed international organisations throughout history (see Ghertman and Allen, 1984). The appearance of the modern MNE, incorporating control over foreign production units, did not occur until the Nineteenth Century (Wilkins, 1977), but early resemblances to the modern MNE appeared in the 1600s and 1700s, when large trading companies from the UK and the Netherlands entered parts of Asia, the Indies and America.[10] The two largest enterprises were the British East India Company and the Dutch East India Company (Carlos and Nicholas, 1988), which dominated the lucrative markets of spices, cottons and silks, and are credited as being the true pioneers of international commercial activities. Investment also later took place in the UK and French colonial territories of Latin America, Asia, Africa and Australia, with most investments being supply oriented, in the form of resource exploitation (Gabel & Bruner, 2003).[11] International companies also emerged with the aim of colonising foreign lands. One of the first was the London-based, British Virginia Company, whose strategy was to profit from the development and colonisation of Virginia in the US. Similar projects across North America were undertaken by the Dutch, the French and the Swedes.

It is generally accepted that the true birth of the modern multinational arose in Europe in the Nineteenth Century (Wilkins, 1986).[12] Examples are the S.A. Cockerill steelworks of England that set up in Prussia; Bayers of Germany that set up chemical plants in the US; and Nobels of Sweden that set up dynamite production in Germany (Tugendhat, 1981). However, it was not until the latter part of the Nineteenth Century that larger-scale foreign direct investment started to emerge. A major motivation for the spread of these firms was the increase in the protectionist behaviour of countries, which in turn was a by-product of increased nationalism. As customers mostly-preferred goods produced locally, as opposed to imported goods, firms had to set-up abroad (Micklethwait and Wooldridge, 2003).

---

[10] For a comprehensive review of the history of multinational enterprise, see Wilkins (1991).

[11] Examples of some of these larger-scale companies include the Hudson's Bay Company, which traded in furs, and the Royal Africa Company, which entered the slave trade.

[12] By 'modern' it is meant that these organisations had production units abroad. See Chandler (1987) for a discussion on the modern multinational enterprise that incorporates ideas on the distribution and the 'governance structure' of MNEs.

Other important reasons for the upsurge in FDI and the growth of MNEs was the search for larger markets, as enterprises began to grow in size, and improvements occurred in transportation and communication, most notably the railways and telegraphs (Wilkins, 1988). These advances not only made it easier for parent companies to control their subsidiaries but to control them over longer distances.

Up until the end of the Nineteenth Century, European firms dominated the MNE scene, but US multinationals were beginning to increase, both in number and size. Examples of US multinationals at this time include Singers, which set up sewing-machine plants in Scotland, and the electrical-manufacturers Thomson-Houston, which set up in England (Atack and Passell, 1994). By the turn of the century, US firms were amongst the world's largest firms and included enterprises such as Rockerfeller's Standard Oil and Ford. The growth of US multinationals continued as they took advantage of the growing size of the American market, which according to Chandler (1987) enabled them to acquire skills such as mass production and mass marketing, and to exploit economies of scale. Factors such as market size, cultural factors, geography and government policy led to the increase in the size of US MNEs (Wilkins, 1991), but despite the increase in the number and size of US MNEs, the UK was still the largest foreign investor by the time of the First World War. However, the majority of international investment was not FDI, but portfolio investment (Jones, 1986), so that the rise of MNEs and FDI did not appear until the Twentieth Century was well under way.[13]

Twentieth Century Investment

The increase in FDI at the turn of the Twentieth Century was halted in the inter-war period both by the destruction caused by the First World War and the threat of another war leading to discrimination against foreigners by the occupants of many countries. The First World War also resulted in European multinationals being forced to sell their pre-war investments, with political upheaval and border changes also impacting on cross-border activities (Dunning, 1983). Other factors leading to a worldwide fall in investment included the Great Depression of the late 1920s and early 1930s and the substantial rise in inflation in Europe (Jones, 1995). By the time of the Second World War, the main stock of FDI was still held by the UK, 40 per cent, while the US held 28 per cent (Jones, 2000). However, after the Second World War a new wave of FDI began to emerge, arising mainly from the US. The factors behind this were improvements in technology and communication systems, greater economic and political stability, the formation of trading blocks and a more liberalised attitude from host governments (Hood and Young, 1999).

The growth of FDI in the second part of the Twentieth Century is explored by Tugendhat (1981). The largest growth in FDI came from the US, with the size of firms an important factor determining the US dominance of industries. Conversely,

---

[13] It is thought that 90 per cent of foreign investment in this period was portfolio investment, although Dunning (1983) calculates FDI at about one-third of world investment.

European firms were hindered by a lack of finance from their governments, who at the time were still recovering from the effects of the Second World War. Despite this, both the US and the European governments welcomed the new wave of FDI into Europe, as it enabled European firms to gain the latest technologies and helped to reduce European dependence on US government aid. In the immediate post-war period, the UK had become the home to the largest share of US investment, mainly as it had a common language, close historical links and could offer access to the Commonwealth market. Yet, by the end of the 1950s there was a shift of US FDI from the UK to Continental Europe, following the establishment of the Common Market. This shift in US FDI provided an opportunity for American firms to gain greater profits from the European market, and was heightened by the superior economic performance of these countries compared with the UK.

It was not until the 1960s that significant European FDI into the US began to emerge, with the availability of capital being the key source for the expansion. Up until this time, the only means European firms had of raising finance was through their respective governments, who were themselves short of capital. However, the introduction of the Euro-currency markets in the 1960s enabled European firms to raise greater levels of finance and engage in higher amounts of FDI (Jones, 1995). The US was the main choice of location for European FDI, as it was the world's technological leader, had the largest market and had the highest level of consumer spending (Young *et al*, 1988). Despite the upsurge of European outward FDI, US firms remained much larger than their European counterparts due to the economies of scale that they accumulated from their own market. While European investment into the US was on a much smaller scale compared to US investment in Europe, it continued to grow, helped by the creation of the European Free Trade Association and an increase in the number of mergers between firms within Europe, with the UK and French firms leading the way.

The Recent Wave

It was not until the latter part of the Twentieth Century that world FDI flows began to increase substantially. This is apparent from Figure 1.1, which shows the global flow of FDI over 1970-2003, measured by outflow at current prices. It shows the extremely strong growth in FDI occurring in the 1990s. There are three periods of growth – the late 1970s, the late 1980s and the late 1990s – which are interrupted by recession, so that FDI follows the movement in the economic cycle.

FDI flows grew steadily in the early 1970s reaching $12bn by 1973, but fell to $10bn in the middle of this decade due to a worldwide recession, protectionism and instability in the dollar.[14] From 1978 to 1981 high economic growth and a merger and acquisition boom led to a rise in FDI, although global FDI in real terms were at a level to that similar to the beginning of the decade. FDI flows followed a rising

---

[14] FDI flows are at nominal prices and calculated using the OECD benchmark technique that is given in Table 1.1. The figures reported here are from UNCTAD's FDI database.

trend from the 1980s onwards and experienced two periods of notable growth. The first increase was from $50 billion to $200 billion between 1985 and 1990, which was interrupted by recession, and the second and much larger increase was the more dramatic rise in FDI inflows from $200 billion in 1990 to nearly $1,500 billion in the year 2000. The annual percentage growth rate in the first half of the 1990s was 20 per cent and later it reached over 30 per cent per annum.

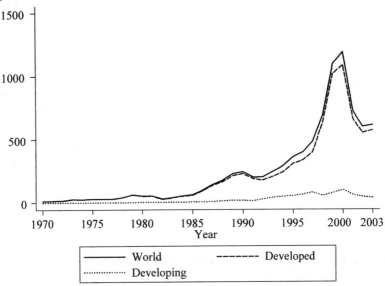

Figure 1.1 Global FDI Flows, 1970-2003

Source: UNCTAD, Foreign Direct Investment Database, 2005.
Note: FDI measured by outflow at current prices.

The early years of the Twenty-First Century saw FDI fall from its record level in 2000 to around $550 billion in 2003. The main reason for the decline was the slowdown in the world economy, which included a recession in the world's three largest economies, as well as lower stock-market valuations and reduced corporate profits (see UNCTAD, 2002, 2003). However, there are signs of a recovery, with flows rising again in 2004 and reaching just over $600 billion (UNCTAD, 2004). There is optimism that the rise in flows will continue to the end of the decade with a report on the prospects for FDI by the United Nations (2004) suggesting that positive macro and micro factors, together with rising confidence in the economic outlook by multinational enterprises, will lead to a growth in FDI between 2004 and 2007. Factors behind this include global GDP growth, low rates of interest in major capital-exporting countries, increased profits and confidence of MNEs and intensified policy efforts by governments to attract FDI.

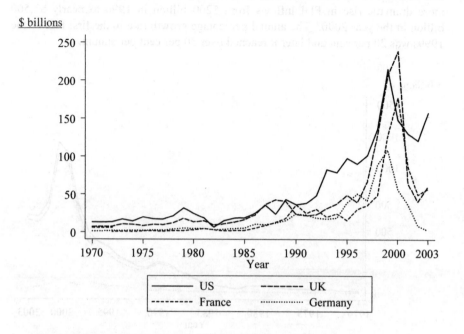

Figure 1.2 FDI Outflows by Country, 1970-2003

Source: UNCTAD, Foreign Direct Investment Database, 2005.

The Current Pattern

The vast majority of foreign direct investment is generated by the developed world. Over 80 per cent of world outflows arose from developed countries in each year over the 1990s, with the concentration increasing further by the year 2003, when the developed world accounted for over 90 per cent of world outflow. Within the developed world, a handful of countries generate most of the FDI. This is apparent from Figure 1.2, which covers the period 1970 to 2003. In fact, the US, UK, Germany and France supplied over 50 per cent of world FDI over the 1990s.[15] The generation of FDI is therefore associated with a small group of countries, and these will be important driving force for future FDI flows (UNCTAD, 2004).

The extreme concentration of FDI outflows by country is not so apparent for FDI inflows, although the developed countries still have a considerably higher level of FDI compared to developing countries. Since 1970 the three periods where

---

[15] The inclusion of Japan increases this to over 60 per cent.

FDI inflows to developed countries vastly exceeded those to developing countries were those of the late 1970s, late 1980s and most notably the late 1990s, indicating that the increase in FDI largely resulted in flows to the developed countries. The

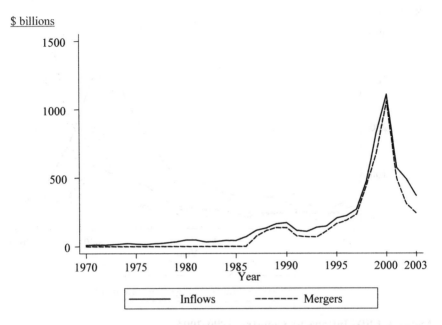

Figure 1.3 FDI and M&A Activity for Developed Countries, 1970-2003

Source: UNCTAD, Foreign Direct Investment Database, 2005.
Notes: FDI measured by outflow at current prices. M&A equals mergers and acquisitions.

main reason for this is that the driver of developed-country FDI inflows, and hence total world inflows, is merger and acquisition (M&A) activity. Figure 1.3 shows the close relationship between FDI inflows and M&A for developed countries, and the massive increase in M&A activity at the turn of the century.

Within the developed world, it is the European Union and North America that account for the bulk of FDI inflows, between them taking over 50 per cent of world inflows per year throughout the 1990s, rising to a peak of 79 per cent in the year 2000. The European Union (EU) has had the greatest increase in inflows since 1990, the result of M&A activity following the completion of the Single Market. On closer inspection, there is a concentration of FDI inflows within these areas with the US, UK, Germany and France being consistently high attractors of FDI. Figure 1.4 shows that the US accounts for the majority of FDI inflows, but outside of the US the UK is the most popular destination of foreign direct investment since the turn of the 1990s.[16] Again, it is M&A activity that is the chief determinant of FDI inflows in these countries, and an issue that is examined later in this chapter. Overall, a pattern of concentration of FDI in the world economy is apparent, with

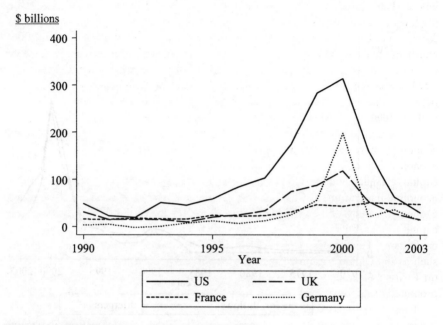

Figure 1.4 FDI Inflows by Country, 1990-2003

Source: UNCTAD, Foreign Direct Investment Database, 2005.

outflows largely generated in the developed world and inflows also largely going to these countries, but to a lesser extent.

The Age of Globalisation

The upward trend in FDI in recent decades is seen by many to be part of a wider and growing phenomenon known as 'globalisation'. The term globalisation throws-up a wide degree of confusion, with no singularly-accepted definition across the different disciplines and authors (Bourguignon *et al*, 2002, Brahmbhatt, 1998).[17]

---

[16] Germany gained higher FDI inflows than the UK in 2000 before falling back again.

[17] Das (2004) claims there are nearly one hundred definitions of globalisation that not only encompass economic and financial issues, but social, environmental and military concepts. Other examples include the World Bank, which defines globalisation as integration through trade and factor mobility, and the Organisation for Economic Cooperation and Development

For many authors, globalisation is seen to represent the increase in cross-border commercial activities that have been a prominent feature of the global economy in the latter part of the Twentieth Century (Greenaway, 1997).[18] These activities not only encompass FDI, but international trade, capital flows and the migration of labour (Das, 2004), with the escalating prominence of these activities increasing the level of interdependence and interconnectedness of the world economy (Weiss, 2002). Yet FDI is commonly seen as an indicator of globalisation (Glyn, 2004), and is the main force behind growing globalisation, with FDI growing faster than not only trade in goods and services, but also faster than world output through the 1990s (Stocker, 2000). Nevertheless, a third of all trade flows consist of payments between companies, again highlighting the importance of multinational enterprises in the process of globalisation and FDI (Micklethwait, 2003).

According to Teeple (2000), the conditions that led to a rise in international economic integration, FDI and 'globalisation' stemmed from changes in the world economy that took place after the Second World War. Before this war, he argues, capital, currency and individuals were tied to nations, which hindered international economic integration. It was only through the post-war re-structuring of the global economy, leading to the growing control of the US in world affairs, which enabled capital to loosen its tie with the nation state, increasing trade and ultimately global capitalism. This process was assisted by the creation of institutions and agencies, such as the United Nations, International Monetary Fund and General Agreement on Tariffs and Trade. Thus, there was a shift in the global economy towards trade, promoted by supranational institutions and heavily dominated by US ideology.

These factors provided a framework for international economic integration, but it was not until the last decade of the Twentieth Century that globalisation became apparent. Thomsen (2000) attributes this to the increase in technological progress and to market deregulation and liberalisation.[19] Scholte (2000) thinks technological progress is the key component of rapid globalisation, which has led to a rapid improvement in infrastructure and communication networks. This has enabled a faster transfer of information at lower cost, facilitating the transfer and diffusion of

---

that defines globalisation as the structure of markets, technologies and communication patterns becoming more international over time.

[18] The concept of globalisation is not a new one and its emergence can be traced back to the 1800s (World Bank, 2000). According to Bourguignon *et al* (2002), trade levels and capital market flows relative to GDP were as high as or higher at the end of the Nineteenth Century than at the end of the Twentieth Century. However, in the present period capital flows cover a wider range of sectors, FDI is larger and global communications are more extensive than in previous historical periods (Scholte, 2000).

[19] The economic performance of the home and host countries involved in FDI is also seen as an important factor. Economic growth in the home country affects levels of outflows, while inflows are affected by the performance of the host country. Thomsen (2000) finds that it is economic conditions in the home country relative to the host that are important in driving FDI flows. The growth of FDI is also not affected by short-term macroeconomic conditions, as the long-term increase in FDI demonstrates.

ideas and enabled much quicker communication between firms located in different countries (Weiss, 2002). According to Miyake and Sass (2000), policy reforms, including privatisation, deregulation and de-monopolisation of national markets, have also led to an environment that promotes globalisation and FDI. National policy reforms have resulted in greater competition within countries, while greater international liberation of trade and investment have resulted in greater competition across world markets.[20] This increased competition has in turn led to a need for firms to invest abroad in order to compete effectively with their rivals.

The above changes in the global economy have resulted in the flourishing of capitalism in an international setting, with consumers and producers from different countries becoming further integrated through trade and foreign direct investment. Overseas production has increased, which in turn has led to greater competition and the need for firms to invest abroad in order to compete effectively with rivals, mostly in terms of keeping place with firms' technological capabilities (Anand and Kogut, 1997). This increased level of competition between firms has ultimately manifested itself in mergers and acquisitions. The importance that M&A activity plays in the rise of FDI in the 1990s is apparent from Figure 1.3.

Cross-Border Mergers and Acquisitions

A cross-border merger arises when the assets and operations of firms located in different countries are combined to form a new legal entity, while a cross-border acquisition involves a firm in a country becoming an affiliate of a firm in another country.[21] The importance of M&As to the growth of FDI flows is evident from Figure 1.3. Between 1987 to 2000 the *World Investment Report* (UNCTAD, 2004) states that the share of total cross-border M&A activity in world FDI flows rose from 52 to 82 per cent. Further, over the same period the value of M&A activity increased from $100 billion in 1987 to over $1,000 billion dollars in 2000.[22] Since the year 2000 there has been a sharp fall in mergers and acquisitions, with the 2003 level standing at $300 billion and impacting on the overall volume of world FDI.

The pattern of M&A activity closely follows that of total FDI outflows, and shows growth in the late 1980s, a recession in the early 1990s, but a strong increase through the rest of the 1990s and a large fall since 2000. Not surprisingly,

---

[20] The *World Investment Report* (UNCTAD, 2000) shows that an average of 57 countries per year undertook some form of regulatory change favourable to FDI over the 1990s giving a total of 974 regulatory changes during the period. The liberalisation of FDI policies continues to occur, with the *World Investment Report* (UNCTAD, 2004) finding a further 244 changes in laws and regulations that affected FDI being made in 2003.

[21] Acquisitions are either minority (the foreign investor holding between 10 and 49 per cent of voting shares), majority (between 50 and 99 per cent) or outright (100 per cent).

[22] Mergers and acquisitions are registered in both the home and host country. Registration of the transaction in the home country is classified as a *purchase*, whereas registration of the transaction in the host country is as a *sale* (UNCTAD, 2000).

the destination of these mergers and acquisitions also follows a similar pattern to FDI inflows. The majority of cross-border M&A activity occurs in the European Union and North America, with these areas accounting for between 70 and 80 per cent of all merger and acquisitions per year since 1990. Within these regions, the

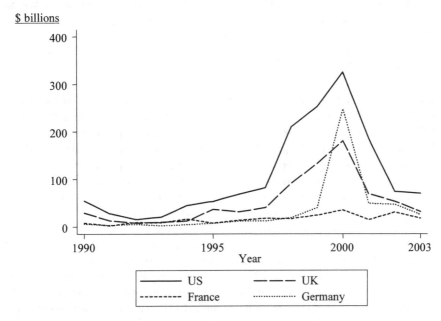

Figure 1.5 Mergers and Acquisitions by Country, 1990-2003

Source: UNCTAD, Foreign Direct Investment Database, 2005.

countries with the largest cross-border M&A activity are those that have the largest FDI inflows: the United States, the United Kingdom, Germany and France. In this group of countries, Figure 1.5 shows the US and the UK are the two countries that have the highest value of mergers and acquisitions, with both experiencing large increases in this activity through the 1990s. Thus, the increase in both world and UK FDI inflows over the 1990s is to a large extent accounted for by the increase in the value of cross-border mergers and acquisitions.

In a comprehensive report, UNCTAD (2000) attribute the growth in M&As in the mid to late 1990s down to the strategic actions of firms and the changing nature of the global economy. Technological advance and the liberalisation process have increased the competition between firms, and M&As are perhaps the quickest way of increasing market share and obtaining market power. It argues that merger or acquisition between similarly technologically advanced firms reduces innovation costs, help the firms gain new processes and technologies and leads to an increase in their competitiveness. Meanwhile, the liberalisation of capital markets has made the process of financing M&As easier, whilst the liberalisation of trade has also increased the amount of global competition. Hence, firms look to M&As as a quick way of providing access to assets, gaining market share and power, enabling firms to diversify, spread risk and grow on a global scale. Further, firms that would not otherwise have undertaken a M&A participate in the process, either as a response to their rivals actions or because they themselves fear being acquired.

UK Inward FDI and Country-Specific Factors

The UK has undertaken outward FDI since the Nineteenth Century, but large-scale inward investment into this country is a more recent phenomenon. In fact, outward UK investment is generally about fifty per cent higher than inward investment. Reasons for this asymmetry are attributed to the problems of traditional relatively low UK growth and government policies. Low growth has reduced the profitability of foreign firms who set up in the UK, while short-term economic policies pursued by successive governments has provided a less stable economic environment, and created uncertainty for those firms wanting to set-up production.

The level of inward FDI to the UK from 1970 onwards is plotted in Figure 1.6. It shows that investment increased in 1973 when the UK became a member of the Common Market, but that it fell over the next two years because of recession. The UK level of FDI rose in the late 1970s, but fell sharply in the early 1980s when the economy was recessed, with a similar cycle following over the next decade. An important factor for the trend increase in inward FDI was the exploitation of North Sea oil. From the mid-1990s, Figure 1.6 shows that FDI increased to peak at over $100 billion in the year 2000. As with world FDI flows, the main propellant of the increase in UK inward investment was the increase in M&A activity. There are three major geographical regions that are a source for UK inward FDI: the US, Japan and Western Europe. The remainder of this chapter considers the motivation for the investment from each of these source regions.

US Investment

The US has been the main source of FDI into the UK since the 1960s. American firms have the advantage of generating large economies of scale, due to their large national market, which according to Thomsen and Woolcock (1993) puts them in a position to expand and reap the profits of other national markets. Acocella (1992a) suggests that other explanatory factors for the initial wave of US FDI into the UK are to gain a foothold into Europe's expanding market and to threaten any potential new competitors from entering their own industry. In the 1960s and 1970s the UK was the richest market outside the US, which together with a common language, made it a natural destination for US multinational enterprise. As the European

Community developed, US firms began to shift their investment to other European countries, such as Germany, France, Ireland and the Benelux countries.

$ billions

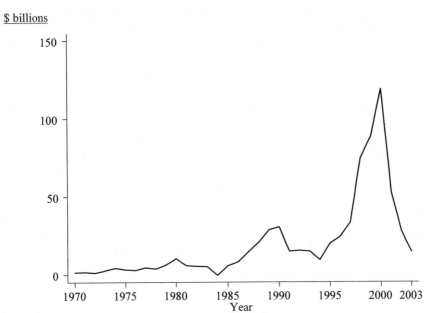

Figure 1.6 UK FDI Inflows, 1970-2003

Source: UNCTAD, Foreign Direct Investment Database, 2005.

Scaperlanda and Mauer (1969) find that an important factor behind the shift of US direct investment to the European Community countries in the 1960s was the growth in the European market, with US firm investing when the market was large enough to produce sufficient economies of scale for the firms producing there. Germany and France also had the advantages of large domestic markets and were politically central to the European market. However, once the UK entered the Common Market it once again became a focal point for US FDI. Its large domestic market, access to the European market and its language, together with a history of US firms locating in the UK meant it retained its pulling power. Even today, the UK remains the focus in Europe for capital expenditure arising from the US.

Japanese Investment

Japanese FDI did not begin to emerge until the late 1960s. According to Sekiguchi (1979), this is down to two main reasons. First, the devastation of the Second World War depleted the managerial resources of Japanese firms, and it took twenty years for these management skills to catch up with rest of the developed world. Second, there was little incentive for Japanese firms to produce abroad as their own wage costs were relatively low. However, as the Japanese economy expanded and wages rose, and as their managerial experience improved, they began to participate in FDI, with the UK being the main beneficiary in Europe. Early FDI ventures were sales agents, distribution companies and trading houses, known as *sogo shosha*, whose aims were to improve trade between Japan and Europe.

A factor leading to the subsequent growth of Japanese FDI was the European Common Market, which imposed discriminatory tariffs on imports, hindering trade between Japan and Europe, and meaning that direct production was the only way to gain access to foreign markets. Further, government policy in certain host countries made foreign production a more attractive proposition for Japanese firms. Thus, the liberal investment policies applied in the UK, Spain and Ireland led to greater FDI than in France, which imposed more restrictive policies. However, it was the UK that attracted the greatest amount of investment due to its language being more widely known in Japan, and its political climate, which was seen as stable.

Despite the investment in the 1960s and 1970s, it was not until the 1980s that Japanese FDI began to grow at a rapid pace, with a sevenfold increase in outflows from Japan in the 1980s reported by Thomsen and Nicolaides (1991). The sudden increase in Japanese FDI is put down to the market-based motives of firms and to the emergence of new globalisation strategies by companies, especially firms with differentiated goods operating in oligopolistic markets. The market-based motives became stronger because of the growing European market, while the globalisation strategies resulted in FDI growing relative to trade. The increase in Japanese FDI in the UK is analysed by Taylor (1993). Factors such as labour availability and the implementation of policies to attract inward investment are found to be the main reasons for the UK being a major destination for Japanese investment.

Western European Investment

FDI between European countries – known as intra-European direct investment – is attributed to the importance of market size and close geographical proximity by Thomsen and Woolcock (1993). Thus, German FDI focuses mainly on Austria; France focuses on Spain; the UK on Ireland; with Scandinavian countries investing between themselves. Over time this FDI has resulted in both inward and outward flows between countries. Thomsen and Woolcock hypothesise that lower wages or less regulation in a particular sector in one country is offset by a reverse flow in a different sector in the other country. However, they find that FDI flows between groups of countries are mainly intra-industry flows, so that market size and market-share incentives are the determinants. Overall, intra-European direct investment results from oligopolistic competition and strategic considerations.

Cantwell & Randaccio (1992) find that technological rivalry plays a role in investment flows within Europe. Industries where FDI is high, such as chemicals, metal products and electrical equipment, are characterised by high technological activity. This investment is also found to be concentrated in the major EU centres of excellence for the industries concerned. This is because innovative activity in an industry is differentiated locationally across countries and therefore the firms have to invest in these leading centres to remain competitive. Examples of these centres include the chemical industry in north-west Germany and Belgium, and the auto-components industry in North-East England (Ernst and Young, 1999). Although regions such as these have been successful in attracting certain types of FDI, other areas have also benefited from increased inward investment flows.

Conclusions

Foreign direct investment is the term given to the cross-border transfer of capital, whereby a firm from a one country generally has at least a 10 per cent share in the equity capital of a firm in another country. This investment is carried out by firms classified as multinational enterprises, i.e. enterprises that consist of entities that are present in two or more countries. This chapter has focused on the history of FDI noting that these flows have been a significant feature of the global economy over the past one hundred years. FDI remains important, if not more so, at the start of the Twenty-First Century due to its dramatic increase over the last twenty years and its role in the process of 'globalisation'. Reasons for the rapid expansion in FDI are attributed to several factors: increased levels and changes in technology, greater liberalisation of trade and investment and de-regulation and privatisation of markets in many countries. These factors have led to increased competition between firms, in turn leading to a massive boom in the number of cross-border mergers and acquisitions as firms seek to reduce their innovation costs and increase their competitiveness in the global economy.

The areas of the world that have consistently been the main generators of FDI have been the United States of America, Western Europe and, more recently, Japan and the Far East. These have also been the areas that have accounted for the recent rise in global FDI flows, due to the participation in merger and acquisition activity. The rise in FDI is especially true of the United Kingdom, where FDI inflows have soared since the early 1990s. The main sources of this investment is the United States, Western Europe and the Far East; areas that have been long-term providers of FDI into the UK. As with the world flow, the recent increase is attributable to the prevalence of firms in these countries engaging in mergers and acquisitions. Thus, inward investment is reliant on the same relatively small group of countries, even though the main form of FDI has shifted to mergers and acquisitions. This reflects the premise that FDI is increasingly being viewed as competition between a relatively small number of firms, but taking place on an international stage.

Chapter 2

Theory

The preceding chapter provided a general background to foreign direct investment setting-out the definition, charting its evolution and examining the current pattern of FDI in the global economy. Notable features of the chapter included recognition of the role of 'control' in defining direct investment and the increasingly important role that FDI has played in the workings of the world economy. As FDI increased in volume from the 1960s, there has emerged a corresponding economic literature on the theory of FDI. Before this time there was no stand-alone theory of FDI, and the concept was treated in the same manner as international capital flows, which neglected many important features of FDI. The new theories were concerned with providing explanations to questions such as why foreign direct investment occurs, when it takes place and where it locates. The purpose of this chapter to review these theories, as they have developed over the past half a century, and outline their contribution to the overall understanding of the process of FDI.

The chapter begins by tracing the development of FDI theory in the 1960s, as it moved from being linked with standard neoclassical theories of capital towards an independent theory encompassing its own unique aspects. The importance of Stephen Hymer in the initial development of theory is discussed before the chapter reviews a number of other authors' contributions to the theoretical literature. As the chapter progresses, the diversity of the theoretical literature on FDI is apparent, with a variety of strands, which highlight different motivations for FDI, dynamic aspects, locational theories and an eclectic theory of foreign direct investment. The chapter discusses the relative merits of the theories, how they have been applied to explain contemporary global patterns of FDI and how they have been updated and adapted to explain the most recent boom in foreign direct investment.

Theories of Foreign Direct Investment

The early attempts to explain why foreign direct investment exists emerged in the 1960s, just as flows of FDI began to increase in volume. Before this time, FDI was modelled as a part of neoclassical capital theory, but as Dunning (1981) notes there are two main problems with viewing FDI this way. First, FDI is more than just the transfer of capital, since just as importantly it involves the transfer of technology, organisational and management skills. Second, the resources are transferred within the firm rather than between two independent parties in the marketplace, as is the case with capital.[1] These factors give FDI its own unique literature, with the key theories often cited as: Hymer's (1960) international operations of national firms; Vernon's (1966) product life-cycle theory; Caves's (1971) horizontal and vertical theories; Buckley and Casson's (1976) internalisation theory; Dunning's (1977) eclectic theory; and Graham's (1978) strategic behaviour of firms. These are now considered briefly in turn, and form the substance of this chapter.

Hymer's Contribution

Up until the 1960s, explanations of FDI were confined to the standard neoclassical theory of capital movements, stating that capital moves from areas with low rates of return to areas with return are higher. Thus, FDI was treated in the same way as portfolio investment, and was seen to depend only on international differences in rates of interest and motivated by rates of return (Hennart, 1994). It was the insight of Hymer (1960), who saw flaws in the prevailing view that portfolio and direct investments were synonymous with one another.[2] Hymer noted that the US was a net exporter of FDI but a net importer of portfolio investment, implying that there were differences in these two kinds of investment. Further, direct investment was mainly carried out by firms in manufacturing, whereas there was a predominance of financial organisations involved in portfolio investment.

Hymer was also puzzled why direct investors should want to invest in a single country when it could spread the risk of investments across different countries (Kogut, 1998). Other confusing aspects were that foreign investors took controlling interests in firms and limited themselves to a narrow range of industries (Hennart, 2001). It was clear to Hymer that existing theories of portfolio investment could not be applied to FDI. According to Hymer's (1960) theory on the international operations of firms, if direct investment is going to be explained then the key concept, which distinguishes it from portfolio investment, is the level of control that it gives the firm over its investment. Specifically, FDI is where the investor has control over the production activities of the foreign enterprise, and this is the basis for his theory (Dunning and Rugman, 1985).[3]

Hymer's theory of FDI draws its influence from Bain's (1956) barriers to entry model of industrial economics (Teece, 1985). Hymer begins by noting that there are barriers to entry for a firm wanting to set-up production abroad. These are in the form of uncertainty, host-country nationalism and risk. Uncertainty gives rise to costs in overcoming informational disadvantages associated with unfamiliarity with local customs. Each country has its own legal system, language, economy and government, which place firms from outside of the country at a disadvantage

---

[1] As noted in Chapter 1, when we are dealing with the transfer of capital then the investment is classified as portfolio investment.

[2] Although Hymer's theory was written in 1960 it was not published until 1976.

[3] The importance of control, as noted by Hymer, can be seen to this very day as it makes up the key aspect of the definitions of FDI discussed in Chapter 1.

compared to firms that are naturally resident to the country. The second barrier is nationalistic discrimination by host countries, which may occur by the government with a protectionist agenda, or by consumers of the host country who prefer to purchase goods from their own national firms for reasons of loyalty or patriotic tendencies. The final barrier manifests itself as an exchange-rate risk. As the firm has to pay a dividend to its shareholders in the home country it has to repatriate the profits back to its own currency.

Given these barriers to international production, the question is why do firms engage in foreign direct investment? According to Hymer there are two reasons, either of which could apply, and both of which are expected to increase its profits. First, the firm removes competition from within the industry, by taking-over or by merging with firms in other countries.[4] Second, the firm has advantages over other firms operating in a foreign country. Examples of the latter are the ability of the firm to acquire factors of production at a lower cost, the use of better distributional facilities, the ownership of knowledge not known to its rivals or a differentiated product that is not known in the other country. Both reasons stress the importance of 'market imperfections' (Dunning and Rugman, 1985), and underlying these the investor has direct control of the investment.

By themselves, these reasons are not sufficient for a firm to engage in direct foreign investment, as what is necessary is that it must enter the foreign market in order to fully appropriate the profits, e.g. a firm could license its product to a firm in the foreign country, so that it need not directly invest in the market. However, there are problems with licensing the product. These include the failure to reach an agreement with the licensing firm over the levels of prices or output, or the costs involved in the monitoring an agreement made between the firms. A firm in the host country may also not be able to fully extract the full potential of the good due to a lack of knowledge about the product and its production process. Moreover, the firm may risk losing the secret of its special advantage and hence its advantage over its competitors. These problems make it less likely that profits can be fully appropriated, and more likely for the firm to undertake direct investment.

Product Life-Cycle Theory

Following Hymer's contribution there was an upsurge in research on international investment by firms. One aspect that was not considered by Hymer was when and where the specific advantages of multinational enterprises would be exploited (Dunning, 1981). This was left to Vernon (1966) and his *product life-cycle theory*. Vernon argued that the decision to locate production is not made by standard factor-cost or labour-cost analysis, but by a more complicated process. The theory drew its evidence from the economy of the United States, of which there were two important features at that time: average income in the US was the highest in the

---

[4] It requires some barrier to entry to the market or that an imperfectly competitive market exists, so excess profits can be earnt.

world, and unit labour costs were higher compared with most other countries. The size of average income is important as it results in an economic climate where new products are offered to satisfy the wants of consumers, while high labour costs will mean that the firms will develop new products where the use of labour is kept to a minimum. The combination of these two features leads to an environment where innovation occurs in order to meet the demands of the market, but where firms try to substitute capital for labour in order to reduce unit labour costs.

According to Vernon, a product has a life cycle that has three main stages. These stages are important as they have implications for the international location of a product as follows.

Stage One: Product development process The nature of the product that the firm is making is not standardised. A product is standardised if the inputs used in the production process can be exactly calculated, so that the general requirements for the product are known with certainty. The lack of standardisation means that there is uncertainty surrounding the product, and therefore communication between the producers, the suppliers and the customers is of utmost importance. These lead to a location decision that results in the product being situated near to its markets.

Stage Two: Maturing product As the demand for the product increases it moves through the product cycle to a greater degree of standardisation.[5] This means that the need for the product to be situated near to its market declines, which allows for economies of scale. These impact on the locational decision of the firm, especially as the demand for the product is likely to grow in other countries, and the firm will have to decide whether it is worth setting up production abroad. This decision will depend on the degree of competition abroad, whether firms in the foreign country have patented the product and if there is a high level of tariffs. If the firm decides to set up a plant abroad and if labour costs are lower, then it will lead to the foreign location being the more cost-efficient plant. This could even mean that the home country experiences exports back to it from the foreign plant.[6] The investment may also precipitate further investment into the country by the firm's rivals as they try to avoid a loss of their market share.

Stage Three: Standardised product This is an extension to the maturing product stage, where the standardisation of the product has reached its 'zenith', and a final framework of the product has been found. The international market will now be well established and sales will be determined by price competition. The low cost of labour in less-developed countries may provide an incentive for firms to reduce costs further and set up in these areas. As less-developed countries do not possess a

---

[5] Product differentiation may begin to take place at this stage but the general requirements of the product will become standardised.

[6] The foreign plant could then be used to produce the good for less-developed countries when demand finally reaches these areas.

large industrial environment, the product should be of a highly standardised nature so that the inputs can be ordered with comparative ease. The product should be a small, high-value item, with a high value-to-weight ratio. This argument may in turn apply to underdeveloped regions of developed countries, so that in principle the multinational firm could set-up production anywhere in the world.

The product life cycle theory of Vernon looks at a dynamic process of FDI in terms of why, when and where it occurs. It was the first attempt to integrate a locational dimension to the theory of FDI. Despite this progress, the analysis was mainly concerned with foreign direct investment by the US, and although this was the main generator of FDI at the time, by the 1970s the dominant role of US had passed and the theory was lacking a truly international explanation.

Caves Theory

Caves (1971) expanded upon Hymer's theory of direct investment, and placed it firmly in the context of industrial organisation theory. The importance of Caves work is that he linked Hymer's theory of international production to the then current theories of industrial organisation on horizontal and vertical integration. Caves distinguished between firms that engage in horizontal FDI and those that undertake vertical FDI. Horizontal FDI takes place when a firm enters into its own product market within a foreign country, whereas vertical FDI occurs when a firm enters into the product market at a different stage of production.

Horizontal FDI According to Caves, a firm will undertake horizontal FDI if it either possesses a unique asset which others do not have or because of the adverse effects of tariffs on its exports. Both reasons are likely to result in FDI occurring in market structures characterised by oligopoly and product differentiation. Where a firm has a unique asset, then according to Caves it must have two characteristics that will enable it to set-up production abroad. The first is that the asset must be a public good within the firm, so that once provided, the sunk cost has occurred and the firm's advantage can be used in other national markets.[7] One such example is the possession of superior knowledge or information. This allows the firm to offset any informational disadvantages that it has compared with foreign local firms, who will have accumulated knowledge on the social, economic and cultural factors in that market. The second characteristic of the asset is that profits made in the host country must depend upon production in that country, as this ensures that the firm has to locate abroad if it is going to be successful in production. Caves argues that both characteristics will be found in a markets with product differentiation, so that the firm can move into these markets at little cost. First, the knowledge about how to serve the market can be transferred with relative ease, and second, uncertainty

---

[7] A public good is non-rival in consumption and non-excludable (Stiglitz, 2000).

about the value of the knowledge makes licensing unattractive. Overall, horizontal FDI is a feature of oligopolistic markets, where products are differentiated.[8]

Vertical FDI Caves also looks at FDI occurring at a different stage of production but within the same industry, i.e. vertical foreign investment. The argument is that it occurs when firms seek to avoid strategic uncertainty, and erect entry barriers to prevent foreign firms from entering the market. Caves argues that vertical FDI is more likely if profits in the foreign market are dependent on long-term prices and investments are large in size, which together ensure that the market structure is characterised by a few suppliers. However, FDI is unlikely to occur when there is no technological complementarity between the stages of production and market is competitive then, as these make the risk of investment high. It is likely when there is a high-seller concentration, the size of the firm is large enough to cope with the size of the investment made and the competitors are small in number.

In conclusion, Caves adapts Hymer's theory of entry barriers and firm-specific assets and embeds this in the industrial organisation literature. He later refined this theory (e.g. Caves, 1982), to encompass theories based on transaction costs and internalisation (Ietto-Gilles, 1992).[9] These theories arose in the 1970s, providing an alternative perspective to why firms produce abroad. They became especially popular for scholars of international business, and they are now discussed.

Internalisation Theory

In the 1970s a further strand to the FDI literature began to emerge, known as the internalisation theory of FDI. It is based on Coase's theory of the firm (1937), and examines the role that transaction costs play in the formation of organisations. In brief, Coase was concerned with why firms exist and why not all transactions in an economy occur in the market? He answered this in terms of the transactions costs involved in using the market, where this is the cost of searching and determining

---

[8] The other way horizontal FDI can occur is if the tariffs imposed by the host country are too high, as this will make the good costly to export. However, market structure again plays an important role, e.g. if the market is highly competitive then the profits the firm can earn will not be high enough to warrant the costs of entry. Conversely, entry is possible if barriers to entry exist, so that long-run profits can be made, and the market structure associated with this is oligopoly. A firm is unlikely to invest abroad whilst economies of scale exist in their home country, so firms engaging in FDI are likely to be large and have few competitors in their home country. Overall, it again leads to the conclusion that the market structure where horizontal FDI occurs will be a differentiated oligopoly.

[9] Caves (1974a) extended his theory to look at multi-plant enterprises and entrepreneurial resources. The multiplant enterprise hypothesis states that in order to capture economies of scale beyond the single efficient-scale plant, firms become multiplants in order to reduce costs. The entrepreneurial resources view states that direct investment will occur in order to maximise the usage of the firm's entrepreneurial talent. This view implies that the firm will hold some intangible assets in the form of human capital.

the market price, or, once the price is found, the cost of negotiation, signing and enforcement of contracts between the parties involved in the transaction.[10] In order to overcome these difficulties and minimise transaction costs, Coase suggests that one owner of a factor of production undertaking a relationship with other factors of production, can engage in a single contract with these factors to define the nature and number of transactions. For this to occur there needs to be an authority figure – known by Coase as the 'entrepreneur'– who directs and manages the resources and transactions. Once this occurs then the birth of a firm takes place, and with it the benefits from acting within the organisation rather than through the market. In this case, we have an internalisation of activity within a firm structure.

The process of internalisation is developed to explain international production and FDI, and one of the leading proponents is Buckley and Casson (1976).[11] They present the MNE as essentially an extension of the multi-plant firm. Buckley and Casson note that the operations of firms, especially large firms, take the form not only of producing goods and services, but activities such as marketing, training, research and development, management techniques and involvement with financial markets. These activities are interdependent and are connected by 'intermediate products', taking the form of either material products or knowledge and expertise. If the markets for intermediary products are imperfect then an incentive arises for the firm to internalise these, provided the benefits exceed the costs.[12] When it occurs across national boundaries a MNE arises, and hence FDI occurs.

A key intermediate product in the internalisation theory of FDI is knowledge. In particular, there are strong reasons to believe that knowledge will not only lead to internalisation but also internationalisation. One reason is that knowledge takes a considerable period of time to generate, e.g. through research and development, but is highly risky, so that futures markets do not exist. Sellers of markets may be unwilling to divulge information, which has uncertain value to the buyer, causing

---

[10] The more parties involved in the contract and the longer the period of time the contract extends over the larger will be the costs of the contract as the exact specifications of the contract become more difficult to determine.

[11] Other authors on internalisation are McManus (1972) and Hennart (1977). As Hennart (2001) points out, not all theories of internalisation are harmonious with each other, with Hennart's theory for example differing from that of Buckley and Casson.

[12] Market imperfections that are believed to give incentives for internalisation include time-lags, discriminatory pricing, unstable bargaining situations and inequality of knowledge between buyers and sellers (Buckley and Casson, 1984). Costs of internalisation include the extra accounting and control required to monitor the product and its overseas operations, as well as the increase in communication costs within the organisation (see Williamson, 1981). These will be higher the greater the distance between the countries and the greater is the difference between the social systems and languages of the countries. A way of reducing these costs is through adopting an appropriate internal structure for the organisation, such as the M-form structure, where the organisation as a whole is split into components each with a degree of independence. According to Williamson (1981), this may have been a factor why US firms first engaged in FDI, as it was US firms that first adopted the M-form structure.

markets to fail. Further, buyers and sellers of knowledge can often hold a degree of market power, which leads to a 'bilateral concentration of power' (see Williamson, 1979), and to uncertain outcomes. These problems indicate the severe difficulties in licensing and contracting where information is crucial.

As regards internationalisation, the public good property of knowledge means it is easily transmitted within the firm, regardless of whether it is inside or across national boundaries. This creates internal markets across national boundaries, and as Buckley and Casson state, as firms search for and exploit knowledge to their maximum potential they do so in numerous locations, with this taking place on an international scale, leading to a "network of plants on a world-wide basis" (p. 45). Thus, MNEs arise because they are in industries with incentives to internalise and where knowledge is an important intermediate product. The internalisation theories of FDI played an important role in developing and advancing the theory of FDI in the 1970s and have remained popular since that time. However, while they answer questions on why FDI occurs, they neglect to answer where it occurs. A locational aspect to foreign direct investment theories also began to emerge in the 1970s.

Locational Determinants

This literature generally assumes that the firm specific and internalisation motives discussed in the previous sections are given, so that it focuses on locational factors when analysing why firms decide to set-up production abroad (Wei *et al*, 1999). An early paper is by Horst (1972), who examines US investment in Canada. He found that one of the most important reasons for firms investing in Canada was the prevalence of natural resources. These resources gave the firm an advantage over those firms that remained in the US. Despite this finding, the locational dimension of FDI was generally ignored as part of the mainstream FDI theory.

Wheeler and Mody (1992) place the main factors that determine the location of FDI into two categories; ergodic and non-ergodic systems (Arthur, 1986). An ergodic system always returns to its initial state when the exact conditions that led to the initial state are reproduced, but a non-ergodic system will never return to its initial state even if the initial conditions are reproduced. In a non-ergodic system the role of history is important, as small changes will lead to irreversible outcomes (Arthur, 1990, and David, 2001). Applied to the theory of FDI, the ergodic system results in location being primarily determined by what are known as *classical variables*: geographical features, labour costs, transport costs and market size.

The reason that the distinction between the two types of systems is important is that agglomeration economies imply a non-ergodic system. Guimaraes *et al* (2000) define agglomeration economies as, "economies that are external to a firm, but internal to a small geographic area" (p. 116). It means that compared to firms elsewhere, the firms experiencing agglomeration economies have a higher level of output for any given levels of capital and labour. To understand the implications of ergodic and non-ergodic systems, and their role in explaining spatial patterns of FDI, it is necessary to look at the different types of agglomeration economy. These can occur either within an industry or across industries. The former are known as MAR externalities, after Marshall (1890), Arrow (1962) and Romer (1986), and are assumed to arise from labour-market pooling, the occurrence of demand and supply linkages or the presence of technological spillovers. Those that occur across industries are known as Jacob's externalities, after Jacobs (1969).[13]

In the case of the MAR externalities, labour-market pooling is based on the notion that when there are a large number of firms in an area, then benefits arise for the workers, which are in turn passed onto the firms. For example, David and Rosenbloom (1990) argue that as long as the profitability of firms is not perfectly correlated, then workers should be able to gain employment when some firms lay-off staff as the other firms will utilise their skills. This will mean that workers will have an incentive to learn skills as it will help them gain employment and in turn this will improve the level of human capital. This concentration of skilled workers results in a specialised workforce and the creation of an area where the chance that an MNE will experience a labour shortage is reduced. MAR externalities also arise from the creation of linkages between suppliers and purchasers (Krugman, 1991). Venables (1996) argues that in an industry that is vertically linked, downstream firms create a market for upstream firms, and a cluster of upstream firms emerges. The downstream firms will want to locate close to the buyers in order to reduce transport costs and to gain a foothold through the local market linkages. Finally, technological spillovers are more likely to flow through firms in an industry when clustering in a small area is present. This is because knowledge can often only be passed on via direct contact, which becomes more likely the smaller is the physical distance between firms.

Jacob's externalities arise when technology becomes diffused across firms in a range of industries. Jacobs (1969) suggests that firms in one industry will benefit from technological advances in a different industry as long as the industries are in close proximity to one another. It is the variety of industries within a locality that is important, and which in turn creates the agglomeration economy. Whether the firms initially locate in an area by accident, due to beneficial classical variables or due to the agglomeration economy, firms provide benefits for other firms located there. In this way, location creates "further expansion by increasing the supply of the factor that made the location attractive in the first place" (Head *et al*, 1995, p. 226). The growing number of firms results in a process of circular causation, and a growing concentration of firms will begin to emerge (Krugman, 1991).

Both the ergodic and non-ergodic systems can lead to the clustering of firms, which has been a focus for recent policy initiatives (Potter *et al*, 2002). However, only with non-ergodic systems will agglomeration economies arise, as the presence of other firms contributes to the attractiveness of the area. Therefore, according to the non-ergodic approach, agglomeration effects become more important over time in attracting FDI compared to the classical variables such as labour availability and geographical endowments. It is these classical variables that the ergodic approach

---

[13] They are also called urbanisation economies (Devereux *et al*, 2003).

relies upon. The empirical evidence for the competing explanations is considered in Chapter 3, where the issue of location is discussed in much greater depth.

Modern Theories

So far, the discussion of the theory of FDI has ranged from explanations as to why it occurs to explanations as to where it will occur. The eclectic approach to FDI is now considered. This suggests that all of the above theories are important in some way, and it has provided the basic outline for FDI theory since its emergence over twenty-five years or so ago.

The Eclectic Paradigm

Reflecting upon the history of the theory of FDI, Dunning (1977) noted that it was very much couched in terms of either the structural market failure hypothesis of Hymer and Caves or the internalisation approach of Buckley and Casson. Dunning provided an eclectic response to these by bringing the competing theories together to form a single theory, or paradigm as it is more often referred. The basic premise of Dunning's paradigm is that it links together Hymer's ownership advantages with the internalisation school, and at the same time adds a locational dimension to the theory, which at the time had not been fully explored. Although in many ways the core of the paradigm shares similarities with the previous research, Dunning does manage to introduce some new considerations, such as the impact that different country and industry characteristics have on each of the ownership, locational and internalisation advantages of FDI.[14]

The eclectic paradigm of FDI states that a firm will directly invest in a foreign country only if it fulfils three conditions. These are necessary rather than sufficient conditions. First, the firm must possess an ownership-specific asset, which gives it an advantage over other firms and which are exclusive to the firm. Second, it must internalise these assets within the firm rather than through contracting or licensing. Third, there must be an advantage in setting-up production in a particular foreign country rather than relying on exports.

Different types of ownership (*O*), locational (*L*) and internalisation (*I*) factors are given in Table 2.1 (collectively known as *OLI*). The ownership advantages are defined by Dunning as particular assets that are specific to the firm that give it the potential to earn greater profits in the future. They include the size of the firm, the level or quality of management, access to factor inputs, access to product markets and technological capabilities. They may reinforce themselves over time to include advantages created from economies of joint supply and through the possession of greater knowledge and information. Thus, a large multinational will have a large

---

[14] The theory has been amended and updated over the years, but the general framework is much the same. For a review of this work see Dunning (2002a, 2002b).

Table 2.1 The Three Conditions of the Eclectic Theory

Ownership-specific advantages (internal to enterprises of one nationality)

Size of firm
Technology and trade marks
Management and organisational systems
Access to spare capacity
Economies of joint supply
Greater access to markets and knowledge
International opportunities such as diversifying risk

Location-specific advantages (determining the location of production)

Distribution of inputs and markets
Costs of labour, materials and transport costs between countries
Government intervention and policies
Commercial and legal infrastructure
Language, culture and customs (i.e. psychic distance)

Internalisation-specific advantages (overcoming market imperfections)

Reduction in search, negotiation and monitoring costs
Avoidance of property right enforcement costs
Engage in price discrimination
Protection of product
Avoidance of tariffs

Source: Dunning (1981).

number of ownership-specific advantages. Location advantages are the assets that a country possesses that make production attractive, as opposed to exporting. They include input prices, transportation costs, communication costs and government incentives. Stable political and legal systems, a commercial infrastructure and language and culture are also relevant. Internalisation advantages are the ways that a firm maximises the gains from their ownership advantages to avoid or overcome market imperfections. Internalisation-specific advantages results in the process of production becoming internal to the firm. Reasons for internalisation include the avoidance of transaction costs, the protection of the good, avoidance of tariffs and the ability to capture economies of scale from production, marketing and finance.

Not all of the *OLI* conditions for FDI will be evenly spread across countries, and therefore each condition will be determined by the factors that are specific to individual countries. Links between the *OLI* advantages and the country-specific characteristics are summarised in Table 2.2. For example, the ownership-specific

Table 2.2 Characteristics of Countries and *OLI*-Specific Advantages

Ownership-specific advantages	Country characteristics
Size of firm.	Large markets.
	Liberal attitudes to mergers.
Technology and trade marks.	Government support of innovation.
	Skilled workforce.
Management and organisational systems.	Supply of trained managers.
	Educational facilities.
Product differentiation.	High income countries.
	Levels of advertising and
	Marketing.

Location-specific advantages	Country characteristics
Costs of labour and materials.	Developed or developing country.
Transport costs between countries.	Distance between countries.
Government intervention and policies.	Attitudes of government to FDI.
Economies of scale.	Size of markets.
Psychic distance.	Similarities of countries' languages
	and cultures.

Internalisation-specific advantages	Country characteristics
Searching, negotiating, monitoring costs.	Greater levels of education and
Avoid costs of enforcing property rights.	larger markets make knowledge
Protection of products.	type ownership-specific advantages
	more likely to occur.

Source: Dunning (1981).

advantage of firm size is likely to be influenced by market size in the firm's home country. This is because the larger the market is, the more likely will a firm be able to gain ownership-specific advantages in the form of economies of scale. In terms of location-specific factors, labour costs will vary across developed and developing countries, while transport costs are determined by the distance between the home and host countries. Finally, country-specific factors are likely to affect the degree to which firms internalise their advantages.

Strategic Motivations of Foreign Direct Investment

Despite the advances made by the eclectic approach to FDI, the theory has been criticised for ignoring another aspect of FDI theory. This is the role of strategy, which was first analysed by Knickerbocker (1973), and then advanced by Graham

(1978, 1998). The notable feature of the strategic approach to FDI is that it believes that an initial inflow of FDI into a country will produce a reaction from the local producers in that country, so that FDI is a dynamic process. The response from the domestic producers can either be defensive or aggressive in nature. A defensive response would be a merger or acquisition of other domestic producers to reinforce market power, while an aggressive response would be a price war or entry into the foreign firm's home market. The empirical foundation for the strategic motivation arose from the wave of European FDI into the USA in the 1970s. This occurred mainly in oligopolistic industries, suggesting that it was a retaliatory response by European firms to the initial entry of US firms into Western Europe.

The role of strategy was extended by Acocella (1992b), who suggested that the ability of a firm to engage in strategic behaviour was a measure of its market power. In particular, firms engaged in foreign production have certain features that 'strengthen' their ability to undertake strategic actions, such as better information from a larger array of markets, greater capacity and a large initial size, which gives them a larger market share and greater market power in their domestic country. Firms engage in strategic activity not only to gain extra market share directly, but to threaten potential entrants and other firms from expanding. This is known as an 'exchange of threats', and its purpose is to minimise risk by threatening-off rival firms (Head *et al*, 2002). Another important aspect of strategic interactions is covered by Casson (1987), who looks at the credibility of threats made by firms. Casson argues that due to repeated interactions between firms over time, a firm not carrying out a threat will suffer a loss of reputation. Thus, even a threat that is self-damaging is credible, as a failure to carry it out leads to a dent in its reputation. It leads to FDI taking place not only to exploit firm-specific advantages or to reduce transaction costs (Hughes and Oughton, 1992), but to stop rivals gaining greater advantages, even though it may lead to a reduction in profits (Graham, 1998).[15]

Strategic theories of FDI have recently been extended to reflect the growing rise in the number of strategic alliances between multinational firms. The growth in global strategic alliances has been noted by authors such as Harrigan (1987), Dussage and Garrette (1995) and Dunning (1995). Global strategic alliances are defined as collaborative projects that occur between firms in different countries and involve cross-border flows and linkages, but where the firms maintain their autonomy (Parkhe, 1991). Reasons for strategic alliances include economies of scale, the reduction of risk and access to knowledge and expertise (Inkpen, 2001).[16]

---

[15] Strategic behaviour can determine the location of MNEs through herd behaviour. If one firm sets-ups in a specific location then others may locate there for no other reason than because its rivals did so (Banerjee, 1992). Strategic behaviour of FDI can be aimed at the home country's government, e.g. threatening to move production abroad to get preferential treatment in terms of taxation, credit or subsidies.

[16] Examples of strategic alliances include franchising, production arrangements, marketing arrangements and non-equity cooperative arrangements for research and development. The benefits of undertaking a strategic alliance must outweigh the costs of the alliance and also

The types of sector that have experienced a growth in strategic alliances are those characterised by a high degree of knowledge intensity (Hagedoorn, 1996), with a rapid growth in the number of 'technology' alliances (Lundan and Hagedoorn, 2001).[17] Strategic alliances are arrangement for multinationals to finance the large amounts of investment involved in technological research and development, which are necessary to remain competitive (Cantwell and Narula, 2001).

A Critical Review

The growth in the interest in foreign direct investment is reflected by the number of disciplines that have become involved in postulating theories of FDI (Dunning, 2001a). These disciplines not only include economics and international business, but organisational theory, political science and economic geography. This section briefly reviews the relative merits of the competing theories of FDI, as they have progressed since the 1960s, and relates them to the temporal and country pattern of FDI that was described in Chapter 1.

Before Hymer, there was no theory of foreign direct investment as such, with FDI treated in the same way as any other cross-border transfer of capital. Hymer realised that FDI was distinct in terms of the level of control of the investment, but his insight went further in providing motivations and explanations for its existence. These were couched in terms of market imperfections that placed barriers to entry, the removal of competition and the exploitation of firm-specific advantages as the key factors in foreign-based production. However, there are a number of criticisms of Hymer's theory. One of these is that it over-emphasises the role of structural market failure and ignores the transaction-cost side of market failure (Dunning and Rugman, 1985). Other criticisms are the lack of a locational dimension and a lack of a dynamic aspect to the theory to indicate what determines the timing of the foreign investment. A more recent objection is whether it is local firms that hold advantages over foreign firm, when multinationals enterprises have advantages in a range of areas, including better access to capital, labour and technology (Dicken, 1994). Despite these criticisms, Hymer provided the first theory of FDI, although it was neglected until the 1970s, not being published until 1976, at which point it was adapted by authors such as Caves (Dunning, 2001a).

In the 1960s, the dominant theory of FDI was the product life-cycle. The main reason for the dominance and popularity of this theory was that it was based on the behaviour of US multinationals, which were the main source of FDI at that time. However, while this made it popular in the 1960s, it hindered the theory in the

---

outweigh the net benefits of other forms of international production such as subsidiaries, mergers or market-based contracts (Inkpen, 2001). The subsequent performance of the alliance will depend on its ability to maintain internal stability (Parkhe, 1993).

[17] Typical of these sectors are the pharmaceutical biotechnology and information technology sectors (Lundan and Hagedoorn, 2001).

1970s, when FDI began to emerge from Europe, and later Japan (Kogut, 1998). Vernon (1979) admitted weaknesses in the life-cycle theory at this time, due to the increasing implausibility of the key hypothesis that firms face different conditions in their own home markets compared to foreign markets. As a response, some authors adapted the theory, so that it could encompass the characteristics of other countries, e.g. Stopford (1976) for the UK, but it still showed signs of redundancy. The mass-production stage of the theory became increasingly outdated because of flexible production techniques (Aoyama, 1996), while the international production and marketing of products began to follow patterns different to that predicted by the life-cycle model (Giddy, 1978). Even so, despite the drawbacks, the product life-cycle model has remained a popular approach to FDI, and it has at times been adapted to encompass other aspects of FDI theory, such as the strategic and internalisation theories (Belderbos and Sleuwaegen, 2001).

As the 1970s progressed there was an increase in the awareness of the rising presence of multinational enterprises in the global economy, and consequent a shift in theory towards the role of these enterprises (Dunning, 2001a). Most notably, this prompted a rise of the internalisation theories of FDI that stressed transaction costs, in contrast to the market imperfections that were the domain of Hymer, and who had neglected transaction costs.[18] The internalisation theory of FDI identifies the accumulation and internalisation of knowledge as the motivation for FDI, which bypasses intermediate product markets in knowledge, (Tolentino, 2001). As such, and according to Buckley and Casson (1976), this theory is key to explaining the rise in FDI in the post-war period, when the important feature is the acquisition and use of knowledge, such as through research and development.[19]

The 1970s witnessed an increase in the number of multinational enterprises in the global economy, but also a growth in cross-border competition and the onset of globalisation. The result of this was an increased interdependence of firms on a global scale, causing some authors to look at the role of strategy in the theory of FDI. Knickerbocker (1973), Flowers (1976) and Graham (1978) were the main proponents of this theory whose basis was in the 'new' industrial organisation and game-theoretic literature of the 1970s, although they also followed in the tradition of Hymer and Caves by focusing on structural as opposed to transaction-based market failures.[20] As FDI has become increasingly concentrated in the hands of a few countries and as MNEs have grown larger, the role of competition and strategy in the global economy remains just as visible in the present day, and especially so given the dramatic rise in mergers and acquisitions in the 1990s.

By the end of the 1970s a number of strands had emerged for the existence of FDI. Of which the internalisation and structural-based theories were both popular explanations. They were incorporated into Dunning's (1977) eclectic paradigm of

---

[18] This was rectified in later versions of Hymer's writings.

[19] See Kogut and Zander (1993) for an alternative view of the role of knowledge in FDI.

[20] The perceived importance of competition and strategy led to Vernon (1974, 1979) to revise his earlier product life-cycle theory (Voutilainen, 2005).

FDI, which turned out to be the dominant theoretical framework of FDI (Cantwell and Narula, 2003). However, the eclectic approach is not without its critics, who have challenged the paradigm on a number of fronts. One, is that the paradigm covers such a range of theories and employs such a large number of variables to explain FDI that in effect it is taxonomy rather than a theory of FDI (Ietto-Gillies, 1992). Dunning himself admits that the paradigm should be seen as an analytic framework for FDI, rather than as an all-encompassing theory, with no-one theory satisfactorily explaining all types of FDI (Dunning, 2001b).

A further criticism of the eclectic paradigm stems from the proponents of the internalisation theory of FDI who claim that Dunning's ownership advantages are theoretically redundant, as they originate from the internalisation process (Itaki, 1991).[21] Early versions of the eclectic paradigm also failed to include a strategic motivation for FDI, although it was later incorporated. Indeed, a criticism of the eclectic paradigm is that it has been modified over time to incorporate new ideas and reflect contemporary trends in FDI. These include the increased importance of knowledge in a global economy, greater liberalisation of cross-border markets, the emergence of non-equity strategic alliances and the increase in M&A activity.[22] The latter was incorporated into the framework through the ownership advantages, so that they not only consist of advantages that are generated internally but depend on the ability of multinationals to obtain advantages generated by other agents, be they competitors, suppliers or customers (Dunning, 1995, 2001b). The advantages of M&A entry into a foreign market are given as the improvement in learning, transfer of knowledge (Lundan and Hagedoorn, 2001) and increased firm-specific assets in terms of technological capabilities (Horn and Persson, 2001).[23] Indeed, knowledge and technology are seen as the most strategically significant resources of the firm and the major driving force of the global economy (Simonin, 1999), and as such the key factors in the theory of FDI (Bresman *et al*, 1999).

Conclusions

This chapter has reviewed the theoretical literature on foreign direct investment. The theory emerged in 1960, when Hymer attempted to give FDI its own place in the literature, and his study on the international operations of national firms is now

---

[21] For further discussion of the disagreements between the different schools of thought see Rugman (1981) and Tolentino (2001).

[22] See Dunning (2000) for the detailed evolution of these.

[23] Strategic and efficiency motives are the main reasons used to explain the rationale behind M&A activity. Strategic reasons are to create and exert market power by the removal of competition (Iranzo, 2004), while efficiency gains result from a reduction in costs through technology transfer, economies of scale and synergy effects (Neary, 2004). Explanations for M&A activity arise from the industrial organisation literature and focus mainly on mergers *per se*, rather than cross-border M&As, for which the theoretical literature is limited.

one of the cornerstone theories of FDI. Prior to this time, explanations of foreign investment were based on theories of international capital movements. Since Hymer, there have been attempts to address a number of issues, such as why FDI occurs and where it locates. The literature has taken on-board developments in economic thought, such as theories of industrial organisation and transaction costs. It is given expression in Dunning's over-arching eclectic paradigm of FDI, which not only encompasses ownership and internalisation advantages of multinational enterprise, but the role that location plays in a firm's decision to invest abroad. Locational factors had been touched upon previously, but Dunning managed to weave these into a more general theory of FDI, where they were treated along with the structural market and internalisation hypothesis of FDI.

Since the time of the eclectic paradigm, other theories have emerged that have stressed the importance of the role of strategy in FDI in the face of 'globalisation' (see Chapter 1) and a corresponding growth in competition between firms. In this, the role of the traditional barriers to entry across countries, such as the differences in the legal, linguistic and economic environments, have become less important, and FDI is now be viewed as competition between a few firms on an international stage. It is evident from the recent large-scale increase in FDI that has been fuelled by the merger and acquisition wave amongst countries in the developed world. The M&A boom has also highlighted the importance of knowledge as a crucial firm-specific asset and a driver of greater FDI flows in the global economy. Such contemporary issues have been incorporated by the eclectic paradigm, and as such the paradigm has managed to remain as one of the most popular frameworks and theoretical tools in explaining the workings of foreign direct investment. In the next chapter we examine the locational determinants in greater detail, including at the regional level, leading to the discussion of regional development in Chapter 4.

Chapter 3

Location

The preceding two chapters have examined both the spatial and temporal pattern of foreign direct investment at a global scale, and reviewed the theory of. FDI. In this chapter the location of FDI is examined. Since the United Kingdom has been, and continues to be, an important destination for FDI, the chapter focuses on location in the UK context, specifically at the regional level. The chapter has two purposes. The first is to review the reasons and empirical evidence on why one area attracts FDI compared to another area. The second purpose is to investigate the location of FDI at the UK regional level, focusing on the main periods of investment since the Second World War. Studies of FDI at the UK regional level are considered in some detail to see what these reveal about location. It leads to the discussion in the next chapter on the implications of FDI for regional development.

The chapter begins by looking at the motivation for FDI location. The factors that are traditionally believed to influence the location decision of a multinational enterprise are known as the classical variables, and include such things as the size of the market that the enterprise is entering, or labour costs, which signal the likely production costs. However, more recently, research has focused on another kind of location factor, which is known as the agglomeration reason for FDI location.[1] It is the external effect or externality, perhaps in the form of a 'spillover', which gives rise to an agglomeration economy, and may encourage a foreign-owned firm to set-up in an area where firms in a similar activity are already present. In the case of these agglomeration economies the existence of an external effect or externality is usually taken as given, but possible sources of 'spillover' are explored in the next chapter. Much has been written on the classical and agglomeration location factors and this chapter reviews this evidence.

Finally, a considerable amount of the FDI that has been attracted to the UK has gone to the peripherally parts of the country, especially in manufacturing. The chapter gives a detailed account of the regional pattern of FDI in the UK, using data for projects and jobs collated by *UK Trade and Investment*.[2] It explores the explanations for this pattern, based on the numerous empirical studies that have

---

[1] In general, the literature on location is characterised by loose terminology, but McCann and Sheppard (2003) formally distinguish an agglomeration from an industrial complex and a social network (the latter is often referred to as a 'cluster'). An agglomeration involves firms in competition that are co-located in an urban area. The nature of relations between the firms is transient, perhaps explaining why they are non-specified in empirical work.

[2] This is the former *Invest UK*, which before that was known as the *Invest in Britain Bureau*.

been conducted at the UK regional level, offering insights on the location decisions of multinational enterprises.

The Locational Determinants of FDI

Many researchers have theorised about the potential determinants of FDI location, which when taken together identify many possible factors.[3] These factors are now considered, along with a brief rationale for their importance. In the next section the empirical evidence for these variables is reviewed.

Market size and growth   The size of the market is argued to have a positive effect on FDI location (Billington, 1999). This is because a large market will attract firms that have outgrown their own domestic market and/or are looking to expand into other markets to gain greater sales or market share. The growth of a market may also influence FDI location, as firms will enter markets where they can grow.

Labour market   The availability of labour is expected to exert a positive effect on FDI location, as a large amount of available labour provides the firm with a pool of workers from which it can choose its labour force. However, there are a number of other considerations. The cost of labour will have an inverse effect on investment (Mudambi, 1995), while more-productive labour will yield productivity gains. The cost of labour is often used in studies of FDI location to test the effect of the labour market, but this is mistaken as it also reflects the level of productivity. Thus, both productivity measures and labour costs should be used (Hill and Munday, 1991).

The degree of labour unionisation is also sometimes used to measure the state of the labour market, whether it is 'strong' or 'weak', but this can have ambiguous effects on location. Strong unionisation can lead to higher wages (which should be captured by the labour-market variables mentioned above), and to stricter rules and regulations on firms, making it a less attractive location for a firm. Conversely, it may create a more contented and productive workforce (Friedman *et al*, 1992), and have a positive influence on FDI location. Other labour market conditions, such as hiring and firing costs and general employment legislation, may also impact on location (Leahy and Montagna, 2004). Gorg (2002), for example, finds that lower redundancy and severance payments play a positive role in the location decisions of US multinational enterprises over the period 1986-96. In a theoretical paper that examines the role of a country's labour market in determining its attractiveness for FDI, Haaland and Wooton (2003) show that labour market 'flexibility' is a key positive determinant on the choice of location for foreign-owned firms.[4] However, where firms act strategically, an 'inflexible' labour market may attract FDI (Dewit *et al*, 2003). This is because firms must commit to a high level of future output, so

---

[3] A theory of MNE location is not considered, for which readers are referred to Chapter 2.

[4] Labour market flexibility reflects the ease of hiring and firing.

that there is some optimal level of 'flexibility'. Further, a switch from a flexible to an inflexible labour market may lock-in or anchor previous FDI, making it more costly to exit (Dewit *et al*, 2004).

Macroeconomic policy The most common macroeconomic effects that are included in the literature are the corporate tax rate and the exchange rate. A high tax rate should have a negative influence on FDI location, as it reduces the profits that can be made (Cassou, 1997), but the effect of the exchange rate is more complicated. A depreciation of the host country currency will make it cheaper for a foreign firm to set-up production in that country, but it will also reduce the value of repatriated profits. Blonigen (1997) points out that FDI does not always involve the transfer of currency, as under a broader definition the 'investment' can be in firm-specific assets, such as knowledge. Further, when the foreign investment is meant for re-exporting out of the country, a depreciation of the exchange rate may lead to a net increase in FDI, as exports out of the host country become cheaper (Radulescu and Robson, 2003). It is to be expected that restrictive policies, such as trade tariffs, will lead firms to substitute production in the country for exports.

Inward investment policy Aside from general macroceconomic policies and labour market regulation, the government and its agencies can use explicit inducements in order to attract FDI, of either a financial or a non-financial nature. One difficulty with these inducements is that they have to be carefully constructed, as either they have no effect on FDI or they may attract more marginal investment that is unable to prosper. A key inducement is grants, which seem to play a substantial role in the international competition for FDI. However, non-financial policies operate at regional and local levels to encourage plants to locate in areas, including the laying-out of industrial estates and business parks, advance-factory provision, labour training and specific items of infrastructure, such as roads (Culem, 1988).

In the case of grants, at the European Union level, Article 87 of the European Treaty makes state aid unlawful if it distorts or threatens to distort competition or impacts on trade between Member States. The European Commission publishes Guidelines and Frameworks for aids that it is prepared to approve. Generally, this allows horizontal supports, such as assistance to small and medium-sized firms, but the support for large firms is really only permissible under the regional policies of Member States. Regional grants are therefore very important in attracting FDI (see Wren, 2005a). In the UK, for example, over the last twenty years, half the regional aid budget has been on grants awarded to foreign-owned plants, under the Regional Selective Assistance discretionary grant and related schemes.

Infrastructure Other than specific measures of infrastructure support, the general level of infrastructure is a potential attractor for inward investment. It encompasses the general state of transport and communication networks in an area or region. It improves the distribution of goods and services and the ability to recruit labour and to communicate with suppliers and purchasers. However, as with many of these factors, it may pick up other effects. For example, a high degree of infrastructure may imply a high level of urbanisation and therefore a large number of consumers.

Industrialisation The level of industrialisation is expected to be associated with a high level of FDI, since a country or region that is highly industrialised will have a large number of firms, potentially increasing the possibility of beneficial spillovers. This is an agglomeration economy, which is discussed further below. Certainly, the evidence in Chapter 1 was that most FDI goes to developed countries, where the level of industrialisation is greatest.

Pre-existing FDI Other potential sources of agglomeration economy are the stock of foreign-owned capital in an area or the level of foreign imports (Culem, 1988). It increases the potential for spillovers, and increases the likelihood that other firms will set-up production or that existing firms will re-invest (Phelps *et al*, 2003). It may also signal to other foreign-owned firm the relatively low risk associated with a particular region. An area that has attracted imports may be susceptible to FDI, as foreign firms will have gained a foothold in this economy and have information on its customs and potential. However, again, the amount of pre-existing FDI in an area could signal other factors, such as the success of inward investment policies, good infrastructure or labour-market conditions.

Information Firms engaged in FDI have an adverse information asymmetry relative to their domestic rivals (Wei *et al*, 1999), and the further the firm is from its home market in terms of geographic distance, the higher will be the asymmetry, and the more disadvantaged will be the investor. To overcome this disadvantage a foreign investor may locate in the 'core' of a country (as opposed to the 'periphery'). The core is likely to have better infrastructure and administrative capabilities compared to the rest of the country, and is a place where better information about the country and market is available, (Mariotti and Piscitello, 1995). It suggests why FDI may locate in the core rather than the periphery of an economy.

Empirical Evidence

The factors outlined above give an indication of the many possible determinants of FDI location. These factors are not mutually exclusive to one another, and can be mutually reinforcing. In terms of the empirical work they are often grouped into 'classical variables', which are the traditional location factors; and 'agglomeration variables', which are not firm specific, but arise out of advantages from location close to other firms. Classical factors directly affect a firm's demand or production costs (e.g. market size, labour costs or taxes), but the distinction between these and the agglomeration factors is not always clear-cut. A further difficulty arises in attempting to measure the agglomeration economies. Studies use infrastructure or the level of industrialisation, but these impact on a firm's costs, and so can also be designated as classical variables. Further, terms that measure the classical factors (e.g. size of the economy) may be correlated with agglomeration economies, so that there are problems of interpretation.

The issue of whether it is the classical or agglomeration variables are relevant in determining location of FDI has been a passion in the literature, but this is not purely an academic matter, as it has important implications. If classical variables are relevant it suggests that policy should operate on the traditional location factors in order to attract FDI, but if the agglomeration factors are significant, then not only may the classical variables and policy have no effect, but it suggests that FDI is self-perpetuating, i.e. the arrival of FDI may attract further FDI. Of course, it is essentially an empirical matter, and attention now turns to this. In so doing, it is apparent that there are a large number of studies on FDI location, and as we see the evidence is not always consistent. In this section we consider the evidence in the round, and in the next section focus on that for the UK.

Empirical investigations into the locational determinants of FDI commenced with the study by Scaperlanda and Mauer (1969), who examined US investment in the European Community. Subsequent studies of the European Union include Pain (1997) and Barrell and Pain (1999a), while there is research on specific Member States as a source of entry into the EU. Mariotti and Piscitello (1995) look at FDI in Italy, Guimaraes *et al* (2000) examine Portugal, and Billington (1999) the UK. The United States is a focus for research, including Coughlin *et al* (1991), Head *et al* (1995) and Hines (1996). Other research is carried out across countries in order to gain a broader perspective, including Wheeler and Mody (1992), Braunerhjelm and Svensson (1996) and Kravis and Lipsey (1982). Most studies ignore the hierarchical structure that may be behind the location decision of a multinational enterprise. For example, a particular country may well be chosen before a decision is made to locate at a particular region or site within that country. However, it is recently been remedied by Mucchielli and Puech (2004), who first on a number of European countries, and then the alternative regions within these countries.[5]

Classical Explanations

Gross domestic product is used as a measure of market size. Kravis and Lipsey (1982), Wheeler and Mody (1992) and Braunerhjelm and Svensson (1996) make comparison across countries, and they all find that market size has a positive effect on FDI. Coughlin *et al* (1991) find that market size has a positive influence when using the USA as the host country. Billington (1999), Barrell and Pain (1999a) and Wei *et al* (1999) find that the growth rate of market size, instead of the level, has an influence in determining FDI location. However, Scaperlanda and Mauer (1969) find that this did not affect the location decision.

---

[5] They use a nested logit model. This approach has been used to test the location decisions of firms within regions and sub-regions of individual countries. For example, Hansen (1987) and Crozet *et al* (2004).

Productivity and the cost of labour have also been found to have an impact on FDI location. Labour costs, measured by the average hourly wage rate, are found to have an adverse effect on FDI by Wheeler and Mody (1992), but as Billington (1999) notes, higher labour costs could be offset by higher productivity levels. To get around this, Friedman (1992) uses labour costs and productivity separately. He finds that labour costs impact negatively, but that labour productivity has a positive impact on FDI. Another way to overcome the problem is to use labour costs per unit of output. Coughlin *et al* (1991), Barrell and Pain (1999a) and Wei *et al* (1999) all use this measure, and find it has a negative effect on FDI.

Turning to the availability of labour, Billington (1999) argues that the rate of unemployment can be used as a proxy for labour availability, as an area with high unemployment will have a larger labour force for firms to choose from. A high unemployment rate may also mean that workers put more effort into keeping their jobs, and are willing to work for a lower wage rate, again making the area more attractive. Billington (1999), Friedman (1992) and Coughlin *et al* (1991) all find that the unemployment rate has a positive effect on FDI location, but evidence in Taylor (1993) suggests that too high a rate can be a disincentive.

Finally, several studies examine the effect that taxation plays in attracting FDI. Billington (1999) finds a negative relationship between tax rates and FDI, which is the case for Coughlin *et al* (1991) when examining state taxation in the US. Hines (1996) finds that high tax rates in states within the US have a negative impact on FDI levels, and that the firms that cannot claim tax credits from their home country reduce their level of FDI within high tax areas of the US. However, both Glickman and Woodward (1989) and Wheeler and Mody (1992) find that the relationship between state taxation and FDI is not statistically significant. The evidence for grants is considered below, so that the final term of interest is the exchange rate. In their reviews, Blonigen (1997) and Gorg and Wakelin (2001) generally find an insignificant relationship between the exchange rate and FDI location. Gorg and Wakelin find a negative relationship for acquisitions, which they attribute to the firm-specific asset motivation for FDI.

Agglomeration Explanations

Whether measured by the infrastructure of an area, the level of industrialisation or the amount of previous FDI, Wheeler and Mody (1992), Billington (1999) and Wei *et al* (1999) all find a significant positive effect between these and FDI location, which they attribute to agglomeration economies. Wei *et al* (1999) look at foreign investment into China, and also use the ratio of population to land area to measure agglomeration within a region and find a positive relationship, although this could just as easily measure market size or transport costs. Agglomeration effects from lower information costs, as proxied by locating in the 'core' of an economy, are found to have a positive effect. Finally, Coughlin *et al* (1991) use the density of manufacturing activity as a proxy for agglomeration in their study of US locational decisions, and find a positive influence for this on location.

A distinction was made in Chapter 2 between agglomeration economies that occur between industries (called Jacob externalities) and those that occur between firms in the same industry (known as MAR externalities). Most studies operate across industries, although several studies consider a single industry. Braunerhjelm and Svensson (1996) measure agglomeration by using the number of employees in a given manufacturing industry relative to total employees in manufacturing. They find that this has a positive effect on FDI, especially in industries characterised by a high degree of technology. Similarly, Barrell and Pain (1999b) find the presence of agglomeration economies in technology-related industries, using the relative scale of production and the relative size of the research base within industries to measure the agglomeration economy. A recent analysis of firm location decisions by Devereux *et al* (2003) also suggests that firms tend to locate near to other firms in the same industry. This study, like many of the others, includes both classical and agglomeration terms, but it finds that the inclusion of the agglomeration terms affects the significance of the classical terms, so that these two kinds of variable should really be considered together.

Agglomeration versus Classical Factors

Head *et al* (1995) argue that it is not possible to list all possible classical variables in the specification of an industrial location model, so that there is a problem of omitted variables. This will give rise to correlation between the error term and the agglomeration variables, and mean that the significance of the latter could arise from omitted terms. In their study of Japanese investment in the US at the state level, Head *et al* use a single state effect variable in an attempt to capture *all* of the classical variables potentially influencing a Japanese investor's location decision.[6] The model expresses the profitability of location as a function of: a state effect, capturing all of the classical factors determining the attractiveness of a state, and a group of agglomeration terms. The latter consist of industry-specific variables, measured by the number of US and Japanese plants in an industry, and variables for the agglomeration of both industrially-related groups and across states. Head *et al* find that Japanese investors prefer locations where a concentration of previous Japanese FDI in the same industry already exists. These agglomeration effects are not contained within states, but they cross into nearby states. Of interest, is that for firms in the auto-related industries, previous Japanese investment across a range of industries is significant in attracting FDI to the state. Finally, they conclude that no state-specific effects are significant in determining the location of Japanese FDI in the US. That is, that the classical variables have no effect.

Despite the advance made by Head *et al* (1995), Guimaraies *et al* (2000) argue that US states are too large a geographical unit to capture an agglomeration effect.

---

[6] As the Japanese investors in the 1980s are a sample of entirely new investors, then the existing pattern of US establishments can be used as a proxy for the locational attractiveness of a specific industry, for example the abundance of factor endowments in a given state.

They examine FDI at the level of a Portuguese Concelho, which is a much smaller administrative unit. They split agglomeration economies into four categories: industry-specific effects, business-service effects, total manufacturing and foreign-specific effects.[7] The classical variables in their analysis are the costs of land and labour. They find that the industry-level, business-level and manufacturing effects have a positive role in attracting FDI, while foreign-specific effects (i.e. the share of employment in foreign-owned firms) are insignificant. Both classical variables are insignificant. Using a hierarchical structure, Mucchielle and Puech (2004) find that the significance of the classical variables depends on whether the analysis is at the country or the regional level, whereas agglomeration effects are significant at both levels of analysis, although stronger at the level of the region. This suggests agglomeration effects occur in relatively close proximity, which is plausible.

In a similar vein, Devereux *et al* (2003) examine the location of new plants in the counties of Great Britain over 1986-92, including a term for Government regional grants and agglomeration terms. These are MAR externalities, as proxied by the number of plants in the same industry (possibly foreign owned), and Jacob externalities, as measured by a Herfindahl diversity index between plants across industries. Their results show that other things equal, the regions where the grants are available are less attractive for FDI, but that a grant has a significant effect on location (see below). However, the effect of this is extremely small, so that a 1 per cent increase in the grant increases the probability of location by only between 0.04 and 0.13 of one per cent. When calculated at the mean a £100,000 increase in the regional grant increases in the probability of location in an area by only 0.0001! Again, it offers little support for the classical location factors. Devereux *et al* find that FDI tends to locate near to other plants in the same industry, which is a MAR externality, and similar to that found by Head *et al* (1995) for the US.

Finally, Taylor (1993) examines Japanese manufacturing FDI in the UK over 1984 and 1991.[8] Unlike Devereux *et al*, which is at the firm level, this study is conducted at the county level, including terms for the areas in which grants are available. Agglomeration terms are the population density and employment in both manufacturing and services to capture supplier networks. The number of Japanese plants in the UK increased many-fold over the study period, and the agglomeration and grant terms are each significant. It suggests a different effect for the classical factors in early-stage FDI, perhaps before the agglomeration effects take hold.

Overall, the studies find that agglomeration economies play an important role the attraction of FDI. While the classical variables, such as market size and labour-market conditions, seem to explain FDI location, the studies of Head *et al* and Guimaraies *et al* suggest that they are dominated by the agglomeration factors. The evidence appears conclusive, but caution should be exercised for several reasons. First, as indicated above, it may be difficult to distinguish the agglomeration and

---

[7] After Rivera-Batiz (1988), business-specific effects are agglomerations within the service sector of urban regions.

[8] This study is considered in greater detail below.

classical factors empirically. For example, measures of industrialisation may just be capturing market size. Second, it is likely that there is relatively little variation in the classical variables for a single country (e.g. taxes are fairly homogeneous), but much more variation in agglomeration. Evidence at the international level would be more compelling, but there is a paucity of studies operating at this level. A recent study at this level, by Mucchielle and Puech (2004), finds that classical variables are stronger at the country level. Finally, classical variables may explain early-stage FDI, while different processes may work for mature FDI, when there is a build-up of foreign-owned plants in a particular locality.

Locational Determinants in the UK

The studies of the locational determinants are now considered in detail, focusing on FDI in the UK. When looking at the UK, there are only a handful of studies examining location, most of which are referred to above.[9] These include Hill and Munday (1991, 1992), Taylor (1993), Billington (1999) and Devereux *et al* (2003). These are now considered to see what they reveal about location in the UK.

Hill and Munday (1991) This study examines the locational determinants of FDI in Wales between 1983 and 1989. As proxies for the volume of Welsh FDI, Hill and Munday use each of the Welsh share of UK capital investment and the shares of FDI projects and jobs in Wales. Four determinants of location are considered: labour costs, output growth, regional incentives and infrastructure (expenditure on roads and road improvements), each of which are measured relative to that of the UK. They find that output growth is the main determinant of FDI into Wales for each of the three possible measures of FDI. Infrastructure has a positive effect, but only when the number of jobs is the dependent variable. Similarly, the grants have a positive effect, but only when investment is the dependent variable. However, there is an endogeneity issue, leading to a potentially spurious causal relationship. This is because greater FDI will lead to more grant being disbursed, so that the coefficient may be picking up this relationship.

Hill and Munday (1992) In this study, Hill and Munday look at the determinants of FDI in the eleven regions of the UK (the South-East of England includes London). Three variables are now used to explain the location of FDI: labour costs, regional grants and the level of infrastructure (expenditure on road transport). Each region's labour cost is calculated as the ratio of average male weekly gross earnings relative to the UK average, while the grant amount and infrastructure are calculated relative to the share of UK employment. The data are pooled for the regions to analyse the determinants of FDI in the UK, including regional and time fixed effects (but the

---

[9] Guimaraes *et al* (2000) note that most studies on the locational determinants of FDI are for the US, leaving a "dearth of empirical location research on other countries (p. 118).

latter are always insignificant). When the infrastructure term is excluded, regional dummies are significant, but the converse is also true. It suggests that the regional differences in FDI levels can be explained by differences in infrastructure, which supports the agglomeration explanation. The grant term is significant, but again there is an endogeneity issue.

Taylor (1993) This looks at the geography of Japanese manufacturing FDI in the UK between 1984 and 1991, using data from the former *Invest in Britain Bureau*. In this period, Japanese firms were beginning to increase their investment abroad, with the number of Japanese establishments in the UK increasing from 40 to 219. Taylor looked at Japanese investment at the sub-regional level, and found seven locations where the number of manufacturing employees in Japanese plants was greater than 10 per cent of the region's total manufacturing employment. Four of these areas were in Wales and another two in North-East England. A feature is that these areas were designated for regional grants, and Taylor sought to analyse the role of these as a locational determinant of Japanese FDI.

Working at the county level, Taylor uses a Poisson distribution to model the number of Japanese firms setting-up production in the UK. Explanatory variables are included for the labour market (earnings and unemployment for labour costs and availability), population density to proxy infrastructure and employment in both of manufacturing and services to proxy agglomeration effects from supplier networks. Dummy variables for Development and Intermediate Area status under regional policy are included to pick up the effect of the grants. To capture a policy change in 1988, two sub-periods are considered: 1984-1988 and 1989-1991.[10] Four terms are significant in both periods: Development and Intermediate Area status and the manufacturing and service terms. In the second sub-period, the level of unemployment has a positive effect on FDI, but the percentage unemployed has a negative effect. This marked the end of an economic boom, and Taylor believes that firms prefer to locate where there is a plentiful supply of labour, but where unemployment is are not too high so that the area is depressed. Labour costs, population and levels of transport are all insignificant. The study is interesting as the way the grants are modelled avoids the endogeneity problem. Further, in this study, infrastructure is included as a classical variable, while agglomeration effects that occur through firm linkages are measured more directly.

Billington (1999) This study uses project-based data, much like that used in the second part of this book, to examine UK FDI over the period 1986-93. Again, the study is at the regional level, but it uses a broader range of variables, encompassing infrastructure, labour availability (as measured by unemployment), labour costs, market availability (as measured by population density), regional grants and levels of industrialisation and infrastructure, as well as regional and time dummies. Most

---

[10] In 1988 there was a shift from automatic grants to a discretionary-based system, whereby firms had to apply for financial support and the grant rate was variable.

variables are insignificant, although labour costs and its availability are significant. However, in the case of the latter, Billington thinks it may pick-up those areas that are designated for regional grants. The significance of the population density term implies that agglomeration plays a role in attracting FDI. Dummy variables for Scotland and Wales are positive and significant, suggesting that these areas get a level of FDI above that which can be explained by other factors. For the North and Northern Ireland these variables are insignificant.

Devereux et al (2003) Finally, this study looks at the location of new plants in ten areas of the UK between 1986 and 1992.[11] The largest proportion of new plants (45 per cent) located in the South of England over this period, with the Midlands and the North each receiving about 20 per cent of plants, but Wales and Scotland each having less than 10 per cent. All regions, except the South of England (which had limited Assisted Area designation over this period), received most of the new plants in the regional policy Assisted Areas. Devereux *et al* match information on regional grant offers to the plant data (see Data Appendix). The North received the highest grant offers, but Scotland gained the largest average grant offer per firm, of nearly £700,000. A location model is developed by this study, based on the firms' profit-maximising behaviour, including firm characteristics, the expected grant rate and industry, region and time fixed effects. For agglomeration effects it includes industry-specific, region-specific and region-industry variables.

An interesting aspect of this study is that it attempts to solve the endogeneity problem that is inherent in estimating the effect of discretionary grant schemes.[12] As Devereux *et al* note, not all plants will be offered financial assistance and "those plants offered grants may be the ones most likely to accept those offers and locate in a particular region" (p. 3), therefore making the grant term endogenous. In order to combat this problem the predicted grant rate offer is calculated for each firm in each region.[13] It was noted above that the results show that the effect of the grant largely disappears when agglomeration term are included. The first iteration of the model included dummy variables only, and showed that the firms were more likely to locate in a non-assisted region, but this is because nearly 50 per cent of the plants chose to enter in the non-Assisted Areas of the South of England. After including the predicted grant rate, it was found that a higher grant rate leads to a greater likelihood of a firm setting-up production in a region. However, when the agglomeration terms are introduced, the effect of the grant is extremely small.

---

[11] The regions are the South of England, the North of England, the Midlands, Wales and Scotland. These are split into assisted and non-assisted areas.

[12] Even where the grant rate is pre-determined the grant amount is endogenous, as it depends on the amount of investment being undertaken. In the case of discretionary assistance the grant rate may also be endogenous, although it is not the issue here.

[13] This depends on a range of variables (size, industry, region, ownership structure), and a Tobit estimation takes into account observations where the grant offer is zero.

Overall, and despite there being only a few studies for the UK, the presence of agglomeration economies appears to be the important factor in the attraction of FDI. In some studies the classical variables are significant, such as market growth and the state of the labour market, while the grants appear to have effects on early-stage FDI. However, as noted above, a difficulty in considering a single country is that the variation in the classical variables may be weak. Moreover, it could be that the primary effect of regional grants is to determine location across countries (e.g. between the UK and France) rather than across regions, especially as the large grants are determined in London. This is a consistent finding of the Government evaluations of regional grants, which finds that for the plants reporting that a grant changed its location decision, two-thirds say it was at an international level (Wren, 2005a). As an alternative, it may be better to look at the actual distribution of FDI between regions to see what this reveals, and attention now turns to this.

The UK Regional Distribution

The discussion begins by considering the temporal pattern of FDI, focusing on the post-War period and the recent boom period of FDI. Two main studies cover this earlier period: Dicken and Lloyd (1976) and Hill and Munday (1992), while for more recent period we analyse data supplied by *UK Trade and Investment*.

The Post-War Period

The early post-War period was dominated by FDI from the United States (Chapter 1). Indeed, three-quarters of foreign companies in the UK in this period originated from the United States, which means that it provides a good indication of the total flow of FDI. Dicken and Lloyd (1976) examine the distribution of FDI within the UK using data for US manufacturing companies over 1945-65. In this period, US FDI concentrated in the South East and East Anglia, which together had more than two-thirds of the UK manufacturing employment in foreign ownership. Using location quotients, each region's share of foreign employment is measured relative to its share of UK employment. The South East had a location quotient greater than unity, which was also the case for Scotland and Wales.

Focusing on US start-up companies, Dicken and Lloyd find that nearly half of the jobs created in manufacturing between 1945 and 1965 were in Scotland, with 15 per cent in the South East. For any other regions it was less than 10 per cent. They note that the timing of the new investments differs from region to region in the early post-War years. From 1945 to 1951, Scotland attracted the main share of employment by US firms, with two-thirds of the jobs going there. However, after 1951 the shares of employment became more evenly spread out, with Scotland and the South East both being the largest beneficiaries, each with around a quarter of total employment in US-owned firms. There are some problems with the data used by Dicken and Lloyd, as they include start-up plants only, and therefore exclude expansions by existing US plants, but it gives a very good indication of the flow of FDI in the early post-War period.

The story is picked-up by Hill and Munday (1992), who use regional data for various points of time between 1963 and 1990. Over this period the absolute level of manufacturing employment in foreign-owned plants was broadly constant, as closures and job losses from earlier FDI were matched by a similar level of jobs in new investment. However, within this, the regional distribution of the FDI changed substantially. The regional pattern of foreign-owned manufacturing employment in the UK for the period 1963 to 1997 is shown in Table 3.1.[14] It reveals a steady shift in FDI away from South-East England to other regions of the UK since the mid-1960s.[15] The share of foreign-owned manufacturing employment in the South East fell from 51 to 28 per cent over 1963-90, and by 1997 it stood at only 13 per cent. Other UK regions experienced an increase in FDI, including the peripheral regions, but also the South West, East Anglia, the East Midlands, and especially the West Midlands since 1981. In fact, if the share of each region's manufacturing employment in foreign ownership is examined for each region (not shown), then there was a distinct shift in the 1980s to the regions with Assisted Area status – the biggest increase was for the North East of England (whose share of manufacturing

Table 3.1 Foreign Manufacturing Employment in the UK, 1963-2003

	1963 %	1971 %	1981 %	1990 %	1997 %	2003 %
South East	51.4	41.1	36.2	28.4	12.6	17.7
South West	0.8	2.6	5.0	5.1	6.5	8.8
East Anglia	3.2	4.1	4.3	4.4	9.7	8.5
East Midlands	3.4	3.5	4.8	5.8	6.9	8.4
West Midlands	8.5	9.0	7.9	11.6	15.3	14.4
Yorks and Humber	3.8	3.3	5.8	7.2	6.1	9.8
North West	13.1	13.2	13.4	11.8	10.2	11.5
North East	1.6	3.3	4.9	6.4	5.3	6.7
Scotland	8.5	11.1	9.5	10.0	8.9	7.2
Wales	4.4	4.8	5.3	6.4	7.1	7.3
Northern Ireland*	1.3	4.0	2.9	2.9	2.7	-
United Kingdom	100.0	100.0	100.0	100.0	100.0	100.0

Source: Hill and Munday (1992) and *Business Monitor*, PA1002, HMSO, London.
Note: The regions are subject to boundary changes over time. *Data are not available for 2003.

---

[14] The data originates from the former Central Statistical Office and has been updated to 1997 after which time the series is no longer published.
[15] It accords with Vernon's theory that as the product becomes more standardised plants locate away from the core and locate in the periphery (see Chapter 2).

employment in foreign ownership increased from 12.5 per cent to 17.3 per cent over the decade) – but possibly reflecting the closure of UK-owned industry. A similar picture emerges when location quotients are calculated, in the same way as Dicken and Lloyd (1976). These show a shift in FDI to the regions with substantial Assisted Areas, with Wales, the North East and West Midlands having the largest location quotients in 1990. Interestingly, the West Midlands, which was designated for regional grants in 1984, had the largest share of foreign-owned manufacturing employment by 1997 (Figure 3.1).

There are some potential drawbacks to the analysis of Hill and Munday. The data concentrate on manufacturing, and therefore do not reflect the changes in FDI occurring in the expanding service sector. When data are used for all sectors there are three regions that stand out as prime attractors of inward investment relative to their size; the North of England, Wales and Scotland. Hill and Munday (1992) use a Relative Regional Performance (RRP) measure of inward investment. This is essentially a location quotient, and gives a region's share of FDI projects relative to its share of UK employment. An RRP above unity therefore implies that a region has been relatively successful in attracting FDI projects, and conversely. They find that the North, Wales and Scotland have the highest RRPs over 1982-92. This is also the case if FDI is measured by the number of new jobs. The lowest RRP is for the South-East region, whether measured in terms of projects or jobs.

The Recent 'Boom'

The Hill and Munday study takes us up to the year 1990, but Chapter 1 shows that there was a phenomenal growth in FDI over the 1990s. To examine the regional pattern of FDI in this period we use data similar to Hill and Munday, which were obtained from *Regional Trends* and from *UK Trade and Investment* (formerly the *Invest in Britain Bureau*). These data refer to the number of inward FDI projects in manufacturing and non-manufacturing, and give information on the number of jobs. *UK Trade and Investment* also collect data on the investment scales, but these data are much less comprehensive in their coverage. Before proceeding, a word of caution is required concerning use of the data. As Hill and Munday (1992) and Stone and Peck (1996) both point out, the data are based on projected jobs and include only those projects that are notified to *UK Trade and Investment*. Thus, the figures may give an under-estimate of FDI if the projected projects and jobs are not carried out (see Hood, 1991). However, it is essentially the same data that is used in the second part of this book, and it is believed to be reasonably comprehensive (see Data Appendix), although the jobs may not be realised, especially in larger projects (see Chapter 7). In examining the regional pattern of FDI over the recent period, we separately consider the numbers of projects and jobs.

Projects   The increase in world flow of foreign direct investment in the last twenty years has been matched by an increase in the number of FDI projects to the UK. Figure 3.1 shows a more than four-fold increase in the number of FDI projects by

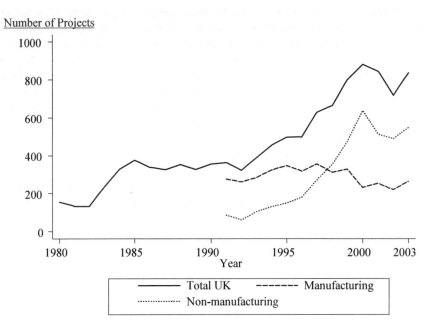

Figure 3.1 UK FDI Projects, 1980-2003

Source: Hill and Munday (1992), *Regional Trends*, Office for National Statistics and *UK Trade and Investment*, London.

investors between 1980 and the peak in 2000.[16] It also shows the subsequent fall-off in projects in 2001 and 2002, reflecting the global downturn in FDI, although the decrease in projects is not as dramatic as the fall in FDI inflows, as witnessed in Chapter 1. Further, in 2003 the project levels have returned to a level close to the peak of 2000.[17] Figure 3.1 gives a breakdown between the manufacturing and non-manufacturing sectors, although only from 1991 onwards. It shows that the non-manufacturing sector accounts for the growth in FDI projects over the 1990s, overtaking those in manufacturing from 1998 onwards. Over the period 1991-2003, the number of manufacturing projects fell slightly from 276 to 265, while those in non-manufacturing increased dramatically from 86 to 546 projects in the year 2003, reaching a peak of 637 projects in the year 2000.

The geographical distribution of FDI projects across the nine regions of Great Britain from 1980 to 2003 is shown in Table 3.2. Over this period, all regions had an increase in the number of FDI projects, but by far the largest increase was in the South East region, from 23 projects in 1980 to 373 in 2003, peaking at 472 projects in 2000. This growth occurred in the late 1990s, reversing the trend of the 1960s

---

[16] In 1980 there were 155 FDI projects into the UK compared to 800 projects in 2000.

[17] In 2003 the number of new projects into the UK was 835.

and 1970s, but reflecting an increase in non-manufacturing projects. This is clear as manufacturing employment in the South East fell over this period (Table 3.1). Referring back to Chapter 1, it means the mergers and acquisitions boom of the 1990s, as it affected the UK, was heavily concentrated in the non-manufacturing sector of the South East region. Other regions experienced an increase in the number of FDI projects over the period 1980-2000, albeit on a much smaller scale. These are the West Midlands (3 projects in 1980 to 103 in 2000), the North West (15 and 39 projects) and Scotland (31 and 74 projects).

Table 3.2 FDI Projects by GB Region, 1980-2003

	1980 No. (%)	1985 No. (%)	1990 No. (%)	1995 No. (%)	2000 No. (%)	2003 No. (%)
South East	23	84	7	89	472	373
	(17.0)	(23.8)	(2.1)	(18.8)	(55.0)	(46.1)
South West	6	15	3	17	39	42
	(4.4)	(4.3)	(0.9)	(3.6)	(4.5)	(5.2)
East Midlands	5	19	15	22	16	31
	(3.7)	(5.4)	(4.5)	(4.7)	(1.9)	(3.8)
West Midlands	3	63	73	77	103	64
	(2.2)	(17.8)	(22.0)	(16.3)	(12.0)	(7.9)
Yorks & Humber	17	16	26	44	36	26
	(12.6)	(4.5)	(7.8)	(9.3)	(4.2)	(3.2)
North West	15	28	53	37	39	64
	(11.1)	(7.9)	(16.0)	(7.8)	(4.5)	(7.9)
North East	19	26	44	62	35	63
	(14.1)	(7.4)	(13.3)	(13.1)	(4.1)	(7.8)
Scotland	31	57	41	72	74	74
	(23.0)	(16.1)	(12.3)	(15.2)	(8.6)	(9.2)
Wales	16	45	70	53	39	67
	(11.9)	(12.8)	(21.1)	(11.2)	(4.5)	(8.3)
Great Britain	135	353	332	473	858	809
	(100.0)	(100.0)	(100.0)	(100.0)	(100.0)	(100.0)

Sources: Hill and Munday (1992), *Regional Trends*, Office for National Statistics and *UK Trade and Investment*, London.
Note: Figures in parentheses are regional shares. Five projects not known in 2000 & 2003. East Anglia is included with the South East region.

Given the dramatic increase in the number of FDI projects to the UK, a better indicator of the distribution is given by the regional share of projects. Table 3.2 shows that half the regions experienced a decrease in their share of FDI projects over 1980-2003, despite having an increase in the absolute number of projects. Of the regions that increased their share, only the South East and the West Midlands saw a substantial increase in their share. In 2003 the South East attracted nearly 50 per cent of GB's foreign investment projects, up from 17 per cent in 1980, while the West Midlands managed an 8 per cent share in 2003 compared to 2 per cent in 1980. Although all regions of Great Britain have experienced an increase in the number of FDI projects, only the South East and the West Midlands managed to substantially increase their share of projects.

The distribution of FDI projects within Great Britain can also be examined by looking at the Relative Regional Performance (RRP) of FDI projects in Figure 3.2.[18] It is used by Hill and Munday (1992), and gives a region's share of FDI projects relative to its share of UK employment. The best-performing regions, which have consistently attracted more inward investment projects relative to their share of employment are Scotland, Wales, the North East and West Midlands. Yorkshire and Humberside and the North West have RRP's that indicate they attracted a share of FDI comparable to their share of employment, while the South East and South West have been under-achievers. Figure 3.2 shows the natural

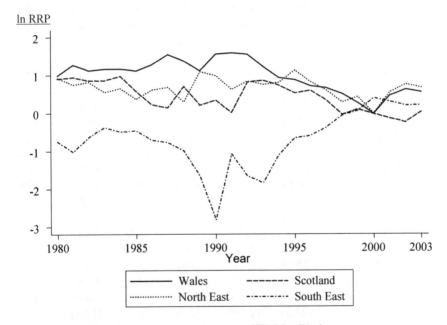

Figure 3.2 Relative Regional Performance of FDI by Projects

Sources: Hill and Munday (1992), *Regional Trends*, Office for National Statistics, and *UK Trade and Investment*, London.

Note: The figure uses the natural logarithm of the index of Relative Regional Performance.

---

[18] The natural logarithm is used, i.e. ln RRP, to aid graphical representation.

logarithm of RRP for four regions over 1980 to 2003. A value of ln RRP that is greater than zero implies a region has been relatively successful in attracting FDI projects, and conversely. Two points emerge from Figure 3.2. First, it highlights the consistently successful performance of the peripheral regions of the North East, Scotland and Wales. Second, it shows the strong performance of the South East over the latter half of the 1990s, particularly as it attracted service sector projects over the M&A boom.

Jobs A similar analysis can be undertaken for the number of jobs promised by the foreign investors, although these data are more volatile because of the influence that large projects can have. In considering the jobs, caution should be exercised, as in Chapter 7 it is shown that not all of the promised jobs are realised, especially in the larger projects, although there is no reason to believe that this differs across regions. Table 3.3 gives a breakdown of the annual number and share of promised jobs in the regions of Great Britain over 1980-2003.

Table 3.3 Jobs in FDI Projects by GB Region, 1980-2003

	1980 No. (%)	1985 No. (%)	1990 No. (%)	1995 No. (%)	2000 No. (%)	2003 No. (%)
South East	1,047 (6.6)	3,649 (14.7)	610 (2.4)	8,345 (19.2)	29,225 (44.1)	6,008 (24.8)
South West	1,010 (6.3)	1,281 (5.2)	580 (2.2)	1,718 (3.9)	4,109 (6.2)	2,162 (8.9)
East Midlands	277 (1.7)	778 (3.1)	820 (3.2)	1,437 (3.3)	2,020 (3.1)	1,982 (8.2)
West Midlands	1,042 (6.5)	5,197 (21.0)	4,410 (17.1)	7,074 (16.2)	4,867 (7.3)	2,391 (9.9)
Yorks and Humber	892 (5.6)	2,263 (9.1)	2,464 (9.5)	1,764 (4.0)	4,061 (6.1)	935 (3.8)
North West	914 (5.7)	2,271 (9.2)	1,810 (7.0)	3,622 (8.3)	3,187 (4.8)	3,162 (13.0)
North East	2,928 (18.4)	1,987 (8.0)	2,714 (10.5)	6,075 (14.0)	4,959 (7.5)	1,919 (7.9)
Scotland	4,482 (28.1)	4,971 (20.0)	9,799 (37.9)	9,092 (20.9)	9,314 (14.1)	1,632 (6.7)
Wales	3,338 (21.0)	2,416 (9.7)	2,636 (10.2)	4,429 (10.2)	4,520 (6.8)	4,064 (16.8)
Great Britain	15,930 (100.0)	24,813 (100.0)	25,843 (100.0)	43,556 (100.0)	66,262 (100.0)	24,255 (100.0)

Sources: Regional Trends, Office for National Statistics and UK Trade and Investment.
Note: Jobs are prospective and may not arrive. Figures in parentheses are regional shares.

Overall, similar conclusions can be drawn to that of the pattern of FDI projects. Every region experienced an increase in the annual number of jobs associated with FDI from 1980 until to the end of the boom in 2000, although the largest gainers are not just the South East and the West Midlands, but the North West of England and Scotland. The South East attracted nearly 30,000 jobs in the year 2000 compared to just over 1,000 jobs in 1980, while the respective figures for the West Midlands were 5,000 and 1,000 jobs, for the North West they were 3,000 jobs and 1,000 jobs, and for Scotland they were 9,000 and 4,500 jobs. The table shows a large fall-off in the number of jobs after the year 2000, and the failure of virtually all regions to make a recovery in terms of the number of proposed jobs.[19] This is contrary to the number of projects, and suggests that the regions are no longer able to attract the very large projects in employment terms.

The figures do not tell the whole story about how successful each region has been in attracting jobs over the period relative to other regions, as the total number of inward investment jobs in Great Britain increased from just under 16,000 jobs in 1980 to over 66,000 in the year 2000 (Table 3.3). In fact, when looking at the regional job shares it is only the South East and East Midlands that have managed a substantial increase in their share. The South East is the most successful region, as it increased its share of jobs to nearly 45 per cent in 2000 from only 6 per cent in 1980, although this fell back to 25 per cent in the year 2003. By comparison, the other regions that gained in share managed only small increases. The biggest losers were Scotland, Wales and the North-East region, which have all suffered large percentage falls in the share of new jobs. It partly reflects the reduction in their of new projects (Figure 3.2).

As with the number of projects, the Relative Regional Performance coefficients can be calculated for the project jobs. The best-performing regions, which have consistently attracted more projects relative to their share of employment, are Scotland, Wales and the North East (and the West Midlands also after 1984). Other regions have failed to attract comparable shares of jobs, although, as with the projects, the South East has managed an improvement in its RRP over the period. Figure 3.3 highlights the superior performance of Scotland, Wales and the North East in attracting jobs over the period 1980-2003 by plotting the natural logarithm of RRP. It shows that each region has a ln RRP above zero across the whole period, and so while they may each have experienced a sharp fall in the share of jobs over 1980-2003, each region has consistently attracted greater levels of FDI relative to its employment. Figure 3.3 also plots the ln RRP of the West Midlands and the South East. The rise in the ln RRP of the South East reflects the massive rise in FDI jobs in the region over the 1990s, and noted in the previous section. Finally, the performance of the West Midlands shows a marked improvement after 1984. This is the year in which it was designated for regional grants. Overall,

---

[19] The number of proposed jobs in Great Britain has fallen in each year since 2000 and thus failed to incorporate a recovery in the year 2003, contrary to UK inflows and new projects.

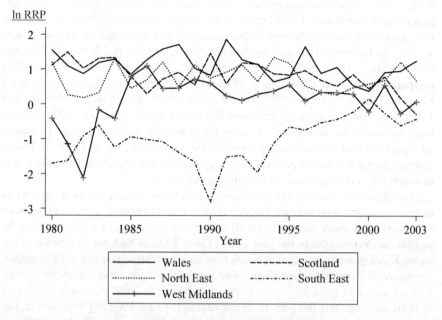

Figure 3.3 Relative Regional Performance of FDI by Jobs

Sources: Hill and Munday (1992), *Regional Trends*, Office for National Statistics, and *UK Trade and Investment*, London.

Note: The figure uses the natural logarithm of the index of Relative Regional Performance.

relatively more FDI jobs appear to go to the regions with substantial Assisted Areas, but Table 3.3 shows a deterioration in their position over time.

Overview

The South East of England is the region that attracts most FDI, both in terms of the number of projects and the number of jobs. It experienced a dramatic increase in these over the 1990s, being a major recipient of the boom in FDI due to mergers and acquisitions, which mainly affected the service sector. However, relative to its share of UK employment it has attracted the smallest number of projects and jobs, so that relative to their size the major beneficiaries of FDI are North-East England, Wales and Scotland. A major reason for this seems to be because these regions have substantial Assisted Areas, with regional grants available to attract projects. There was a substantial shift in FDI away from the South-East region in the 1960s, when regional policy was actively pursued, while the West Midlands has received a much greater share of FDI since being designated for grants in the mid-1980s. Further evidence is provided for this by the surveys of assisted establishments (see

Wren, 2005a). It suggests that policy, and in particular grants, can be a powerful instrument for attracting FDI to the regions. It runs counter to the evidence of the econometric studies, which stress the importance of agglomeration factors.

Regional Studies of FDI

Relative to their employment share, North-East England, Wales and Scotland have been the major beneficiaries of FDI in terms of both projects and jobs. This is also the case for the West Midlands more recently. Detailed studies of FDI have been carried for these regions, which potentially offer further insights on the locational determinants of foreign investment, so that these are now considered. The regional studies differ in several respects. Some make comparison across regions, some focus on a single region, while others examine investment arising from a particular country. These different kinds of study are now considered in turn. As we see, the studies also differ in the activities considered, so while they typically concentrate on the manufacturing sector, some examine particular activities within this sector.

Cross-Regional Studies

Stone and Peck (1996) This is perhaps the most detailed regional study of FDI. It examines the foreign-owned manufacturing sector (FOMS) in the peripheral parts of the UK, comprising the North of England, Wales, Scotland and Northern Ireland over the period 1978 to 1993. The data draw from a number of sources, including development agencies, industrial directories and local authorities. They are broader than just the number of projects and jobs, as not only do they include information on the number of foreign plants, but they distinguish between start-up, acquisition and expansion projects.[20] The experience of the regions differs sharply over 1978-93. Whereas the employment in FOMS relative to all manufacturing increased in the North and Wales, by 13 and 15 per cent respectively, in Scotland and Northern Ireland it fell by 20 and 7 per cent respectively. Stone and Peck (1996) carry out a 'components of change' analysis, the results of which are presented in Table 3.4. It shows that the experience of the North and Wales (N&W) differs from that of Scotland and Northern Ireland (S&NI). It shows that not only does N&W benefit from greater numbers of plant start-ups and acquisitions than S&NI, but they have a smaller number of plant closures.

---

[20] Stone and Peck find that the location quotient for the share of manufacturing employment in foreign ownership in each region relative to that for the UK is above unity in each case at 1993. This is similar to that exhibited in Figure 3.4. The location quotients for Scotland and Northern Ireland were unchanged over the period, while the North moved from a quotient below unity at the beginning of the period to above unity by 1993. The highest quotient was recorded for Wales.

Table 3.4 Components of Change of FOMS, 1978-1993

Components	North	Wales	Scotland	N. Ireland
New plants	30	30	18	14
Acquisitions	38	31	18	16
Closures	(21)	(11)	(39)	(49)

Source: Stone and Peck (1996).

Note: Figures show percentage change in employment of the foreign-owned manufacturing sector (FOMS) from each of three possible sources. Negatives in parentheses.

Stone and Peck examine the country of origin of the inward investors in order to analyse differences between the regions. The USA, Europe and Far East account for most FDI, with the North and Wales again sharing a similar pattern compared to Scotland and Northern Ireland. In the early 1970s the USA dominated FDI, with between 63 and 75 per cent of FOMS employment in the regions, but its influence diminished over the period 1978-93. In its place N&W gained much larger shares of employment from the Far East compared to S&NI, but smaller shares from the European Community.[21] It seems that investment arising from different sources not only is different in nature (i.e. start-ups or acquisitions), but it may have different trajectories in terms of plant survival. These issues are explored on the second part of the book. As a further point, the North was the only region that was successful in attracting FDI from European countries outside the European Community, with this mainly coming from nearby countries such as from Scandinavia.

Brand, Hill and Munday (2000) This study examines the West Midlands, Wales and Scotland, assessing the impact of FDI on the manufacturing sector in the years 1994 and 1995. Using data from the former Census of Production they focus on the five activities in the manufacturing sector that account for the largest output shares of these regions; these are: rubber and plastics; metals; engineering; electronics and electrical equipment; and transport equipment. The foreign-owned sector's share of regional output in these five activities combined is the largest in Scotland (52%), with Wales and the West Midlands having 39 and 23 per cent respectively. This points to a substantial concentration of FDI in certain activities, but which varies between regions. In Scotland it is electronics and electrical engineering (at 80% of output), but in the West Midlands it is transport equipment (60%), while in Wales there are three sectors: electronics (38%), metals (28%) and transport (21%). It is suggestive of agglomeration economies in the form of MAR externalities, with the firms locating near other plants in the same industry.

---

[21] For N&W compared with S&NI the respective FOMS employment shares for the Far East are 40 & 52 and 30 & 21, and for the European Community they are 23 & 21 and 37 & 33 (all figures are percentages).

Single Region Studies

Hill and Munday (1991) This study focuses on Wales. It shows that FDI has been increasing in scale since the 1970s, with foreign firms employing a total of 21,000 more people in 1990 compared with 1971. Employment is concentrated in a few plants. In the late 1980s eight companies accounted for 20 per cent of employees in the foreign-owned sector, whilst the top 25 companies accounted for 40 per cent. The main activities of these companies were electrical, electronic and automotive components. In terms of the country of origin, over 50 per cent of the investment is from the US, 25 per cent from the EU and 24 per cent from Japan. Again, this pattern changed from the early 1980s when the US had a 68 per cent share and the EU only 4 per cent, reflecting the increased investment from the EU and Japan during the 1980s. This trend is borne out by the *Invest in Britain Bureau* data, with the number of new projects increasing to nearly sixty in 1988 from sixteen in 1980, and the number of new jobs increasing from 1,000 to 6,000 over the same period.

Collis, Noon and Edwards (1998) These authors focus on the West Midlands; a region that experienced a sharp decline in economic activity in the late 1970s and early 1980s, but which has since been one the more successful regions in attracting FDI. Collis *et al* use data from a survey of 344 foreign-owned companies in 1992, of which 112 entered through acquisition. The main reasons given by the firms for acquiring companies in the UK were the potential for increased market share and increased sales. They examine the investment type, its concentration within various activities and the country of origin, but a similar pattern emerges as elsewhere. In the early 1980s, North America had the largest proportion of foreign-owned firms in the region (42%), followed by the EU (34%) and the Far East (12%). By the late 1980s, US investment had fallen to 37 per cent, and the EU was marginally the dominant investor, with a 39 per cent share. There was also FDI from elsewhere in Europe, accounting for 14 per cent of foreign-owned plants in the late 1980s. The main sectors for FDI are distribution, metal goods, engineering and vehicles.[22]

By Country of Origin

Kirchner (2000) Kirchner undertakes a study of German-owned manufacturing in the North East of England. Germany is the largest European investor in the UK, and the second largest of all countries after the USA. According to Kirchner, this is the first detailed analysis of FDI into a UK region by a European country. Using data supplied by the *Northern Development Company*, Kirchner finds 29 German manufacturing companies in the region at 1999, employing around 6,000 people. The vehicle-parts sector accounts for 2,000 of these, and the other two important activities were chemicals, with 1,200 employees, and mechanical engineering, with

---

[22] Distribution was mainly arose from Germany, and metal goods, engineering and vehicle activities originated mainly from the US and Japan.

1,050 people. The majority of this FDI was through acquisition. Kirchner surveys the companies, and finds that market penetration is the main reason for FDI in the region. The presence of a skilled workforce, infrastructure levels, a good customer and supplier bases, cheap industrial sites and financial incentives are also given as reasons. According to Kirchner these reflect market orientation, geographical and cost-related factors, but there is no mention of agglomeration factors.

Hood and Taggart (1997) This is another study of German FDI, but for the UK. It identifies 409 German-owned manufacturing companies in the UK at 1994.[23] It again uses a survey approach, which involved sending a questionnaire to all 409 companies, from which 102 useable responses were obtained. Fifty per cent of the firms were in the mechanical engineering, chemicals or vehicle-related sectors, with employment in the generally between 11 and 500 persons per plant. However, a third of plants were small, with less than 50 employees. Eighty per cent of the firms chose the UK to locate because of the presence of a large base of existing customers in the country. Labour costs and the size of the UK market also figured in the companies' location decisions.

Overview

The regional studies focus on the areas that have been relatively successful in attracting FDI over the past twenty years, especially in manufacturing. Although US investment is the main source of FDI up to the 1980s, the studies show the growing importance of FDI from elsewhere, especially the European Union and the Far East. However, it has affected regions differently, such that employment in foreign-owned manufacturing has increased in the North and in Wales, but actually fallen in Scotland and Northern Ireland. In the case of Scotland, our review of historical trends in Chapter 1 shows that this country was a major recipient of FDI in the immediate post-war period, so it is likely to have an older stock of plants. The studies also point to the concentration of this investment in a relatively small number of activities, like chemicals, electronics and transport equipment. Again, the pattern varies between regions, so in Scotland it is electronics and electrical engineering and in the West Midlands it is transport equipment, but in Wales it is more broadly based. These could point to agglomeration economies, or may be the location of major suppliers or buyers, or reflect the existing structure in the case of acquisitions, but this issue is unexplored, both in these studies and elsewhere.

---

[23] These are all known German companies in the UK. The German Chamber of Industry and Commerce and the Industrial & Development Agency were used as sources.

Conclusions

This chapter is concerned with the location decisions of multinational enterprises regarding foreign direct investment, focusing on the distribution of this investment at the UK regional level. Traditionally, the decision on where a foreign investor decides to locate was thought to be determined by factors such as market size and labour costs; known as the classical variables. More recently, attention has turned to agglomeration economies, implying that firms locate to take advantage of these external effects. However, there is uncertainty on the relative importance of these factors. Econometrics-based studies find evidence for the classical factors, such as market size and labour market conditions, which directly affect the firm's sales and costs, but these are insignificant when agglomeration factors are included. All the same, there are many reasons to be cautious about this finding.

First, there is the problem of distinguishing empirically between the classical and agglomeration factors. Agglomeration economies are often measured by the infrastructure of an area, but this directly affects the firm's costs and is a classical factor. Agglomeration economies are also measured by the existing FDI in an area, but the importance of this could just reflect existing supplier or buyer relationships, which strictly are not an agglomeration economy.[24] Second, it may be that the econometric studies are biased against the classical explanation, as the studies tend to be for a single country, where there is relatively little variation in these classical variables. A good example are the grants for FDI in the UK Assisted Areas, which are determined centrally for large projects, and are used to compete internationally for projects. The actual location pattern suggests the regions where the grants are applied tend to do better at attracting FDI, particularly in manufacturing where the grants are taken up. Indeed, the Assisted Area regions did much better after 1960 when the grants commenced, and the West Midlands did well after 1984 when it was designated for the grants. A third reason to be sceptical about the findings of the econometric studies is that a sizeable proportion of FDI is by acquisition, which is likely to reflect the industrial structure of an area, e.g. vehicle manufacture in the West Midlands, and is not an agglomeration economy. Finally, existing FDI may just signal to potential investors that an area is a good place to 'do business', given that information is a major barrier to entry for FDI under the market-imperfection motivation for FDI discussed in Chapter 2.

Agglomeration economies aside, most inward FDI in the UK continues to go to the prosperous South-East region, although relative to their size, the North, Wales, Scotland and the West Midlands have all been major recipients of FDI projects and jobs. Studies of these regions find that the FDI is highly concentrated in a number of ways. Unlike the South East, it is mainly in the manufacturing sector, although it originates from the US, Western Europe or Far East, and the jobs are in a small number of plants. However, there are important differences in the way the regions attract FDI. In Scotland it is concentrated in electronics and electrical engineering,

---

[24] McCann and Sheppard (2003) argue that these should involve transient relationships.

and in the West Midlands it is in transport equipment. In Wales, FDI is much more broadly based across activities, and this region is more similar to northern England in the pattern of FDI compared to either Scotland or Northern Ireland. This may reflect the existing industrial structure, with a sizeable proportion of FDI through the acquisition of existing plants. Whatever the reason, it is clear that while there are similarities in the regional distribution of FDI there are also differences. In the next chapter we look at the evidence on the beneficial effects of FDI for regional development and the potential costs of this investment.

Chapter 4

Regional Development

The preceding chapter showed that the peripheral parts of the UK have received a disproportionate amount of foreign direct investment relative to their size. Each of these areas has inward investment agencies, at national, regional and sub-regional levels, which like other regions, seek actively to attract FDI, but why should this be so? Of course, a simple answer to this question is that these investments bring jobs to areas with relative high unemployment, and indeed these regions are designated for regional grants for this purpose. Multinational enterprises are also believed to bring many other benefits to these areas that are advantageous to both regional and national economies. These include firm-specific assets, such as superior production techniques and knowledge, which are believed to 'spillover' to domestic firms in the local economy. However, despite this, FDI is believed by some authors to have harmful effects on the economies of these regions. These include the possibly low-quality jobs associated with FDI, and the 'footloose' nature of these plants, which destabilises the economies of these areas. The purpose of this chapter is to review the fast-accumulating evidence on the benefits and the costs that FDI is believed to provide to the host economy and specifically for regional development.

As we see, major potential benefits of FDI are the increase in jobs and income, with various multiplier effects, which can boost the regional economy. However, perhaps perversely, both the theoretical and empirical literatures on FDI focus on the potential 'spillover' effect of this investment. As possible explanations for this, it could be that FDI simply displaces domestic activity, so that when measured in net terms there are no new jobs to the regional or national economy. In this case, and given its 'footloose' nature, the potential efficiency effects of this investment on the domestic economy may be its major benefit. However, any consideration of the case for attracting FDI must weigh this potential benefit against the costs, both to the agencies and more broadly to the economy, so that a net calculation must be made in considering its contribution to regional development.

The purpose of this chapter is to review and critically appraise the voluminous evidence on the benefits and costs of FDI, focusing on the regional economy. The discussion has three parts. It begins with a review of the theoretical literature on 'spillovers', and then secondly it assesses the empirical evidence for these effects. Finally, it considers the potential costs of FDI. As we see, the empirical studies generally seek to establish an increase in productivity in firms or sectors where the multinationals are prevalent, which is taken to imply the existence of 'spillovers'. This chimes well with the productivity agenda of UK Central Government (HM Treasury, 2000). However, arguments for the costs of FDI generally ignore these 'spillovers', and concentrate on the loss of control of assets, the displacement of employment from the domestic sector and the high closure rates of these plants. Nevertheless, despite all this, policymakers seek to attract FDI, which is perceived to be important for regional development. The chapter closes by considering the role of the agencies, serving as an introduction to the second part of the book.

The Benefits of FDI to the Host Economy

According to Hanson (2001), when compared with a domestic firm, the typical view of a multinational enterprise (MNE) is that it is larger, more capital intensive, has more skilled labour, higher technological knowledge and a greater productivity level. Given this, it is not surprising these investments are highly prized, and that the economic development agencies spend substantial sums in attracting them. The benefits are not only the direct investment, employment and output of these plants, with resulting income flows, but MNEs are thought to have other benefits that are transferred to indigenous plants, known as 'spillovers'. The spillovers are of two types; either a productivity or a market-access spillover (Markusen, 1998). The former is when a MNE enters a local economy and increases the productivity of domestic firms. A market-access spillover is when domestic firms are able to gain knowledge about markets that the MNE is active in, such as distribution networks or export markets, and to use this information to their own advantage. These are external effects, although they are sometimes referred to as externalities.[1]

These spillovers may have positive effects on the host economy, which are not taken into consideration by the MNE when it makes its investment decision. The academic research has tended to focus on these to the exclusion of the direct effects. As we indicated, a possible reason for this is that if the inward investment serves only to displace activity that would otherwise occur, then any net impact on the host economy will have to be measured in terms of its efficiency effect. On this view, and given the vast literature on the subject (Gorg and Greenaway, 2004), then this section focuses on the spillover effects. It deals with the different types of spillover that arise from MNE activity in the domestic economy, beginning with an overview of the productivity and market-access spillovers. Underlying these are a number of transmission mechanisms in the form of competition, knowledge and technology effects, and these are subsequently discussed. Finally, the likelihood of a spillover occurring is examined in terms of the receptiveness of domestic firms.

---

[1] Spillovers could be externalities, but can arise through other mechanisms, so that this is an incorrect use of the term. This is because spillovers are either pecuniary or technological in nature, where only the latter is an externality. The former operates through markets (e.g. the hiring of labour from a domestic plant by a foreign plant or a supply linkage), but the latter is non-marketed (e.g. an information flow). These are each examples of an external effect, but the nature of these depends on the precise transmission mechanism.

Productivity and Market-Access Spillovers

Blomstrom and Kokko (1998) identify four transmission mechanisms underlying a spillover: purchase and supply linkages between MNEs and domestic firms; the movement of labour between MNEs and indigenous plants; imitation of MNE-specific technology by domestic firms; and competition effects that force domestic firms to become more efficient. The first two of these enable both productivity and market-access spillovers to occur, while the latter two are solely concerned with the productivity benefits of FDI. They are now considered.

Linkages, whether they are backward towards suppliers or forward towards customers, enable domestic firms to learn directly from a MNE that is present in the local economy (Markusen, 1995). First introduced by Hirschman (1958), a forward linkage is where a firm uses another firm's output for its inputs, while the opposite is the case for a backward linkage. The movement of labour from a MNE to a domestic firm may enable the latter to benefit from the training and knowledge that the employee would have acquired from their time spent at the MNE (Gorg and Strobl, 2001). Both of these mechanisms allow productivity and market-access spillovers to take place. For example, when there are linkages between a MNE and a domestic firm, such as a backward linkage, then the domestic firm has to meet the production process and technological requirements of the MNE. It means it is acquainted with the superior knowledge of the MNE, which, it is argued, increases its capabilities and productivity. Further, this knowledge may include information on the distribution networks and export markets of the MNE, so the spillovers may take the form of greater market access (Blomstrom and Kokko, 1998).

Similar productivity and market-access spillovers are argued to occur through the movement of labour between local producers and MNEs. When a high-skilled employee from a MNE moves to a domestic firm, a level of awareness about the knowledge that the MNE possesses is transferred. This knowledge may consist of information about the technology, production process or distribution network of the MNE, so that productivity and market-access spillovers arise (Fosfuri *et al*, 2001). The other spillover mechanisms in the form of technology and competition are concerned solely with the productivity benefits for domestic firms. The first of these is an imitation of technology, or what is often called a 'demonstration effect', whereby the domestic firm becomes more efficient. On the second, the arrival of an MNE can induce productivity spillovers, even though there is no formal linkage, employee transfer or imitation of technology, as it increases competition. On this argument, the least efficient firm is pushed out of the industry, so that the domestic firms have an incentive to use their existing capabilities more efficiently or search for more efficient production techniques (Markusen and Venables, 1999).

Of course, some of these arguments do not rely on the 'foreignness' of the entrant firm, and could equally apply to new domestic firms setting-up in an area. However, what they do rely on is that the entrant is in some way superior to the incumbent firms, and in the case of FDI this tends to taken as a stylised fact.[2] The underlying mechanisms whereby the productivity and market-access spillovers can transmit to the host economy are now considered in detail. Since competition and linkage effects are closely related, then these are often considered together.

Competition and Linkage Effects

Markusen and Venables (1999) examine the competition and linkage effects that FDI can have on local producers in the host economy. In their model there are two industries, one producing an intermediate good and the other a final good. They find that there are two effects that the FDI has on the host economy, which are akin to substitution and output effects. The first is a 'competition effect', by which the MNE displaces domestic producers in the final-goods industry. This reduces the domestic firm's sales and causes some firms to exit the industry.[3] The second is a 'linkage effect', which is beneficial to domestic firms producing the intermediate good. The backward linkage occurs because the MNE creates extra demand for the intermediate goods. It may lead to a forward linkage effect if the intermediary-goods producers achieve economies of scale, which lowers their price, leading to the attraction of new entrants into the final-goods sector.

The size of the effects depends upon whether the MNE increases production in the final-goods sector or if it entirely replaces the domestic production, in which case there will be no backward linkage to the intermediary producers. Further, if the multinational is a less-intensive user of inputs compared to the local firms that it displaces, there could even be a reduction in the output of domestic intermediary-goods producers. Even if there is no displacement, the MNE may source its inputs from elsewhere so that there are no linkage effects. A further possibility is that the multinational enterprise displaces foreign firms in the home economy who were exporting to the host country. As long as the MNE uses some of the intermediary-goods producers then its arrival will increase the output of domestic intermediary producers, which in turn will increase other local firms in the final-goods industry via the linkage effects. All of this points to the uncertain and highly complicated effect that FDI can exert on the output of domestic producers through competition and linkage effects. It is compounded by further backward and forward linkages that may arise between the final and intermediate-goods industries, and the process can be self-reinforcing (Markusen and Venables, 1999).

---

[2] Given that there are barriers to entry into a foreign market, then one view is that, whatever advantages a MNE possesses and for whatever reason it undertakes FDI, it must have a productivity advantage over firms in the host economy (Driffield, 2001). This stylised fact is a simplification, and other views are taken (Fosfuri and Motta, 1999), which acknowledge the other motives for FDI discussed in Chapter 2.

[3] Irrespective of spillovers, higher exit rates will result in an improvement in the average productivity of the industry (the 'batting-average' effect), and clearly this is a problem that confronts empirical work.

Knowledge-Capital Effects

According to Markusen (1995), the spillover effects are relatively more important in industries where there is a prevalence of intangible, firm-specific assets, known as knowledge capital. These include production or process techniques, reputations and trademarks. Much like the internalisation theory of FDI outlined in Chapter 2, Markusen argues that knowledge can cause a MNE to undertake FDI, so that where knowledge capital is important the market structure will be characterised by large foreign-owned MNE plants, which have a substantial productivity advantage over domestic firms. This is because knowledge capital is transferable across space, and can be supplied to other production facilities within the firm at little cost. It gives a multi-plant firm a cost advantage over smaller single-plant firms, as it only has to make a single investment in knowledge capital between the plants, whereas single-plant firms each have to undertake the investment independently of each other. It arises from the jointness of supply characteristic of information, and it differs from physical capital, which is a private good, and where the economies of scale result in geographical co-location to obtain the cost-efficiency gains. The spillover is that knowledge capital transfers to the domestic sector.

Markusen (1998) finds MNEs are prevalent in industries where knowledge capital is important. In much the same way as the internalisation theory of FDI, knowledge capital gives strong incentives to internalise this advantage and engage in FDI, rather than by licensing it to other firms. An example of where knowledge capital is important is industries characterised by high technology. The spillovers arising from technological effects are now discussed.

Technological Effects

The ways in which technology is transferred from MNEs to the host economy are considered by Blomstrom and Kokko (1998) and Driffield (2001). These spillovers are either direct or indirect. A direct transfer of technology occurs when a MNE sets up production in the host country and licenses the technology to a host-country firm, or when the MNE is engaged with local firms as suppliers. One possibility is that the MNE passes on its technological knowledge to upgrade the capabilities of a host-country firm, so that it can meet its requirements. An indirect technological transfer occurs when the technology is learnt or copied by competitors in the same industry (horizontal spillovers), or when the MNE transfers technology to the firms supplying inputs or distributing its products (vertical spillovers). Alternatively, as mentioned above, the MNE may lead firms to search for new technologies in order to compete (Blomstrom, 1986), and thereby in increase their productivity.

Kokko (1996) argues that one of the most likely ways for the domestic firm to gain the technology of an MNE is by hiring the former employees the MNE. These may have the specialised skills necessary for the understanding of a technological process. For this reason, MNEs may development and operate these technologies in teams, in order to protect their specific advantage from poaching. Blomstrom and Kokko (1998) suggest that FDI tends to take place in industries characterised by scale economies, high-capital requirements, advertising and technology. These industries have high barriers to entry and levels of concentration, but a low level of competition. They suggest MNEs find it easier to enter these industries, and hence they bring increased competition and ultimately higher productivity.

Finally, spillovers are a source of agglomeration economy (McCann, 2001), encouraging other firms to set-up in a locality, and giving rise to clusters of firms.[4] This can magnify the spillover, compounding the benefit to the host economy, and leading to a process of cumulative causation. Given that a distinguishing feature of MNEs is their technological capability, the presence of MNEs can attract similar firms, and according to Driffield and Munday (2000) create a spatial concentration of technologically-advanced industries. It leads to the notion of a 'growth pole'.

Absorptive Capacity

Given that the MNE has a productivity advantage over firms in the host-economy, then according to Findlay (1978) a 'catching-up' of productivity by the local firms ensues. However, there is disagreement on the conditions under which this occurs. Findlay defines relative backwardness as the 'distance' in technological ability between the MNE and the host economy. The greater this is, the stronger will be the pressure for technological change, so that the spillovers are transferred quickly. However, Glass and Saggi (1998) point out that the extent to which productivity is transferred depends on the 'absorptive capacity' of the host economy. The greater is this gap, implying lower levels of human capital and infrastructure, the less likely is the economy to absorb large productivity spillovers. This points to a non-linear effect, with some optimal 'distance' between the MNE and the economy. It suggests that developed countries will tend to locate their FDI in other developed countries, for which ample evidence was found in Chapter 3.

A similar point is made by Markusen (1995, 1998), who believes that in order for FDI to take place the home and prospective host economies should be similar in terms of size, per capita income and relative factor endowments. This is because multinationals exploit their specific advantages in countries where the conditions are similar to the home country. For example, if the prospective host economy is relatively large, has lower factor costs and higher productivity then the MNE may find it hard to compete against the firms in this country. Conversely, if the host economy is relatively small then there is little incentive for the MNE to incur the costs of setting up abroad as the country will not provide sufficiently large profits. Of course, an issue is whether it is the regional or national economy that is relevant to the MNE, or indeed whether these relevant at all given that MNEs operate in global markets. In truth, this discussion tells us about the generation and location of FDI, but little about the likelihood of spillovers. For this, we now turn attention to the substantial recent and substantial empirical literature on spillovers.

---

[4] See Chapter 3 for a discussion of agglomeration economies.

Empirical Evidence on Spillovers

There has been an upsurge of research investigating the spillover effects of FDI on domestic firms (Proenca *et al*, 2001). By and large, the econometric studies seek to determine evidence for an increase in either labour productivity or output growth when foreign firms enter an industry.[5] These studies are carried out for different kinds of country using different kinds of dataset. It includes developing countries, like Mexico, Morocco and Venezuela, and developed countries such as the UK. A comprehensive review of these studies is given in Gorg and Greenaway (2004), which also considers the more recent evidence for transition countries. Geography is an important aspect to these studies, since many of the transmission mechanisms (i.e. linkages, labour movement, imitation and competition effects) are expected to operate over relatively short distances, which given data limitations means that the spillovers tend to measured at the regional level. Prior to the mid-1990s the studies used cross-sectional data, but since then most researchers use panel data. This is potentially more informative, and it has led to differences in the results obtained. The two kinds of study using the different kinds of data are now briefly reviewed, after which possible reasons for the differing results are considered.

Cross-Sectional Studies

The empirical literature on spillovers commenced with Caves (1974b), who looked at the impact of MNEs on the Canadian and Australian manufacturing economies. He tested the hypothesis that as the proportion of foreign firms in an industry gets larger, the higher is the likelihood of a transfer of technology to domestic firms. He found that as the share of foreign employment in an industry increases, the level of disparity between the productivity of foreign and domestic firms reduces, implying the presence of positive spillovers being generated by the foreign sector. Using the same model, Globerman (1979) looked at manufacturing industries in Canada and also found that spillovers occur when the presence of foreign firms in an industry increases. Since this time, the studies using cross-section data have mainly been carried out for less-developed countries.

Mexico, which also borders the US, has been a focus of a number of studies. Both Blomstrom and Persson (1983) and Blomstrom and Wolff (1989) find higher productivity rates in industries where either employment in foreign-owned firms or the number of foreign-owned firms in an industry is relatively high. However, Blomstrom (1986) fails to find evidence that the presence of foreign firms raises the rate of technological transfer to the domestic sector. Instead, it is the level of competition in an industry, as measured by the Herfindahl index that has a positive effect on the productivity of domestic firms, implying that competitive forces are more important than technological spillovers. Kokko (1994) uses data for Mexico, and finds evidence that foreign firms improve the productivity of domestic firms.

---

[5] This review focuses on the econometric studies. An alternative is the case-study approach.

Contrary to Findlay, this study finds that spillovers are smaller in industries where the 'technology gap' is large, but also where there is a large share of foreign firms. As an explanation, Kokko argues that for the industries characterised by product differentiation and economies of scale, the foreign firms tend to produce in what are called 'enclaves', which are separate from the rest of the industry.[6] Finally, for the UK, Driffield (2001) finds positive intra-industry spillover effects.

Panel Studies

The first study to utilise panel data in the empirical investigation of spillovers was Haddad and Harrison (1993), and since then most studies have used kind of data. The potential advantage of panel data is that is allows unobserved or unmeasured effects to be controlled for. Haddad and Harrison examine spillovers for domestic Moroccan firms, and find that the disparity in productivity levels is lower for those industries where there are a greater number of foreign firms. They condition on the size of the 'technology gap' to examine technological spillovers, but find this is insignificant. Aitken and Harrison (1999) apply a panel-data analysis to Venezuela, and find positive spillovers from MNEs to domestic firms in the same region, but negative spillovers to firms in the same sector but any region, i.e. increased foreign presence in an industry reduces the productivity of other producers.

These studies focus on developing countries, but recently there are studies of spillovers resulting from FDI in the UK economy. Barrell and Pain (1997) find that a 1 per cent increase in the stock of FDI in manufacturing raises technical progress in this sector by 0.26 per cent, and overall that it increased domestic productivity by about 1 per cent per annum between 1981 and 1995. However, using the panel data to control for industry-specific effects, Girma *et al* (2001) find no evidence of spillovers at the UK aggregate level. Spillovers do occur at a smaller geographical scale, but only for domestic firms in the same sector and region as the investor. It is especially the case for sectors with a low 'technology gap' between foreign and host firms and with a high level of competition. For firms in the same sector but located in different regions the spillovers are much reduced. Thus, spillovers occur in sectors with low 'technology gaps' and are geographically confined. A similar result is found for the UK by Liu *et al* (2000). Finally, Driffield *et al* (2004) examine productivity spillovers from forward-linkage effects for 20 manufacturing sectors. They use input-output tables for the UK to construct the linkage variables, and while there is some evidence of linkage effects, it is regarded as tentative.

These studies operate at the aggregate industry level, but recent UK studies make use of Annual Census of Production Respondents Database (ARD).[7] This is

---

[6] Kokko (1996) defines an 'enclave' as an isolated sub-section of industry where the level of technology is different and the product is differentiated from the rest of the industry.

[7] For more information concerning the ARD see Griffith (1999) and Oulton (1997). Since 1998 the Census of Production was superseded by the Annual Business Inquiry, which is not strictly a census, as it samples a proportion of smaller firms, focusing on manufacturing.

an establishment-level panel database. There are three studies of interest, but which obtain very different results, perhaps indicating the sensitivity of the results to the choice of methodology.[8] In the first of these, Harris and Robinson (2002a) test for intra-industry, inter-industry and agglomeration spillovers in manufacturing over 1974 to 1995. The results are mixed, as in one-third of industries there is no evidence of intra-industry effects, whereas in the remaining industries there are spillovers, but both positive and negative in nature. For inter-industry spillovers the effects were just as likely to be positive as negative, while in over two-thirds of the industries examined there was no evidence of spillovers due to agglomeration effects, although for the remaining industries the effects could again be positive or negative. Haskel *et al* (2002) examine spillovers in manufacturing industries over 1973-1992 and generally find small, positive effects. A 10 per cent increase in the foreign presence in an industry leads to an increase in domestic productivity of about 0.5 per cent. Finally, Driffield and Girma (2003) focus on the electronics sector, a major source of FDI, and investigate wage effects. They find that wage spillovers are confined to the region where FDI occurs, but that skilled workers are the main beneficiaries at both the intra- and inter-industry level. Wage effects for unskilled workers are more pronounced where grants for FDI are available.

The overall conclusion from these studies is that positive spillovers exist, but the effects are subtle and complex, possibly occurring within the same industry and region, but only where there is a low 'technology gap'. However, a number of studies find evidence of negative spillovers, which are relatively little discussed in the literature. These seem to have a weaker foundation, but a possibility is that the foreign-owned firms harm the productivity of domestic firms by poaching labour. They may also displace output, pushing up the costs of domestic firms by making them operate inefficiently (see Aitken and Harrison, 1999).

Panel versus Cross-Sectional Studies

Panel data sets involve observations on the firms over time, as well as on a cross-sectional basis. This allows the researcher to control for a number of variables that cannot otherwise be allowed for. For example, differences in managerial expertise may play an important role in whether spillovers are transferred to domestic firms or not, but if they cannot be reliably measured then they cannot be accounted for in the studies using cross-sectional data alone. Using fixed-effects or random-effects models with panel data it is possible to control for these unobserved influences that vary between firms, and which may also vary over time as well.[9]

---

[8] Differences in methodology include weighting the data to take account of non-selected observations, the length of lag to take account of spillovers and the level of analysis at either the plant or establishment level. For a discussion of how different methods of analysing the ARD data can bring about different results, see Harris and Robinson (2002b).

[9] Hsiao (2003) classifies the variables as: individual time-invariant (same for each firm across time but varying across firms); period individual-invariant (same for all firms at any

The above review of studies using panel and cross-sectional data reveals that these produce different results. Cross-sectional studies find evidence of positive spillovers, but panel-data studies find that the positive spillovers are much more limited in scope, and can be negative. The issue is considered by Gorg and Strobl (2001). They argue that it is because the cross-sectional studies do not pick up the time-invariant effects across firms (e.g. such as managerial expertise), but which are correlated with the foreign-presence (Aitken and Harrison, 1999), so that there is an issue of attribution.[10] Panel data studies can take account of this unobserved heterogeneity, by including fixed or random effects, and according to Castellani and Zanfei (2002) the more believable conclusion to be drawn from the literature is that there is inconclusive evidence on whether FDI leads to spillovers in domestic firms. This finds support from Proenca *et al* (2001), Gorg and Strobl (2001) and Gorg and Greenaway (2004), so that at best the evidence is mixed.

Overall, the conclusion is that positive spillovers exist, but they are spatially confined and in industries with a small 'technology gap' between the foreign and domestic firms. Further, FDI can have negligible or even negative spillover effects on the host-economies. As a corollary, more recent studies are concerned with bi-directional spillovers, going both from and to domestic firms (Kokko, 1996). As a rationale for these 'reverse spillovers' it is argued that the MNEs locate to take advantage of the superior technologies of host firms, i.e. 'technology sourcing' (Fosfuri and Motta, 1999). This is an about-turn from the traditional view of FDI, which stresses the 'ownership' advantages, and it is perhaps recognition of the weak evidence found for the positive spillovers. Early evidence, such as Liu *et al* (2000), suggests that these reverse spillovers are an important factor, with Driffield and Love (2003) finding evidence for these in the case of the UK.

Implications for Regional Development

The discussion so far has been concerned with the benefits that FDI can bring to an economy through its spillover effects on domestic firms, reflecting the focus of the economic literature. The evidence for these efficiency effects is inconclusive, but fortunately, at the regional level, the spillovers are not the only potential benefit of FDI for regional development. This is because FDI has many direct effects for the regional economy. Not only does it bring direct employment benefits to a region, but it can help diversify and support these economies, making them less prone to adverse economic shocks. In addition it may have indirect pecuniary external effects through supply and demand linkages with other firms and institutions.[11] As

---

given point in time but varying across years); and individual time-varying (vary across firms at any given point in time as well as varying through time).

[10] It must imply that the FDI locates in the activities where there are domestic firms with higher productivities, so that these higher productivities are wrongly attributed to the FDI.

[11] These are different to spillovers, which are technological external effects or externalities.

Markusen and Venables (1999) note, other than as a replacement for trade, little is known about the role played by FDI in the wider economy. The purpose of this section is to attempt to get a broader appreciation of the role of this investment for regional development, again by reviewing the available evidence.

Foreign direct investment can have many potential direct and indirect benefits for a region, but it is clear that it can also have costs. For example, competition can reduce the number of local producers in the region, possible resulting in an overall reduction of regional employment where the MNE has greater scale and economies of scale (Driffield and Munday, 1998). Competition may be played-out in output or input markets, with, for example, higher wages bidding away employees from domestic producers and displacing activity in this way (see Driffield, 1999). While increased competition can result in lower prices, which is beneficial to consumers, it may be of scant value to the regional economy if the output is exported from the region and consumed elsewhere. Nevertheless, in an export-base model, increased exports can boost regional growth (see Armstrong and Taylor, 2000).

Of course, one interpretation of the displacement issue is that it is simply the working of the market economy, and that this 'creative destruction' is beneficial to the regional economy, as it modernises its productive capacity and makes it more efficient.[12] However, there are several reasons to be sceptical of this argument in the case of a regional economy. First, foreign-owned firms in the regions are well-known to be 'footloose', experiencing high closure rates (see Fothergill and Guy, 1990, for detailed case-studies). Indeed, Gorg and Strobl (2003) find that foreign-owned plants in Eire have closure rates that are up to 40 per cent higher than their domestic counterparts. Aside from the adjustments costs this upheaval imposes on individuals, it may well be that regional development is a non-ergodic process (see Chapter 2). It means that once displaced the domestic producers do not return once the foreign-owned entrants have exited. Another reason to be wary of the 'creative destruction' argument is that the high closure rate of foreign-owned plants in the regions suggests that they are inferior in some way, so that they do not modernise the productive stock. A longstanding criticism of FDI in the regions is that they offer relatively low-skill, low-wage jobs (Hudson, 1998).[13] Of course, not all the closed plants are failures, as many are internationally mobile, but this reinforces the argument, as they tend to move to lower labour-cost areas. Finally, as we have seen, FDI tends to agglomerate in certain activities, so that rather than diversifying regions it may make them vulnerable to adverse industry-level shocks.

---

[12] The term 'creative destruction' was coined by Schumpeter (see Wren, 2004) and has been popularised by the work of Davis *et al* (1996). It sees entry and exit as an essential part of economic growth, fostering enhanced productivity.

[13] Not only does it apply to the foreign-owned manufacturing 'branch plants', but a similar argument is extended to the more recent call-centres in the service sector. It may be that FDI in the regions is of a different quality to that in the core, suggesting that there may be different locational determinants. Indeed, the studies reviewed in Chapter 3 suggest that the unemployment rate is an important location factor, which is higher in the regions.

Thus, without prejudging the following discussion, we see that there are many potential costs to foreign-owned investment. Yet, despite this, over recent decades FDI has been seen as a panacea to the 'regional problem', and as an important aid to regional development. Of course, one possibility is that FDI is beneficial to the national economy, and prized by national policymakers, but it has harmful effects on the regional economy. There may also be a temporal trade-off, e.g. it 'mops-up' unemployment in the short-run, but 'knocks-out' domestic producers in the long-run. The remainder of the chapter examines the claims about FDI and regional development. It focuses on two aspects: first, FDI adversely affects employment, and second, that it is associated with high exit rates. It considers the steps that can be taken to 'embed' these plants to forestall exit and the role played by the inward investment agencies. It serves as a prelude to the second part of the book.

Employment

The model of Markusen and Venables (1999), discussed above, finds that a MNE plant has competition and linkage effects, but that these have ambiguous effects on domestic employment. For example, firms may exit the sector if the MNE replaces domestic production, and regional employment will decrease if it is either a less-intensive user of inputs or if it sources its inputs from elsewhere. Conversely, the foreign-owned plant may substitute for imports, and not only bring direct benefits to the regional economy through increased jobs, but indirect benefits through backward and forward linkages, as well as potential externalities. These factors are likely to vary from plant to plant, and may differ by entry mode, e.g. 'greenfield' start-up or acquisition. However, there is a paucity of empirical evidence on the direction and magnitude of these competition effects.

One avenue that has been explored is the potential displacement of domestic employment through factor markets. Since multinationals possess certain specific advantages, which are reflected in higher productivity, then Conyon *et al*, (2002) argue they can afford to offer relatively higher wages. In order for domestic firms to maintain their workforce they must offer higher wages, leading firms to exit the industry. It means that the displacement of jobs in the domestic sector occurs even if there is no direct effect in the output market, i.e. the FDI substitutes for imports. Driffield (1999) explores this issue for the UK over the period 1986-92. He finds that about 20 per cent of jobs created by foreign investors are substituted from the domestic sector. However, in general, there is a paucity of evidence on the net employment impact of FDI. Further, since most of the jobs are in manufacturing, which has been in decline, the issue is whether FDI has displaced employment in this sector or simply replaced it, but on this the literature is mute.

Several issues that have attracted considerable attention, with implications for employment, are the loss of control over regional assets as a result of FDI (Alden, 1997) and the quality of employment in foreign-owned plants (Hudson, 1995). These worries stem mainly from a body of work in the 1970s that investigated the effect of so-called 'branch plants' on the regional economy, not all of which are necessarily foreign owned (i.e. they could be UK plants attracted to the regions by the operation of the then regional policy). Crone (2000) reviews this literature. The argument is that plants controlled from outside the region tend to concentrate on lower-quality functions, such as production activities, and avoid the higher-quality activities like research and development. The bulk of employment is in low-skill activities (Townroe, 1975), resulting in the 'branch-plant economy', which has a large proportion of its employment in low-quality jobs (Firn, 1975). In respect of the MNE branch plant, a perceived change in the organisational structure of these plants (Dicken *et al*, 1994), led to a reappraisal of the theory in the 1990s. This was a perceived change in the structure of firms from a geographical basis to a product-based organisational structure, which potentially gave the branch plants a greater control over functions such as research, technology, engineering and marketing.[14] However, the extent to which these changes have impacted on the quality of the branch plant has not received overwhelming support (Crone, 2000). Thus, the fears attached to the 'branch-plant economy' remains.

Closure

Another potential cost of FDI that has received much attention is that it can induce instability into a region's employment (Hudson, 1998). It stems from a belief that MNE plants are 'footloose' in comparison to their domestic counterparts (Flamm, 1984), which is related to the intrinsic ability of these plants to transfer resources, facilities and production between plants located in different countries (Gorg and Strobl, 2003). When adverse conditions affect an economy (or opportunities arise elsewhere) an MNE can transfer activity across international borders with much greater ease compared with a domestic (single-plant or single-national) firm, which faces entry barriers to setting-up abroad.[15] In any case, the domestic firm may serve regional or national market, rather than international markets, and not want to relocate overseas. It imparts instability to a region's economy (Schuh and Triest, 2000), not least because the incentives for relocation are likely to be accentuated at a time of recession in the domestic economy (see Harris, 1988).

Firm exit and survival are subjects of considerable interest in the empirical literature on industrial organisation (e.g. Audretsch and Mahmood, 1994; Mata and Portugal, 1994), but in fact there are relatively few studies on the lifetime durations of foreign investors. It is an important topic, as exit detracts from the employment gains of these plants and it bears directly on the issue of stability. Two concepts that are central to this literature are the 'survival duration', which is the period of time from entry to exit, and the 'hazard rate', which is the probability of exit at a given time conditional on the firm surviving to that time. The hazard rate exhibits duration dependence, which could be positive (i.e. the exit rate increases the longer

---

[14] It led some to classify these as 'quality plants' (Amin *et al*, 1994).

[15] Baden-Fuller (1989) argues that the operations of the plants are vulnerable to transfer in order to avoid fixed costs and to achieve economies of scale within the company structure.

is the period of time that the firm exists) or negative (i.e. decreases with time). It can also be non-monotonic, e.g. positive to negative duration dependence, where an increasing hazard rate is followed by a decreasing failure rate.

In general, the empirical literature supports an increasing and then decreasing hazard rate, so that firms are less likely to fail early on and also when they have been around for some time. Thus, while Mata and Portugal (1994) and Mata *et al* (1995) find negative duration dependence, Audretsch and Mahmood, (1994) and Holmes *et al* (2003) both find an increasing to decreasing failure rate. These studies are concerned with domestic and foreign-owned plants, but others focusing solely on foreign 'greenfield' entrants find support for an increasing to decreasing hazard rate, such as McCloughan and Stone (1998) and Li (1995). Gorg and Strobl (2003) investigate the exit of foreign plants in Ireland. They find that the exit rate for foreign-owned plants that is about one-and-a-half times greater than that of domestic plants, and conclude that foreign plants are relatively 'footloose'. It holds when taking account of plant size, and suggests that the foreign firms find it easier to move production from one site to another, no matter how large the plant is.[16]

The studies on the survival of foreign-investors can be seen as an extension of the studies on the survival of multi-plant firms. The distinction between single- and multi-plant enterprises has been an important focus for the survival literature since Reynolds (1988), Dunne *et al* (1989) and Ghemawat and Nalebuff (1990). Dunne *et al* find that smaller plants that belong to a single-plant firm are less likely to close compared to multi-plant firms, but that the converse is true for large plants. Watts and Kirkham (1999) look solely at the closure of multi-plant firms and find that the size of the plant matters, with smaller plants facing a greater likelihood of closure. Other studies that find that the ownership structure is important are Audretsch and Mahmood (1995), Mata *et al* (1995) and Colombo and Delmastro (2000), which all find that plants belonging to a multi-plant firm are more prone to exit. Harris and Hassaszadeh (2002) find that plants in multi-plant firms have higher exit rates compared to single-plant firms, but in contrast to Dunne *et al* and Colombo and Delmastro, they find that it is the larger plants that are more likely to exit. This may be because the larger plants are more likely to be foreign-owned. Overall, even allowing for the enterprise structure, it appears that foreign-owned plants are more prone to exit than domestically-owned plants, which may increase the larger is the plant size. This is the case for the 'greenfield' start-up investments, although exit rates are higher for plants that commence by acquisition (Delacroix, 1993; McCloughan and Stone, 1998).

Embeddedness

Notwithstanding the benefits that FDI brings to the regional economy, a substantial part of the literature has focused on the drawbacks of this investment, including the

---

[16] Geography is also important, with Watts and Kirkham (1999) finding that the distance from the parent makes a plant more likely to close.

potential displacement of domestic jobs, the poor quality of these jobs and the high exit rate of MNE plants. In the 1990s, the prevalent view was that FDI was an integral part of the regional economy and its development, and considerable efforts to both attract foreign direct investment to the regions and to retain it by integrating it in the regional economy, thus making recognition of the high exit rates.

According to Cooke (2002) this belief that FDI was beneficial to the regional economy arose from the increased importance of knowledge. This is the driving force behind what is called the 'new regionalism', which in essence examines how regions utilise learning skills to increase their level of development (MacKinnon *et al*, 2002). Regions compete with one another, and the attractiveness of a region depends on how well it is perceived (Lovering, 2003). FDI is an important source of knowledge (Sugden and Wilson, 2001), and according to this theory the capacity of a region for learning and innovation determines its competitive advantage and hence its ability to attract FDI (Morgan, 1997). This implies regional strategies to improve learning and innovation, so that FDI shapes regional development in terms of both policies and outcomes. An important strand to this theory is a 'learning region' (Amin and Thrift, 1994), which makes use of the idea of 'embeddedness'.[17] This argues that economic behaviour is affected by the structure of the relations, or networks, and that these relations are the process by which regional development occurs.[18] In the light of the 'new regionalism' and the nature of FDI, the emphasis on these networks shifted to the 'embeddedness' of foreign investment.

In the context of FDI, 'embeddedness' is defined in terms of the depth and quality of the relationships that exist between inward investors and local agents and organisations, and the extent to which these provide opportunities for development (Phelps and MacKinnon, 2000). A difficulty lies in giving concrete form to these relationships and in forming testable hypotheses.[19] Given this, Phelps *et al* (2003) attempt a more rigorous definition and identify five possible sources by which FDI 'embeds' itself in the regional economy. These are: corporate status; research and development and design (R&DD); supply chains; skills and training; and repeat investment.[20] These embody long ideas of industrial linkages (Rodriguez-Clare,

---

[17] This concept stems from the work of Granovetter (1985).

[18] Examples of networks include inter-firm collaborations, of institutional support for firms and any structures that improves learning (see Amin and Thrift, 1994).

[19] Lovering (2003) criticises it as being 'theoretically fluffy', while Markusen (1999) calls it 'fuzzy', i.e. an "entity, phenomenon or process which possesses two or more alternative meanings and thus cannot be reliably identified or applied by different readers" (p. 702).

[20] In more detail, these are as follows. First, following Young *et al* (1994), corporate status and function is seen as an indicator of a plant's potential to develop within the region. A plant that has both manufacturing and non-manufacturing capabilities signifies that it is not a standard 'branch plant'. Second, R&DD activity signals higher-level functions, but also potential contacts with regional research institutes and universities. A third source of 'embeddedness' is the extent to which a foreign plant uses local sources, which is a standard 'linkage effect', described above. The fourth factor is the skills and training that the investor develops that makes it reliant on the region. Finally, repeat investment signifies commitment

1996; Dietzenbacher, 2002), and a more recent focus on repeat investment (Phelps and Fuller, 2000). However, while the new regionalism is couched in terms of the attractiveness of regions, these factors are about tying plants more closely into the regional economy, i.e. forestalling plant exit rather than entry. They are amenable to policy but to a greater or lesser extent.

While Phelps *et al* (2003) provide a testable definition of 'embeddedness', the empirical results fail to offer much backing for this when examined for Wales and the North East of England.[21] The fact that 'embeddedness' fails to materialise in regions with differing institutional arrangements undermines the new regionalism literature. However, the theory is broader than previous approaches that tended to concentrate solely on the linkages between foreign firms and local suppliers. These are investigated using survey-based approaches (e.g. Crone and Watts, 2000; PACEC, 1995), econometric techniques (Gorg and Strobl, 2002) and input-output tables at the aggregate level (Turok, 1993). However, the support is mixed. Crone and Watts find little support for supply linkages in Yorkshire, but PACEC find stronger links for Japanese manufacturing firms. A similar pattern is evident in the debate between Turok and McCann on the 'embeddedness' of the electronics industry in Silicon Glen in Scotland (Turok 1993, 1997; McCann 1997). Gorg and Strobl find no evidence for supply linkages. While these studies use different methodologies, they are indicative of the inconclusive evidence found for supply linkages and more generally for the 'embeddedness' of FDI.

Inward Investment Policy

The interest in foreign direct investment has not just been an academic matter, but policymakers at national, regional and sub-regional levels have actively sought to attract FDI (Webb and Collis, 2000). We conclude by briefly indicating the nature of these institutions and the role they play in attracting inward investment, focusing on those in the North East of England.

As an explanation for the increase in the number of agencies concerned with FDI at the regional level, Lovering (1999) argues that a shift from the centralised, redistributive Keynesian regional policies of the 1960s and 1970s to the policies of the 1980s and 1990s, neglected the redistributive needs of the poorer regions. As a response these regions have developed their own institutions and organisations in support of regional development. In fact, in the traditionally Assisted Areas, many of the regional organisations were formed from the agencies of the Keynesian-era. They are property-led, which is a legacy from the earliest regional policies of the 1930s, and they tend to be targeted on inward investment, partly reflecting policies

---

by a plant to a region and can re-enforce the other sources of 'embeddedness', such as a local-skills base, so that the factors are not mutually exclusive.

[21] Chapter 7 examines whether re-investing plants have longer survival durations from the time of the re-investment compared to plants that do not re-invest, but again fails to find support for this form of 'embeddedness'.

of the 1960s and 1970s aimed at redistributing industry, of which the main source is now from abroad. In the 1990s the Regional Development Organisations (RDOs) had limited resources, and the attraction of FDI was the prime objective, for which Central Government grants continued to be available in the regions. The functions of the RDOs were subsequently taken on by the Regional Development Agencies (RDAs), set-up in 1999, but with expanded remits and much larger budgets.

In the North East of England there are currently two main agencies concerned with the attraction of FDI; these are the Regional Development Agency (RDA), *One NorthEast*, and the national agency, *UK Trade and Investment*.[22] Along with most other RDAs, *One NorthEast* was established in April 1999, with a remit to further economic development and regeneration; promote efficiency, investment and competitiveness; generate employment; encourage skills; and contribute to the sustainability of the UK economy as a whole. It superseded the RDO, the *Northern Development Company* (NDC), which itself took over the functions of the former *North of England Development Company* in 1986 (see Darnell and Evans, 1995). Funding for NDC was modest, but like other RDOs, its resources were increased in the late 1980s conditional on it co-ordinating the inward investment function in the region, i.e. local authorities and new town development corporations (see Wren, 1996).[23] Although the NDC did not have a strategic remit, it did promote the region as a 'one stop shop' agency for inward investors (Dicken, 1990). For this purpose it established overseas offices in the US and Far East, which now stand at nine, and offered non-financial support. This included the organisation of events, identifying and making presentations to potential investors, project management and follow-up activities with successful investors.

The main national inward investment agency is *UK Trade and Investment*. Prior to 2003, when it merged with the trade function, it was known as *Invest UK*, and prior to that as the *Invest in Britain Bureau*. The *Invest in Britain Bureau* was established in 1977 to boost national employment through inward investment, and its primary functions were to market the UK as a location for FDI and to handle enquiries from potential inward investors (Fraser, 1999). It worked through British Embassies, High Commissions and Consulates to promote the UK overseas, and sought to generate investment leads, manage the inward investment process and realise positive outcomes (Economists Advisory Group, 2000). *Invest in Britain Bureau* was re-branded as *Invest UK* in July 2000, whose primary activities were

---

[22] In addition, each county council in the region has an inward investment office, carrying out promotional work and giving support to foreign-owned plants in their respective areas. The local authorities offer support to FDI, such as works to land and building and training grants. The Government has encouraged the formation of 'regional chambers', comprising representatives of local authorities, industry, unions, and voluntary organisations, but these are consultative and have no statutory basis or direct powers.

[23] The co-ordination of the RDOs was undertaken by an English Unit in the Department of Trade and Industry. Similar arrangements existed for Locate in Scotland and for the Welsh Development Agency.

advice and promotional work on establishing or expanding a plant in the UK.[24] As well as promotional work it undertook specific events, such as the organisation of a regional tour, a tailor-made presentation or site visits.

The relationship between *UK Trade and Investment* and the RDAs is that the former provides the Development Agencies with leads generated from its overseas marketing campaigns (DTI, 2002). As such, the national agency works mainly as a facilitation agency for the RDAs, which play an important role in marketing their regions (Fraser, 1999). The main form of financial inducement remains the grants in the designated Assisted Areas under UK regional policy. In England this is the Regional Selective Assistance scheme, which is little changed since 1984, and recently renamed Selective Finance for Investment.[25] Since the late 1980s around half the regional aid budget has gone to support FDI (Wren, 2005a). Prior to 2002, regional grant offers of up to £2 million were decided by the Government Offices in the regions, but since then have become the concern of the respective Regional Development Agencies, while offers above £2 million are dealt with in London.[26] Other forms of financial support are available from the RDAs, such as equity and loan schemes, but these generally involve relatively small amounts.

Conclusions

This chapter focuses on the benefits and costs that FDI brings at a regional level, and hence its role in regional development. It examines theoretical and empirical research, spanning work in the area of industrial organisation through to economic geography and related literatures. In terms of the benefits of FDI, the economic literature focuses on the efficiency gains that potentially 'spillover' to the regional economy in the form of increased productivity. However, the chapter also spans to consider various costs of FDI to the regions, including potentially low-quality jobs in plants with high closure rates, and with few regional ties.

Anyone new to the area of FDI would wonder why the agencies seek to attract these investments. Not only are the potential benefits of FDI apparently absent in the research findings, but the plants are demonstrated to have higher exit rates. It is the case even when the ownership structure and plant size are held constant, which suggests that the fact that these enterprises operate across international boundaries causes them to be relatively 'footloose'. Further, push factors, such as a recession in the regional economy, is likely to increase the probability of exit, just when the

---

[24] It offered information on locational requirements (e.g. availability of labour, transport links, proximity to customers and suppliers); advice on setting up an operation (legal and regulatory frameworks); information on public and private services (local government, utilities and key private-sector contacts); and on national, regional and local incentives.

[25] Similar schemes operate in Scotland and Wales.

[26] Prior to 1988 National Selective Assistance was also available in the regions, and outside the designated Assisted Areas, but it dealt with very few cases. The Regional Development Grant scheme operated in the regions, but was effectively terminated in 1984.

jobs provided by these plants are most valued. Multinational enterprise gained a poor reputation in the economic development literature of the 1970s, when it was argued that it led to a 'branch plant economy', which had a large proportion of its employment in low-quality jobs. The fresh wave of FDI led this argument to be reappraised in the 1990s, but recently the old argument has returned. A factor in this has been the accession of eastern European countries to the European Union, which has led to flows of outward FDI in order to take advantage of these cheaper labour markets within the EU, both in the run-up and subsequent to membership. However, there has also been a reappraisal arising from the results of academic research, of which there are several strands.

First of all, while research was initially supportive of the claims that foreign investment raises the productivity of domestic firms, as techniques have improved, this evidence has become ambiguous. At best the results emerging from this large body of work can be described as mixed. Second, recent research has focused on 'technology sourcing' as a motive for FDI, resulting in 'reverse spillovers' flowing from domestic plants to foreign-owned firms. In much of the literature, negative spillovers are just as likely as positive spillovers, which again points to the relative inferiority of FDI. Third, the 'new regionalism' that emerged in the 1990s, argues that the structure of relations or networks that exist in a region can 'embed' FDI, serving both to attract and retain this investment. However, the results obtained on 'embeddedness', which includes supply linkages, suggest that these relations are weak, again indicating the 'footloose' nature of FDI. Finally, empirical support for positive wage spillovers shows that in the case of unskilled workers these are most pronounced in the regions, again reflecting the nature of this investment.

Given all of this, the natural question to ask is are the agencies wasting their time and resources trying to attract this investment to the regions? The answer no doubt lies in the direct benefit of this investment, but which is almost completely ignored in the empirical literature.[27] Given the incidence of unemployment in the regions then in any Cost-Benefit Analysis the major benefit of FDI is likely to be the jobs created. This is because individuals taken off the unemployment register have no resource cost – they are otherwise unemployed – so that they have a zero social cost, i.e. a zero shadow wage, and a direct benefit to society. Of course, the situation is complicated, as account must be taken of the indirect and the possible feedback effects in the direct market.[28] Many of the indirect effects are considered under the guise of spillovers (e.g. linkage and displacement through competition effects), but the direct effect is almost wholly ignored. This is despite the fact that employment creation is key criterion of the regional grants that are offered to these plants. One explanation could be unemployment outside the Assisted Area regions is believed to be at its natural level, so that job creation has no social value, and the·

---

[27] The approach to the evaluation of overseas operations, including foreign direct investment is considered in Wren (2005b).

[28] In effect, even the indirect pecuniary external effects should be measured in the direct market (see Sugden and Williams, 1978).

indirect effects are likely to be the major benefits. All the same, job creation in the regions has value, and it is a focus for us in the second part of the book.

Part 2

Inward Investment in a
Regional Economy

Chapter 5

Investment

The purpose of this chapter is to analyse the pattern of investment carried out by foreign-owned plants in the North East of England. The analysis utilises the Inward Investment Dataset, which is described in the Appendix. This dataset is a project-based account of foreign direct investment in this region over the period 1985-98, but which is held at the plant level. Not only does it include investment by start-up, acquisition or joint venture, but it includes re-investment that involve a 'significant' enhancement to a plant's operating capacity. The data at our disposal form the basis of the quarterly returns made to the UK's inward investment agency, *UK Trade and Investment*. These are made by each region and reported for the UK as a whole. The kinds of issue examined in this chapter are the scale, timing, location, activity and country of origin of the foreign direct investment (FDI). The investment is analysed at the project level, but also at the plant level. Much of the analysis is novel, since as the first part of this book showed, regional analyses of FDI typically operate at the aggregate level and rarely consider investment.[1] In addition to shedding light on the nature of FDI within a single UK region, which has been a long-term recipient of FDI, the chapter offers insights on the nature of the data themselves, which are the most widely used figures for UK FDI.

At the outset it is important to be aware of two features of the data. The first is that while the agencies seek a comprehensive account of the number of projects and the jobs, the data on the investment scale is only partial.[2] It reflects a difficulty in obtaining this information, which is known for only two-thirds of the projects in the Inward Investment Dataset. An issue is the representativeness of the known data, and it is examined by making comparison with the project job data, which is known in nearly all cases, revealing the known investment data are broadly representative. A second feature of the investment data is that they are prospective, in the form of commitments given by the investors. It is believed that the projects all went ahead, although they may not have been fully implemented at the proposed scale. The issue is explored in Chapter 7, again in relation to the project jobs, which are also prospective, and it is reported on in this chapter.

---

[1] Production census-type data are much used, e.g. Harris and Robinson (2002), but generally sample only a proportion of smaller companies, and which for the UK 'census' can be as little as 1 in 5 for firms with less than 100 employees (Griffith, 1999). However, we find that three-quarters of foreign-owned start-ups have less than 100 employees on entry, so that this is a major advantage of the project-based data.

[2] For this reason the agencies tend to report the FDI in terms of the number of projects or jobs. This was the kind of information presented in Chapter 3 (see Tables 3.2 and 3.3).

The Inward Investment Dataset identifies investment of about £8.7 billion in the North-East region over 1985-98 (1995 prices). Overall, it suggests total FDI in the region over this period of around £1 billion per annum over this period, which is about 5 per cent of the region's Gross Domestic Product (1995 prices). The analysis shows investment is heavily concentrated in a small number of projects and plants, and these largely determine the overall pattern of FDI. Nearly all of the investment is in manufacturing, and within this it is heavily concentrated in a few activities. In terms of the investment volume the most important source is Japan, although more projects originate from the USA, which is much more broadly based in terms of the activity. In the next section the nature and representativeness of the investment data are explored. The scale and concentration of investment are examined, before the characteristics of the investment are considered, in terms of its location, activity and country of origin. This analysis is mainly at the project level, but, at the end of the chapter, investment is analysed at the plant level. Throughout, and unless otherwise indicated, all monetary sums are at 1995 prices.

The Nature of the Investment Data

The investment data were originally collated by the main inward investment agency for the North-East of England, *One NorthEast*, and its predecessor, the *Northern Development Company*. The method of data collection and nature of the data are described in the Appendix. The investment data are given in Appendix Table 10, and the distribution of scales according to project type is shown in Appendix Figure 3. It indicates that the modal investment scale is in the range £2 to £5 million, but that there are some very large projects.

The investment data are project-based and cover 'significant' investments by foreign-owned plants in the region, including start-ups, acquisitions, joint ventures and re-investments. Of course, what is 'significant' is subjective, but a judgement of this kind cannot be avoided, even in the studies of investment using census-based data.[3] In the case of initial investments (i.e. project by which a plant commences in foreign ownership), any start-up, acquisition, joint venture project can be regarded as 'significant', while the agencies refer to re-investment projects as 'expansions'. These involve an enhancement to a plant's capacity, such as the installation of a new production line or some other plant upgrading. They do not include small-scale activities, like the routine replacement of machinery, but which are not of interest to this study. Of course, it is possible that smaller investments will not come to the attention of the agencies, but this is without real significance.

The investment data are recorded for the calendar quarter in which the inward investor makes a firm commitment to the project, which may pre-date the formal public announcement. Where this is a start-up, re-investment or joint venture, the

---

[3] For example, Nilsen and Schiantarelli (2003) define an episode of investment where the investment rate exceeds 2.5 times the median plant investment rate.

expectation is that the construction work will commence within 12 to 18 months of the commitment. Acquisitions do not involve physical work to land or buildings, and may be notified retrospectively. Otherwise, the data are prospective, i.e. they refer to planned investment, and important issues are whether the investments went ahead or not, and, if so, whether they were fully realised.

Planned and Realised Investment

It is difficult to utilise company accounts for the purpose of determining whether an investment went ahead or not, and at what scale, as the plants are likely to be part of multi-plant enterprises, from which individual plants or investments are difficult to identify, while an investment may be implemented over several years. Also, the conditions under which the RDA, *One NorthEast*, supplied the data prevent the plants from being contacted directly. Each plant in the Inward Investment Dataset existed in the region at some time (see Appendix), which suggests all of the initial investments went ahead in some form. This is the case for start-up, acquisition and joint venture plants, but it is more difficult to determine for re-investments, which were carried out some time after the initial investment.

When making a commitment to an investment, firms also give a commitment to the number of project jobs that it plans to have in place within two years. To the extent that the planned jobs are realised it is reasonable that the investment will also be achieved. Overall, the data show that 86 per cent of the prospective jobs are reflected in plant employment at 1999 for those new plants that have not exited by this time (i.e. plants commencing in foreign ownership after 1985). If an allowance is made for reasonable rates of job loss then at a crude level it suggests that the job targets were substantially realised. However, a more thorough analysis of this issue is undertaken in Chapter 7. This shows that at the mean about 90 per cent of the project jobs are in place at the end of the study period for plants that remain open, but that for very large plants this is only about 50 to 60 per cent. It is problematic, as it suggests that the very large investments are less likely to be realised, which in fact account for the lion-share of total investment. This needs to be borne in mind in the subsequent analysis, which relates to the prospective investment.

Representativeness of the Known Investment Data

Another important issue is the representativeness of the known investment data, as the proposed investment scales are known for only 364 of the 550 projects in the Inward Investment Dataset (i.e. 66 per cent). The issue is whether the 364 projects are representative of the overall pattern of investment in the region, according both to the investment scale and to the different project types.

Part (a) of Table 5.1 shows that the investment scale is known for 63 per cent of the start-up projects and 79 per cent of re-investments. However, the investment is known for only 39 and 50 per cent of the acquisition and joint venture projects respectively, but which together account for only one-quarter of known investment.

Table 5.1 Representativeness of the Known Investment Data

	All	SU	AC	JV	RE
(a) Coverage of Investment Data					
No. of Projects	550	164	93	24	269
Where investment scale known	364	103	36	12	213
Percentage known cases	66%	63%	39%	50%	79%
(b) Inward Investment Dataset					
Investment (£'m)	8,714	2,868	1,410	659	3,778
Percentage of investment	100%	32.9%	16.2%	7.5%	43.4%
(c) Estimated Total Investment					
Investment (£'m)	14,267	4,552	3,615	1,318	4,782
Percentage of investment	100%	31.9%	25.4%	9.2%	33.5%

Note: Part (b) reports known investment data, i.e. for 364 projects, and part (c) estimates total investment (i.e. for 550 projects) using the known average investment scale for each type.   SU = start-up, AC = acquisition, JV = joint venture and RE = re-investment.

The relatively poor information on these no doubt reflects the fact that the inward investment agencies are less likely to be involved with these projects. It suggests that the known data are not a representative sample of investment across the project types, with the start-up and re-investment projects relatively over-represented.

To examine the representativeness of the known investment data according to the scale, it is again possible to make use of the job data. Both the investment scale and total number of jobs are known for 350 projects, and these are plotted on a log-log scale in Figure 5.1. The project jobs include both new and safeguarded jobs (see Appendix). The figure shows a strong positive relationship between the investment scale and the total number of jobs, with a correlation coefficient between these of +0.66.[4] Overall, larger investments are strongly associated with more jobs.

The close correlation between the jobs and investment scale for the projects in which both these variables are known enables the representativeness of the known investment data to be considered. This is because the total number of jobs is known in virtually all cases, i.e. for 511 of the 550 projects. This is achieved by comparing the job distribution for all 511 projects, with that for the 350 projects where the investment scale is also known. The comparison is made in Table 5.2, with the job distributions disaggregated into ten size job groups. Except at either tail, inspection

---

[4] When a few highly capital-intensive projects are excluded, then the correlation coefficient between the investment and jobs increases to +0.70. In fact, Figure 5.1 suggests that the investment scale increases much more sharply than the number of jobs in the case of the very large projects, and this is explored in Chapter 6.

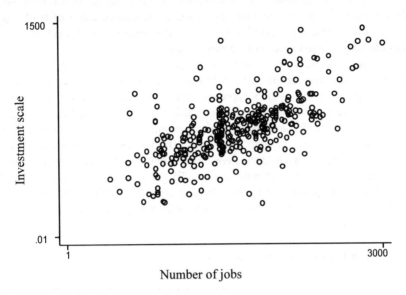

Figure 5.1 Scatter-Plot of Investment and Jobs

Note: The figure plots total investment scale (£'m) against total number of jobs on a log-log scale, for the projects where both these are known.

Table 5.2 Distribution of Project Jobs

Job Range	All Projects		Investment Known	
	No.	**(%)**	**No.**	**(%)**
1 – 5	19	(4)	5	(1)
6 – 10	41	(8)	21	(6)
11 – 25	75	(15)	54	(15)
26 – 50	99	(19)	71	(20)
51 – 100	82	(16)	59	(17)
101 – 200	86	(17)	65	(19)
201 – 500	80	(15)	53	(16)
501 – 1000	20	(4)	13	(4)
1001 – 2500	8	(2)	8	(2)
> 2500	1	(0)	1	(0)
Number of Projects	**511**	**(100)**	**350**	**(100)**

Note: Number of jobs (*JOB*) for projects where this is known and where investment is also known. Investment scale is known for 364 projects, and the jobs for 350 of these.

of Table 5.2 shows that the distributions are very similar. Indeed, standardising the distributions for the number of observations there is no difference between these distributions. A Spearman rank test gives a Chi-square value of 9.14 against a critical value at the 5 per cent level of 16.9. The same pattern is evident for each of the four project types when considered in turn.[5]

Given the close correlation between the investment scale and jobs, then the similar distributions for the 350 and 511 projects in Table 5.2 it suggests the known investment scales are broadly representative of total investment. However, while this holds overall, a close inspection of Table 5.2 suggests that the investment scale is much likelier to be known for projects promising a very large number of jobs, although these projects are small in number. In one sense it is encouraging, as these projects account for most of the investment, although in another sense it means the larger investments are over-represented. To get a view on the overall investment scale (i.e. make allowance for the missing cases), the known investment is now scaled-up *pro rata*, making allowance for the bias by project type.

The Overall Scale of Investment

The Inward Investment Dataset identifies £8,714 million in investment over the period 1985-98 at 1995 prices. This is for the 364 projects where the scale is known. Part (b) of Table 5.1 shows that one third of this investment is in start-up projects, and that 43 per cent is re-investment. Of the re-investment, £1.37 billion is by the start-up plants, so that in total the start-up plants account for £4.4 billion in investment (see Table 5.7 below). It is about half of the total FDI over the period. Investment by the other types is relatively small in scale, so that acquisitions make up 16 per cent of investment and joint ventures account for only 8 per cent.

The start-ups and re-investments are relatively over-represented in the known investment data, and part (c) of Table 5.1 uses the known average investment scale of each project type to calculate the total investment for the types, and hence for all 550 projects. It gives an overall figure for FDI in the North-East region over 1985-98 of £14,267 million (1995 prices). Of course, it is likely to be an over-estimate, as the larger projects are slightly over-represented in the data, and they are less able to achieve their proposed scales. However, it means a ballpark figure for investment of about £12 billion over the whole period, which is £1 billion per annum (1995 prices). To put this in perspective, on an annual basis it represents 4 to 5 per cent of GDP of the North-East region, or about 15 per cent of its manufacturing output (at 1995). It indicates the substantial contribution of FDI to the regional economy.

Of the total of £14,267 million in FDI, Table 5.1 shows that about a third is in the form of start-up investment, a third is re-investment and the remainder is in the form of acquisitions and joint ventures. It differs from the pattern for the known

---

[5] In the case of the start-up projects the Chi-square value is close to significance, due to the relative under-representation of investment data on the smaller start-up projects by job size.

investment data, shown in part (b) of Table 5.1, due to the fact that some types are over-represented in the known investment data. In the remainder of the chapter the focus is on the 364 projects for which the investment scale is known. While these are broadly representative of the overall investment scale, they are biased by project type. Allowance is made for this by disaggregating the analysis by project type. As we see, the pattern of investment is dominated by a relatively small number of very large projects, for which we have complete data, so that, in fact, in most cases the results that are presented are broadly representative of the overall picture.

The temporal distribution of the known investment cases is shown in Figure 5.2. The number of cases is broadly constant, at around 25-35 projects per year. There is a dip in the number of projects in the early 1990s, possibly related to recession or the uncertainty induced the UK's exit from the Exchange Rate Mechanism, and again at the end of the period.[6] The volume of investment is much more variable, with a sharp increase in FDI in the mid-1990s, owing to a small number of very large projects originating from each of Germany, Japan and Korea. In fact, the years 1994 and 1995 account for 40 per cent of the foreign investment over the

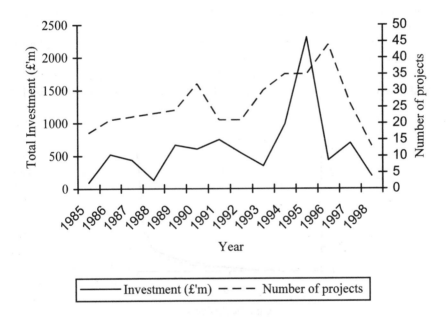

Figure 5.2 Investment by Year, 1985-1998

Note: Total known investment (*INV*) and number of these projects by year (*YEAR*).

---

[6] There is not a full year's worth of data for 1998, although it cannot fully explain this.

period 1985-1998. It may well reflect the keenness of the inward investment agencies to attract these projects at this time. However, in Chapter 7, we find that projects arriving at this time were much less able to achieve their promised scales, so that there was exaggerated optimism about the contribution of these projects.

The Concentration of Investment

The average project investment scale is £23.9 million, but higher for acquisitions and joint ventures (Appendix Table 10). The average scale of a start-up is £28.4m, but for a re-investment it is only £17.6m. The size distribution of the investments is shown in Appendix Figure 3, with a breakdown by project type. Most investments are between £2m and £10 million, but there are a number of very large investments in excess of £150 million. In fact, there are 14 projects, each in excess of £150 million, which account for two-thirds of the total known investment. In total, 28 projects, each in excess of £50m, account for nearly 80 per cent of investment, but which is only 8 per cent of the number of projects. Of course, the large investments are more likely to be observed, but this is still a striking finding. It explains why the mean project investment scale is £23.9m, but the median scale is only £2m to £5m. The concentration is more apparent for some project types: projects in excess of £150 million account for 78 per cent of FDI by start-up and 58 per cent by re-investment, but only 39 per cent by acquisition.

The Lorenz curve in Figure 5.3 shows the heavy concentration of investment in a small number of projects. In total, the 364 known investment projects are carried

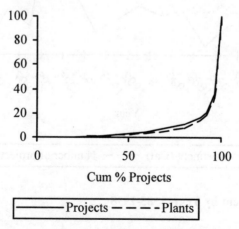

Figure 5.3 Lorenz Curves for Project and Plant Investment

Note: Proposed investment scales (*INV*) for projects and plants.

out by 230 of the 337 plants. A full record of projects may not be observed for any one plant, and this issue is taken up below.[7] Figure 5.3 shows there is a similar level of concentration of investment across plants, but which if anything is slightly higher. This is because the 28 very large investment projects are undertaken by 20 plants. Indeed, 23 plants carried out total investment in excess of £50m over 1985-98, which is 10 per cent of the number of plants for which investment is known, but two-thirds of the known investment over the period. The median plant investment scale is only £5m, which again points to a heavy concentration of investment.

Table 5.3 Characteristics of the 28 Large Projects

	No. of Projects	Investment	
		(£'m)	(%)
Project Type			
Start-ups	5	2,363	34.5
Acquisitions	10	1,236	18.0
Joint Ventures	1	556	8.1
Re-investments	12	2,705	39.4
Location			
Northumberland	1	111	1.6
Tyne and Wear	12	3,235	47.2
Durham	6	1,660	24.2
Cleveland	9	1,854	27.0
Activity			
Chemicals (24)	6	715	10.4
Machinery (29)	1	462	6.7
Communications (32)	6	2,668	38.9
Transport (34)	7	1,610	23.5
Other	8	1,405	20.5
Country of Origin			
Germany	3	1,245	18.2
USA	11	1,851	27.0
Japan	9	2,937	42.8
Korea	1	462	6.7
Other	4	365	5.3

Note: Each project has an investment scale of at least £50 million (1995 prices). The NACE activity codes are given in parentheses.

---

[7] These are plants commencing prior to 1985 or where there is missing data on investment.

The concentration of investment means that the overall pattern of investment is dominated by a relatively small number of projects and plants. It is not possible to identify the individual investors because of the terms on which the data were supplied, but Table 5.3 summarises the main characteristics of the 28 investment projects that are greater than £50 million in scale. It shows that three-quarters of these investments were carried out by start-up or re-investment, even though the acquisitions account for ten of the projects. The large projects are mainly located in Tyne and Wear county, in two or three activities and originating from Japan, and to a lesser extent the USA. The characteristics of the FDI are now analysed. Given the concentration of investment, as we see, that this is largely determined by the pattern of investment in the large projects.

The Characteristics of Investment

The characteristics of the foreign-owned investment is now considered, including the location, activity and country of origin. It is conducted at both the project and plant levels. The 550 projects in the Inward Investment Dataset were implemented by 337 plants, but the analysis of this section focuses on the 364 projects for which the investment scale is known, and which were carried out by 230 plants.

Location

The postcode location of the plants is mapped in Figure 5.4, which shows that the plants are non-uniformly distributed across the study area. In particular, they tend to be located towards the eastern-seaboard of the region, close to the main centres of population. There are no foreign-owned plants in much of Northumberland and County Durham, but concentrations around the former New Towns of Cramlington in Northumberland, Washington in Tyne and Wear, and Peterlee and Newton Aycliffe in County Durham. There are also clusters around the industrial estates of the Tyne Tunnel to the east of Newcastle, along the River Wear at Sunderland, at Consett and Stanley in north-west County Durham, and at Stockton and Billingham on Teesside or Cleveland.

In determining this location pattern several factors seem to be at work. First, there is a corridor for the investment running north-to-south, closely following the A19 and A1 trunk roads to the east of the region. The A19 is of greater importance. It passes through Stockton and Peterlee, runs between Sunderland and Washington, where it links to the A1, continues through the Tyne Tunnel to Cramlington, where it again connects with the A1, which then runs through Northumberland and on to the Scottish border. The advantage of this location is that it gives good road access, both within and outside the region, and easy access to the coastal ports and airports. It runs along the periphery of the main conurbations, from which plants draw their labour. These areas are less important as markets for the output of these plants, as the plants tend to operate in national and international markets.

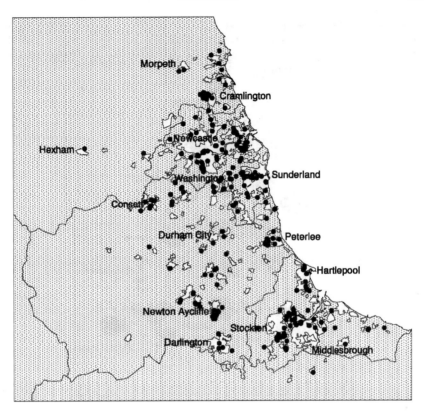

Key:

- **Plants**
- **Built-up Area**
- **Land Area**

Figure 5.4 Plant Locations

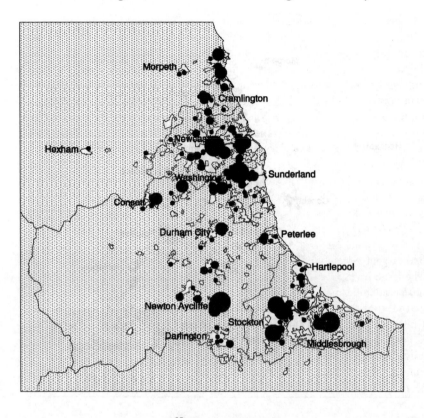

Key:

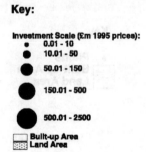

Figure 5.5 The Location of Investment

A factor in plant location is the economic development strategies of the local and regional agencies, and the policies of Central Government. Concentrations of foreign-owned plants exist in the estates set up in the 1960s at the New Towns of Cramlington, Washington and Peterlee, the more modern industrial estates created alongside the rivers Tyne and Wear in the wake of shipyard closures, and the estates in north-west County Durham set-up following steel closure. Finally, while it is not the purpose of this book to investigate the nature of the linkages between firms, there are several clusters of foreign-owned plants in related activities. One is a cluster of the car-component plants setting-up near the Nissan plant to the west of Sunderland. Another is the cluster of plants drawn to Teesside (or Cleveland), which is heavily-specialised in chemicals, offshore and heavy-engineering. Strictly, the plants around Nissan should be described as an industrial complex, as there are strong supplier links between these plants (see McCann and Sheppard, 2003), while the linkages on Teesside are less certain, and the foreign-owned plants may locate here to take advantage of agglomeration economies.[8]

Total project investment is aggregated at the plant level and mapped in Figure 5.5. The large investments tend to occur in the corridor identified above, but there are substantial investments elsewhere in the region, including large investments near the A1 at Newton Aycliffe and Durham City, at Consett and Stanley in north-west County Durham, and Blyth in South-East Northumberland. There would seem to be a good distribution of FDI across the populated parts of the region, but Table 5.4 shows that nearly half the investment occurs in Tyne and Wear (46 per cent), reflecting the large investments shown in Table 5.3. Approximately a quarter of the FDI occurs in each of County Durham (26 per cent) and Cleveland (24 per cent), but only a very small proportion is in Northumberland (5 per cent).

Table 5.4 gives a disaggregation by project type, and shows different kinds of investment going into different parts of the region. Half the start-up investment is in Tyne and Wear, while Northumberland has very little at all of this investment. Many acquisitions (44 per cent) and nearly all the joint ventures occur on Cleveland (or Teesside), reflecting the industrial structure of this area, which is dominated by large plants operating in international markets. Finally, re-investment principally occurs in Tyne and Wear and County Durham, which is because Northumberland gets little start-up investment, while Cleveland has the acquisitions.

Looking at it from the perspective of each county we see that Tyne and Wear and County Durham have similar patterns of FDI. Both receive most investment in the form of re-investment, and to a lesser extent by start-up, while there is relatively little FDI through acquisition. Northumberland has little start-up investment and much more by acquisition. Finally, FDI in Cleveland is more broadly based, but it has a much lower proportion of investment in the form of re-investment. Overall, these patterns are driven by investment in the large projects (Table 5.3).

---

[8] Although, much of the FDI on Cleveland is by acquisition (see Table 5.4).

Table 5.4 Investment by County and Type

	ND		TW		CD		CL		Total	
	£'m	%	£'m	%	£'m	%	£'m	%	£'m	%
Start-ups	26	6	1,511	38	623	28	709	34	2,869	33
Acquisitions	117	28	471	12	246	11	575	27	1,410	16
Joint Ventures	27	6	54	1	21	1	556	27	658	8
Re-investments	257	60	1,961	49	1,312	60	248	12	3,777	43
Total	**427**	**100**	**3,997**	**100**	**2,202**	**100**	**2,088**	**100**	**8,714**	**100**

Note: Project investment scales (*INV*) by county (*COUNTY*). ND = Northumberland, TW = Tyne and Wear, CD = County Durham and CL = Cleveland.

Activity

Of the known investment of £8.7 billion investment in 364 projects, manufacturing accounts for £7.3 billion in 315 projects (84 and 86 per cent respectively). Unlike FDI in the South East, the investment in the region is heavily concentrated in the manufacturing sector. Within manufacturing, there is a further heavy concentration, with four activities combined accounting for £6.5bn of this investment (89 per cent) and more than half the projects in this sector (57 per cent). These activities, along with the amount and number of investment projects, are as follows:[9]

> *Chemicals*: £1,035m (14% of total known investment) in 55 projects;
> *Machinery and Equipment*: £649m (9%) in 36 projects;
> *Radio, Television and Communications Equipment*: £2,895m (40%) in 37 projects; and
> *Transport Equipment*: £1,928m (26%) in 51 projects.

Other UK regional economies show concentrations of investment in these kinds of activity (see Chapter 4). At 1994, Brand *et al* (2000) find five activities – rubber and plastics, metals, engineering, electronics and transport equipment – account for 67, 70 and 88 per cent of foreign-owned manufacturing employment in Scotland, Wales and the West Midlands respectively. However, within this, there are strong variations. Transport equipment is dominant in Scotland and Wales, and followed by metals in Wales, while engineering is dominant in the West Midlands. In terms of the activities that are attracted to regions it seems to reflect the existing industrial structure, which could indicate MAR agglomeration economies.[10] Of course, it is likely to be the case for acquisitions, which account for around a quarter of FDI.

---

[9] The communications equipment activity includes electronic components and the transport equipment activity includes the manufacture of motor vehicles.
[10] But see the discussion in Chapter 4.

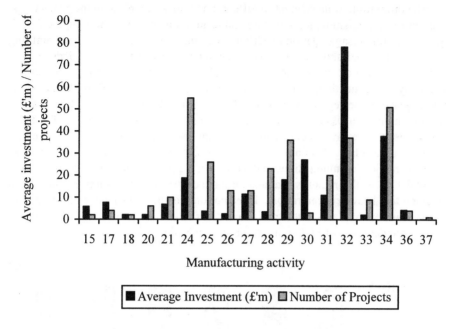

Figure 5.6 Investment by Manufacturing Activity

Notes: NACE two-digit classification, as follows: 15 = Food Products and Beverages; 17 = Textiles; 18 = Wearing Apparel; 20 = Wood and Wood Products; 21 = Pulp, Paper and Paper Products; 24 = Chemicals and Chemical Products; 25 = Rubber and Plastic Products; 26 = Other Non-Metallic Products; 27 = Basic Metals; 28 = Fabricated Metal Products, except Machinery and Equipment; 29 = Machinery and Equipment not elsewhere classified; 30 = Office Machinery and Computers; 31 = Electrical Machinery and Apparatus not elsewhere classified; 32 = Radio, Television and Communication Equipment and Apparatus; 33 = Medical, Precision and Optical Instruments, Watches and Clocks; 34 = Transport Equipment; 36 = Furniture; Manufacturing not elsewhere classified; and 37 =Recycling. Activities with zero investment are not shown.

The remainder of manufacturing outside of the four main activities accounts for only £819m in FDI in North-East England, but in 136 projects. The distribution of this across manufacturing activities is illustrated in Figure 5.6. For each activity it shows the number of projects and the average investment scale. The dominance of the four activities can be seen, as these each have both a high number of projects and a large average investment scale. Other activities where there are a relatively large number of projects are: Rubber and Plastic Products (26 projects), Fabricated Metal Products (23), Basic Metals (13), Other Non-metallic Products (13), Pulp and Paper Products (10) and Medical and Optical Instruments (9).

The proportion of investment in different activities according to the project type (i.e. start-up, acquisition, joint venture and re-investment) is shown in Figure 5.7. It gives a six-fold disaggregation of activity according to the four main manufacturing activities (outlined above), the rest of manufacturing and the rest of industry. It shows interesting differences in the nature of investment. In Chemicals investment is mainly by acquisition, and these account for nearly a half of all the acquisitions taking place in the region over the study period. In Machinery and Equipment and in Communications Equipment it is start-ups and re-investments, while in Transport Equipment it is re-investment by existing plants, with much of it is associated with the Nissan car plant. Combined, start-ups in Communications Equipment and re-investments in Communications and Transport Equipment account for 60 per cent of total FDI in the region's manufacturing industry over the study period, again pointing to a heavy concentration. Thus, not only is the investment concentrated in a small number of plants, but there is a concentration in a narrow range of activities, with particular types of FDI going to certain kinds of activity.

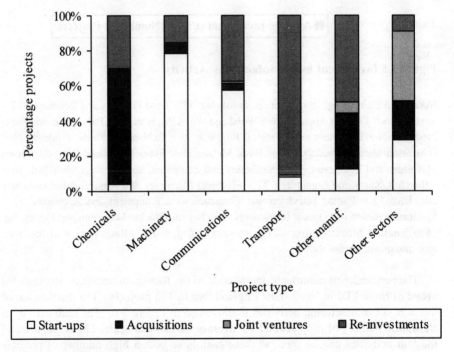

Figure 5.7 Type of Investment by Activity

Note: The figure shows the proportion of project investment by each type according to plant activity. The activities (*IND*) are given in the text.

Country of Origin

The distribution of foreign-owned investment projects according to the location of the ultimate owner is shown in Table 5.5. For the three supranational regions of origin it gives a breakdown by the major countries within. Over the period 1985-98, most known investment projects originate from Western Europe, followed by North America and the Far East.[11] However, by volume, nearly half the investment comes from the Far East (47 per cent), so that the mean project scale is about £41m. For the other two regions the percentage investment and the mean scales are 24% and £14m for Western Europe, and 29% and £22m for North America. Investment from outside these three regions is trivial. The breakdown of investment by major country within each region shows that in fact most investment originates from just three countries. These are Japan (£3.3bn, or 38% of known investment), the USA (£2.4bn, 28%) and Germany (£1.4bn, 16%), which in total represent 82 per cent of the FDI. When one further country is included (Korea) it increases to 88 per cent. Again it indicates a striking degree of concentration, but perhaps it is not surprising given the pattern of the large investments shown in Table 5.3.[12]

Table 5.5 Investment by Location of Ultimate Owner

Region	Total (£'m)	%	Mean (£'m)	Number of Projects
Western Europe	**2,091**	**24**	**14**	**147**
Germany	1,376		34	40
Scandinavia	211		4	52
France	100		6	17
Other	404		11	38
North America	**2,486**	**29**	**22**	**114**
USA	2,403		22	110
Other	83		21	4
Far East	**4,127**	**47**	**41**	**100**
Japan	3,325		49	68
Korea	554		50	11
Other	248		12	21
Rest of the World	**10**	**0**	**3**	**3**
Total	**8,714**	**100**	**24**	**364**

Note: Proposed investment scales (*INV*) by ultimate owner. For each supranational region the table highlights the major countries of origin.

[11] Appendix Table 6 gives a breakdown according to the total number of projects.
[12] In the case of Japan the study excludes the start-up investment for the Nissan car factory, but it includes subsequent investments in this plant.

Table 5.5 shows that four countries (Japan, USA, Germany and Korea) account for 229 of 364 projects (63 per cent), while the other 135 projects originate from a further 25 countries. Germany accounts for £1.4 billion in investment, but the rest of Western Europe accounts for only £715 million. After Germany, the next major European source of investment is the Netherlands, but with just 2 per cent of known investment. The USA is second to Japan in terms of the volume of investment, but it is by the most important source by number of projects. There were 110 projects from the USA over 1985-98, but 68 projects from Japan, 40 from Germany and 11 from Korea. During the 1990s much was made of Korean investment, but there are more investments originating from countries on the near-Continent, such as Norway (21 projects), Denmark (18), France (17) and Sweden (13).

The investment type originating from each of the three supranational regions of origin is shown in Table 5.6. Most investment from Western Europe is by start-up, while from the Far East it is primarily by re-investment. Indeed, the re-investments from the Far East amount to £2.7bn, which is a third of the total investment over the study period. The table shows that investment from North America is more broadly based, with much the same amount of FDI in the form of mergers and acquisitions as in start-ups and re-investments combined. In fact, there were 89 start-ups and re-investment projects from the USA, which is more than that from any other country (61 from Japan, 34 from Germany and 11 from Korea). However, while the US investments include 11 of the 28 large projects (see Table 5.3), they do not include the very large investments, so that on average they are smaller in scale than those originating from the other main sources.

For each of the four main countries of origin (Germany, the USA, Japan and Korea), Figure 5.8 gives a breakdown of investment by activity. It is according to the four manufacturing activities identified above, and for the rest of manufacturing and for the rest of industry. Again, US investment is more broadly based than that from the other countries. Manufacturing. accounts for only half of US investment, and within this a third goes to activities outside of the four main manufacturing

Table 5.6 Project Investment by Origin and Type

	WE		NA		FE		Total	
	£'m	%	£'m	%	£'m	%	£'m	%
Start-ups	1,192	57	466	19	1,208	30	2,869	33
Acquisitions	292	14	998	40	120	3	1,410	16
Joint Ventures	1	0	558	22	99	2	658	8
Re-investments	605	29	464	19	2,700	65	3,777	43
Total	**2,091**	**100**	**2,486**	**100**	**4,127**	**100**	**8,714**	**100**

Note: Proposed investment scales (*INV*) by supranational region of origin (*ORIGIN*). WE = Western Europe, NA = North America and FE = Far East. Investment from the Rest of the World (not shown) is £10 million, of which £2m is in start-ups and £8m in re-investments.

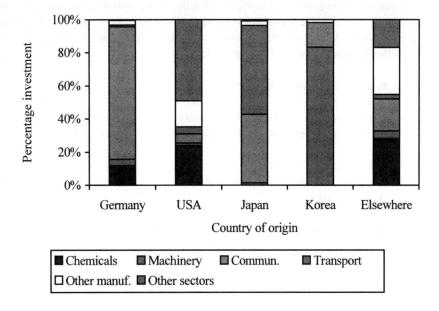

Figure 5.8 Investment by Country of Origin and Activity

Notes: The activities (*IND*) are given in the text.

activities. It is perhaps a reflection of the more mature nature of investment from this source, which is concerned with more-established activities in manufacturing, as well as growth areas in the service sector, such as leisure and entertainment. It is in contrast with the investment arising from the other three countries, which is heavily concentrated. The four manufacturing activities account for virtually all the German investment, 96 per cent of Japanese investment and 98 per cent of Korean investment. However, investments from these countries are in different activities. German investment is in Communications, Japanese investment is split between Communications and Transport, and Korean investment is nearly all in Machinery and Equipment, which includes domestic appliances.

Plant-Level Investment

The re-investment projects account for up to two-fifths of known investment.[13] An interesting issue is the relationship between projects over time, and in particular

---

[13] This is from Table 5.1, part (b). Of course, re-investment projects are over-represented in the dataset, but once allowance is made for this it is reckoned that these projects account for a third of total investment over the study period (Table 5.1, part (c)).

between the re-investments and the projects by which a plant commences in foreign ownership. In Chapter 8 re-investment is analysed in some detail, and the effect of re-investment on plant survival is analysed. In this chapter, the relationship between the different kinds of project is examined.

Project and Plant Definitions

In order to conduct this analysis it is necessary to define certain kinds of project and plant. First, for a given plant, we distinguish between projects as follows:

Initial investment: The first project undertaken by a plant.
Subsequent investment: Any further project undertaken by a plant after the
    Initial investment.

Further, we distinguish between two kinds of plant:

New Plant: A plant commencing in foreign ownership from 1985 onwards.
Mature Plant: Other plants commencing in foreign ownership.

For a New Plant the Initial investment project determines the plant type, so for these there are three types: start-up, acquisition or joint-venture plants. A plant is a Mature Plant if it commenced in foreign ownership prior to 1985. The number of plant types is given in the first row of Appendix Table 3. It shows that of the 337 plants, 72 are Mature Plants and 265 are New Plants (arrived from 1985 onwards), of which 164 are start-up plants, 79 are acquisitions and 22 are joint-venture plants. The table indicates the number of projects per implemented by each plant type, but it shows that these are similar. Two-thirds of 265 New Plants undertake only one project, so that 167 of the 265 plants are not observed to re-invest over the study period. For the Mature Plants the Initial investment project is not observed, so that for these we observe Subsequent investments only. In fact, the data on the Mature Plants are truncated, as only plants that subsequently invest are observed. In the Appendix it is estimated that we have data on three-fifths of the Mature Plants (i.e. plants arriving prior to 1985), which suggests that two-fifths of these failed to make any Subsequent investment by 1998. For the New Plants we believe we have a reasonably complete record of projects, including Initial and Subsequent projects. It enables us to give a classification of the New Plants as follows:

Single Investor: A New Plant that after the Initial investment carries out no
    further significant investment by 1998.
Multiple Investor: A New Plant that carries out a Subsequent investment by
    1998.

From the above, 63 per cent of the New Plants are Single Investors, so that 37% are Multiple Investors. Of course, there is data censoring, as a Single Investor may invest at some time after 1998.[14] We now analyse the pattern of plant investment, distinguishing between Mature and New Plants, and between Single and Multiple Investors. Again, it is for known investments only, but we subsequently examine the overall pattern of plant investment by scaling-up this up at the plant level.

Multiple and Single Investors

The details of the known investments at the plant level are given in Table 5.7. It was mentioned above that the 364 known investment projects were carried out by 230 plants, but for only 172 plants is there a complete record of investment in each project undertaken over the study period. These are shown in Table 5.7, and they

Table 5.7 Plant-Level Investment by Plant Type

	All	Known cases		Investment	
	No.	No.	%	Total (£'m)	Mean (£'m)
Start-up Plants					
Single Investors	100	55	55%	1,827	33.2
Multiple Investors	64	31	48%	2,608	71.6
Acquisition Plants					
Single Investors	53	17	32%	801	47.1
Multiple Investors	26	8	31%	685	65.2
Joint Venture Plants					
Single Investors	14	7	50%	580	82.8
Multiple Investors	8	1	13%	101	34.0
Mature Plants					
One project	38	31	82%	143	4.6
More than one project	34	22	65%	1,969	15.4
All Plants	**337**	**172**	**51%**	**8,714**	**37.6**

Note: Known cases are plants for which there is a compete record of project investment. Total investment is all known investment (364 projects), whereas the mean investment is calculated only for known cases (261 projects). Monetary figures at 1995 prices.

---

[14] In Chapter 8 we find that a plant either carries out a re-investment within a period of 7 to 8 years or not at all, so only some of the Single Investors will possibly invest after 1998.

involve 261 projects. Of course, there could be a bias towards the Single Investors, as the more projects a plant undertakes the more likely it is to have missing data on investments and so not included, although it is not apparent from the table. It shows that plant investment is much more likely to be known for Mature Plants, whereas for the New Plants it varies between 52 per cent for start-up plants, but 36 and 32 per cent for the joint ventures and acquisitions. Thus, the data are a little thin, and it is difficult to know how representative are the known plant investment data, on which more is said below.[15] The table shows the total and mean investment by the plants. In the case of the former it is all projects associated with the plant types (i.e. all 364 projects), but the mean investment scale is calculated for only the plants where there is a full record of project investment (i.e. 261 projects).

The importance of the start-up plants once the Subsequent investments are taken into account is revealed by Table 5.7. These plants carried out a total of £4.4bn in investment over the period, which dominates that of other types of New Plant (the respective figures for acquisition and joint-venture plants are £1.5bn and £0.7bn), and it is much larger than that for the Mature Plants (£2.1bn). Overall, plants that carry out more than one project (including the Mature Plants) account for £5.4bn or 62 per cent of investment over the study period. As regards the mean plant scales, not surprisingly, the table shows that the multiply-investing plants carry out much more investment on average.

A summary of the Initial and Subsequent investment projects implemented by the Multiple Investors is shown in Table 5.8.[16] The vast majority of the Subsequent investments are re-investments, so these terms are used interchangeably. The 64 Multiple Investor start-up plants carried out a total of 160 projects, which is a ratio of 2.5. It is much the same for the acquisitions and joint ventures, at 2.6 in each case. Overall, the three types of New Plant are just as likely to become a Multiple Investor (Table 5.7), and once a Multiple Investor they carry out a similar number of projects per plant. In the case of the start-up plants, Table 5.8 shows the mean scale of the Subsequent investments is the same as for the Initial investments (£31m and £30m respectively). Further, these are similar to the mean investment scale of the Single Investors of £33m, shown in Table 5.7, so that the greater investment associated with the start-up plants does not result from greater investment scales, but because these plants implement more projects. In the case of the acquisition plants there is a different pattern, as the mean scale of the Subsequent investments is smaller (£14m) than the Initial investments, whether the latter is undertaken by a Multiple Investor (£42m) or by a Single Investor (£47m).

---

[15] Comparison could be made at the plant level with the total number of jobs in projects implemented by each plant, but it is not attempted. The representativeness of the data is most problematic for the joint ventures, with just a single observation on Multiple Investors.

[16] Single Investors implement Initial investments but not Subsequent investments, so that details of the projects implemented by these can be found in Table 5.7.

Table 5.8 The Projects of Multiple Investor New Plants

	Number of cases		Investment (£'m)	
	Total	**Known**	**Total**	**Mean**
Start-up Plants				
Initial investment	64	31	1,042	30.0
Subsequent investments:	96	41	1,566	31.4
Re-investment	(90)	(37)	(1,370)	(29.6)
Acquisition	(5)	(3)	(187)	(61.4)
Joint Venture	(1)	(1)	(8)	(8.2)
Acquisition Plants				
Initial investment	26	8	407	42.4
Subsequent investments:	42	13	278	14.1
Re-investment	(38)	(12)	(273)	(14.8)
Acquisition	(3)	(1)	(5)	(5.2)
Joint Venture	(1)	(0)	(0)	(0.0)
Joint Venture Plants				
Initial investment	8	1	71	32.0
Subsequent investments:	13	1	30	2.0
Re-investment	(12)	(1)	(30)	(2.0)
Acquisition	(1)	(0)	(0)	(0.0)
Joint Venture	(0)	(0)	(0)	(0.0)

Note: Known cases are plants for which there is a complete record of project investment. Total investment is all known investment (364 projects), whereas the mean investment is calculated only for known cases (261 projects). Monetary figures at 1995 prices.

The Scale of Plant Investment

The above analysis relates to the known investment data. In order to determine the relative significance of the different plant types in terms of the overall scale of plant investment it is necessary to allow for the fact that a third of the investment data are missing, while there is a complete record of investment for only half the plants (see Table 5.7). A correction for the missing data is carried out in Table 5.9, based on a *pro rata* allocation at the plant level.[17] Part (a) of the table presents the known investment data in respect of all 364 projects, with a disaggregation according to the Initial and Subsequent investments. Again, it shows the importance of the start-

---

[17] It therefore differs from that undertaken in Table 5.1, which was at the project level.

Table 5.9 Initial and Subsequent Investment by New Plants

	SU	AC	JV	New Plants
(a) Inward Investment Dataset				
Initial investment (£'m)	2,869	1,208	651	4,728
Subsequent investment (£'m)	1,566	278	30	1,874
Total investment (£'m)	4,435	1,486	681	6,602
% Total investment	67%	23%	10%	100%
% Subsequent investment	35%	19%	5%	28%
(b) Estimated Total Investment				
Initial investment (£'m)	5,470	3,817	1,788	11,076
Subsequent investment (£'m)	3,666	900	394	4,960
Total investment (£'m)	9,136	4,717	2,182	16,036
% Total investment	57%	29%	14%	100%
% Subsequent investment	40%	19 %	18%	31%

Note: A New Plant entered into foreign ownership over the study period 1985-98. Part (a) reports the known investment data, while part (b) estimates the total investment in each category. SU = start-up plant, AC = acquisition plant and JV = joint-venture plant.

ups, although investment is more likely to be known for these plants (52 per cent against 36 and 32 per cent for the other plant types – see above). Part (a) of Table 5.9 also shows the importance of re-investment in the case of start-up plants.

To allow for the missing cases, part (b) of Table 5.9 scales-up the data to get a sense of the total investment undertaken by the New Plants. This uses the mean investment scale for each of the three types of New Plant and according to Initial and Subsequent investments. It gives an estimate of total FDI for the New Plants of £16,035 million over 1985-98. It is much higher than the estimate that was arrived at in Table 5.1, and which included the Mature Plants. The scaling-up is now done according to the plants rather than projects, and the discrepancy arises because of the high proportion of missing data on the acquisition plants, on which the known investment scales are very large. Reflecting this, it suggests the acquisition plants undertake a greater proportion of total investment (29 per cent against 23 per cent in part (a)) and that the start-ups undertake a much smaller proportion of this (57 per cent compared with 67 per cent). Thus, the scaling-up of investment at the plant level is not very successful, and the figures in Table 5.1 are preferred.

Plant Dynamics

Before closing this chapter it is worth briefly considering the characteristics of the Multiple Investor plants compared to the Single Investors. This is in terms of the size distribution of the plant investment. For the New Plants for which there is a complete record of investment, Table 5.10 shows investment according to three size levels.[18] Again, it shows that the overall pattern of investment is dominated by the large investments and by start-up plants. However, the split between the Multiple and Single Investors reveals something about plant dynamics. First, it shows the Single Investors tend to be small plants. Of the total of 79 Single Investor plants, 61 (77 per cent) have total investment of less than £10m. Second, plants that enter small tend to stay small. Of the total of 80 plants that have total investment of less than £10m, only 19 (24%) are Multiple Investors, going on to implement at least one Subsequent investment. Finally, in the case of the start-ups it suggests that the number of large plants (> £50m) that re-invest is relatively small, so only 5 of the 86 start-up plants are Multiple Investors in this size range.

Table 5.10 Plant Investment Scales for New Plants

	< £10m		£10m - £50m		> £50m	
	£'m	(No.)	£'m	(No.)	£'m	(No.)
Start-ups						
Multiple investors	75	(17)	161	(9)	1,983	(5)
Single investors	121	(47)	144	(6)	1,562	(2)
Acquisitions						
Multiple investors	13	(2)	35	(2)	474	(4)
Single investors	45	(9)	58	(3)	698	(5)
Joint Ventures						
Multiple investors	0	(0)	34	(1)	0	(0)
Single investors	4	(5)	19	(1)	556	(1)

Note: Total known investment in plants for which all the project investment scales are known. Plant numbers are given in parentheses, which sum to 86, 25 and 8 for the plant types respectively (119 in total for New Plants), and can be reconciled with Table 5.7.

Conclusions

This chapter has analysed the pattern of foreign-owned investment in North-East England over the period 1985-98. It utilises the Inward Investment Dataset, which identifies around £8.7 billion in investment. The investments are prospective, but it is believed that every project went ahead in some form, and the data are believed to be representative of the overall volume of investment undertaken in the region over

---

[18] In total there are 17 plants with investment totalling more than £50 million. Earlier it was indicated that 23 plants carried out investment in excess of £50m over 1985-98, so that the other six plants are Mature Plants.

the period. The level of investment over the period is about £1 billion per annum (1995 prices), representing about 5 per cent of a region's GDP, or around 15 per cent of its manufacturing output (at 1995). About a third of this is in the form of start-ups, a third through re-investment (possibly by plants existing prior to 1985) and the remainder is through acquisitions and joint ventures. The analysis reveals many interesting findings about the nature and pattern of inward investment.

First and foremost, the chapter finds that the investment is heavily concentrated, with 28 projects, each in excess of £50 million (1995 prices), accounting for 80 per cent of total FDI in the region over 1985-98. These 28 projects are just 8 per cent of projects, and implemented by 20 plants. There is a similar level of concentration across the different project types, so that projects in excess of £150m account for 78 per cent of start-up investment and 58 per cent by re-investment. Thus, the pattern of investment is dominated by a small number of projects. In addition, investment is heavily concentrated in terms of its spatial distribution and activity. It tends to be located towards eastern-seaboard, close to the centres of population, reflecting good market access, access to labour and the operation of public policy in the laying-out of estates, either under regional policy, the New Town programme or in the wake of industrial closures. This appears to be evidence of classical location factors and industrial complexes, rather than agglomeration economies *per se*. Further, there is a striking sectoral concentration of investment, with three-quarters of investment in four two-digit manufacturing activities. These four activities account for more than 95 per cent of the investment coming from each of Germany, Japan and Korea.

Overall, much of the analysis is novel, as for the first time it analyses the pattern of investment by foreign investors in a region and over a long period. While other aggregate-level regional studies point to a concentration of FDI by activity, this chapter shows that the concentration is more deep-rooted. In particular, there is a heavy concentration of investment in projects and plants, which largely determines the overall pattern of FDI, especially since the typical inward investor is actually quite small (a median investment of not much more than £2 million). The chapter also points to the importance of the start-up plants in the regions. These account for half the investment over the study period, while the start-up plants that multiply invest on average carry out twice the investment of a singly-investing plant. Indeed, plants that enter small tend to be Single Investors, and hence stay small. There are also differences by country, since while virtually all the German start-up investment is by Single Investors, in the case of Japan it is nearly all by Multiple Investors, so that these are much more likely to stage their investments.

Chapter 6

Project Jobs

The purpose of this chapter is to examine the pattern of jobs associated with foreign direct investment in the North East of England. These are the jobs that the inward investors plan to have in place within two years of project commencement. It can be seen from Chapter 4 that pre-existing research on the jobs provided by FDI tends to be aggregative in nature, either at the regional level, e.g. Hill and Munday (1994) and Brand *et al* (2000), or examining specific issues, such as a 'components of change' analysis (Stone and Peck, 1996), so that relatively little is known about the pattern of jobs in the round. The chapter has two objectives. The first is to describe the characteristics of the jobs, according to the type, timing, number, location and so on, linking these to the pattern of investment described in the previous chapter. The second aim is to undertake an analysis to determine the nature of the projects that generate relatively greater or fewer jobs. An issue is whether the projects that generate more jobs simply represent the intrinsic project characteristics (e.g. type or activity) or whether they reflect the nature of FDI arising at different times, from different countries or locating in different parts of the region.

Unlike the investment data, the number of project jobs is known in virtually all cases, so that the issue of representativeness does not arise. In total, the Inward Investment Dataset identifies about 80,300 project jobs, and this chapter builds up a picture of the pattern of these jobs. It begins by looking at the relationship between the jobs and investment. It shows that large investments generate proportionately many fewer jobs, but that there is a concentration of jobs across projects, although much less so than was the case for investment in Chapter 5. As with investment, the jobs are prospective, and in the next chapter the relationship between the project jobs and actual plant employment is considered. The chapter begins by considering the pattern of the project jobs promised by the investors.

The Pattern of Project Jobs

The 511 projects for which job details are known promised a total of 80,318 jobs over 1985-98 (Appendix Table 11). Most of these jobs are in manufacturing, and their contribution is substantial, as at 1999 manufacturing employment in the North

East region was only 176,000 jobs.[1] It is also very high by historical standards, as Hudson (1995) reports that there were no more than 8,500 jobs in foreign-owned plants in the region in 1963, increasing to 53,000 by 1978 and to 80,000 in 1993.

The Inward Investment Dataset distinguishes between new jobs, which do not pre-exist the project, and safeguarded jobs, which do. In some ways, the distinction between these is artificial as both kinds of job depend on project implementation. A safeguarded job may otherwise be lost, and so is dependent on implementation, although a new job may be preferred, as job 'additionality' appears more clear-cut. Appendix Table 11 shows that half the 80,318 jobs are associated with re-investment projects (45 per cent), a quarter with start-ups (24), and that much of the remainder arise in acquisition projects (27). It is different to the pattern of total investments in part (c) of Table 5.1, where the respective percentages are 34, 32 and 25 per cent. It suggests re-investments are relatively labour-intensive, but that start-up projects are much less so. However, the start-ups are more or less exclusively associated with new jobs, whereas only 60 per cent of the jobs in re-investment projects are new (Appendix Table 11). Overall, 45,684 of the total project jobs (57 per cent) are new jobs, and the other 34,634 jobs are safeguarded.

Relative to Investment

The number of jobs relative to investment (known investment cases only) is shown in Appendix Table 11. Overall, 9.2 jobs are associated with each £1 million of investment. It is similar for re-investment projects, at 9.6 jobs, but smaller for start-ups, at 6.7 jobs, although start-ups are much more likely to be associated with new jobs. In Chapter 5 a strong positive correlation was reported between the investment scale and total project jobs. This relationship was plotted in Figure 5.1, and it was suggested that the larger projects were associated with proportionately fewer jobs. It is now investigated by regressing the variables in log form, but with a quadratic term included to allow for the possibility of a non-linear relationship:

$$\ln JOB_i = 3.645 + 0.523 \ln INV_i - 0.007 [\ln INV]_i^2 \quad (6.1)$$
$$\quad\quad (55.6) \quad (11.0) \quad\quad\quad (0.7)$$

$$R^2 = 0.44, n = 350, \text{t-statistics in parentheses.}$$

The coefficient on the ln *INV* term indicates that a 2 per cent increase in the investment scale is associated with a 1 per cent increase in the number of project jobs. It means that the proportion of jobs falls quite sharply with an increase in the investment scale. Thus, on average, a £5m project is associated with 90 jobs, but a £50m project has 300 jobs and a £500m project has a 1,000 jobs (ratios of 18, 6 and

---

[1] Further, our figures exclude jobs in foreign-owned plants existing prior to 1985 (Mature Plants). At 1999 the Inward Investment Dataset comprises 282 surviving plants, but there are estimated to be 475 foreign-owned plants in the region at this time (see Appendix).

2 respectively). Figure 5.1 suggests that there is a different relationship for the very large projects, but the quadratic term is unable to capture this. However, when it is excluded, and instead spline terms are entered on the ln *INV* and constant term for the investments of more than £50 million, then both of these are also insignificant. It suggests that the relationship between the jobs and investment scale is the same for the larger investments as for other projects, but in a logarithmic form.

Temporal Distribution

The time profile of the 80,318 projects jobs is given in Figure 6.1, which shows an increasing number of jobs with time, especially from mid-1990s onwards. Indeed, the years from 1994 to 1998 account for half the jobs (and there is not a full year's worth of data for 1998). While there is an increase in the number of projects in the late 1990s, it is clear that it cannot explain for the increase in the number of jobs. It arises from a small number of very large projects in the years 1994 and 1995 from Germany, Japan and Korea. In some respects the profile of jobs is similar to the profile of investment (see Figure 5.2), but less variable, since whereas nearly 40 per cent of total investment occurs in the years 1994 and 1995, only around 20 per cent of the total jobs are in these years. The time profiles of the new and safeguarded jobs (not reported) shows that while a quarter of the new jobs occurred in the years 1994 and 1995, over half of the safeguarded jobs occur over 1994-98. It is perhaps not surprising, as the safeguarded jobs are more likely to occur later on in time, when plants re-invest subsequent to the Initial investment.

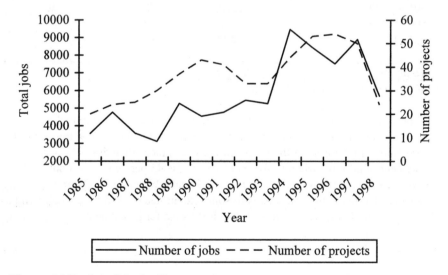

Figure 6.1 Project Jobs by Year

Note: Number of proposed project jobs (JOB) by date of commitment.

Size Distribution

The mean project size is 157 jobs (i.e. 80,318 jobs in 511 projects), but the median number of jobs associated with the projects is just 61, so that as with investment the distribution of jobs is skewed. The first point about this is that many projects are in fact quite small (i.e. half promise fewer than 61 jobs). The other point is that the skewness is much less than is the case for investment, as the large investments are much less labour-intensive. The distribution of the project jobs is reported in Table 6.1. It shows that 29 projects have more than 500 jobs associated with them (i.e. 5.6 per cent of projects account for 35.6 per cent of the jobs). This compares with 28 large investment projects (7.7 per cent of known projects) that account for 78.7 per cent of investment.

Table 6.1 Concentration of Project Jobs

	No. Jobs	Cum. %	No. Projects
1 – 5	73	0.1	19
6 – 10	359	0.5	41
11 – 25	1,324	2.2	75
26 – 50	4,091	7.3	99
51 – 100	6,264	15.1	82
101 – 200	12,909	31.2	86
201 – 500	26,700	64.4	80
501 – 1000	13,490	81.2	20
1001 – 2500	12,108	96.3	8
>2500	3,000	100.0	1
Total	80,318		511

Note: Total number of proposed project jobs (*JOB*).

The distribution of the project jobs by size class can also be examined by project type (not shown). Project jobs are most concentrated for the acquisitions, but also for start-ups. In the case of the latter, projects with more than 500 jobs account for 40 per cent of all jobs, whereas for acquisitions it is 45 per cent. For joint ventures and re-investments the respective figures are 20 and 29 per cent. Overall, it can be concluded that the pattern of jobs is to some extent determined by a small number of projects, but that it is much less so than is the case for investment.

Location

The geographical distribution of the jobs by county is shown in Table 6.2, which also gives a disaggregation according to new and safeguarded jobs. Nearly half the

Table 6.2 Distribution of Project Jobs by County

	Total Jobs		New Jobs		Safeguarded Jobs	
	No.	**%**	**No.**	**%**	**No.**	**%**
Northumberland	10,349	13	3,468	7	6,971	20.
Tyne and Wear	34,590	43	22,669	50	11,921	35
Durham	21,920	27	12,135	27	9,785	28
Cleveland	13,369	17	7,412	16	5,957	17
Total	**80,318**	**100**	**45,684**	**100**	**34,634**	**100**

Note: Number of total, new and safeguarded jobs (*JOB, JOBNEW* and *JOBSAFE*).

total jobs are in Tyne and Wear, with half of the remainder in Country Durham. It is in line with the distribution of the investment shown in Table 5.4. However, while Cleveland (or Teesside) has 24 per cent of investment it has only 17 per cent of the jobs, and Northumberland has 5 per cent of investment but 13 per cent of the jobs. The new and safeguarded jobs occur in different parts of the region. The new jobs are located in and around the Tyne and Wear conurbation, while the safeguarded jobs are more evenly distributed across the region.[2] The large number of new jobs in Tyne and Wear reflects the concentration of start-up investment in this county (see Table 5.4), but the high number of safeguarded jobs in the other parts seems to reflect a number of considerations. Northumberland has 20 per cent of safeguarded jobs, but only 8 per cent of new jobs, which is because of the relatively large amount of re-investment and acquisition activity taking place in this county. County Durham has a high number of safeguarded jobs arising from re-investments, while in Cleveland it reflects the acquisitions.

Activity

The number of project jobs by broad sector of activity is given in Table 6.3. It also gives the percentage of the total jobs that are either new or in start-up projects, and the number of jobs per £1 million of investment (known cases only). It shows that the manufacturing sector accounts for the majority of jobs (87 per cent), but which is similar to the proportion of investment undertaken by this sector (84 per cent). The next largest sector is Construction with 5 per cent of jobs, while Wholesale and Retail Trade and the Real Estate and Business Activities each have 3 per cent of the jobs. As a whole, the service sector has a very small share of the jobs (8 per cent), although jobs in this sector are almost always new and by start-up. By contrast, less than a quarter of manufacturing jobs are in start-ups and just over half are new. In total, a million pounds of FDI is associated with nine jobs, of which about half are

---

[2] A sub-regional analysis shows there is also a concentration of new jobs at Stockton in the Teesside conurbation (i.e. Cleveland).

Table 6.3 Distribution of Project Jobs by Industrial Sector

	Total jobs			Jobs / Inv.
	No.	% New	% Start-up	
Mining and Quarrying	190	0	0	0.1
Manufacturing	70,156	56	24	7
Electricity, Gas and Water Supply	141	81	0	12
Construction	3,887	35	6	51
Wholesale and Retail Trade	2,051	96	18	11
Hotel and Restaurants	179	49	49	8
Transport, Storage and Communications	48	100	85	4
Financial Intermediation	232	100	100	82
Real Estate, Renting and Business Activities	2,069	73	31	13
Education	25	100	100	3
Community, Social and Personal Services	1,350	93	73	2
Total	**80,318**	**57**	**24**	**9**

Note: Total jobs (*JOB*) by NACE two-digit headings. The final column shows the jobs per £1 million in investment (1995 prices) for known cases only. New jobs and jobs in start-up projects are known for 511 projects, but investment for 364 projects.

new jobs. This is much the same for the manufacturing sector (which dominates the overall job pattern), although on average the utilities, construction and financial services tend to be much more labour intensive.

The bulk of the jobs are created in manufacturing, and a breakdown of these is given in Figure 6.2. As with investment, there is a strong concentration of proposed jobs in a few two-digit manufacturing activities, and these are the same activities as before. These are: Transport Equipment [NACE code 34]: 22% of jobs (and 26% of known investment); Communications [32]: 21% (40%); Chemicals [24]: 13% (14%); and Machinery and Equipment [29]: 12% (9%). Together they account for two-thirds of manufacturing jobs (against 89 per cent of manufacturing investment), and 59 per cent of total jobs. Since 54 per cent of the projects are in manufacturing, then to an extent the jobs reflect the distribution of projects.[3] After these activities, the next most important manufacturing activities, according to the number of jobs, are Electrical Machinery (7% of manufacturing jobs), Metal Products (5%), Rubber

---

[3] There are differences in the nature of the jobs occurring in the four main manufacturing activities (not shown). In Chemicals only 7 per cent of jobs are as a result of start-ups and 19 per cent are new, reflecting the large number of acquisitions in this sector. In Transport Equipment while 19 per cent of jobs are in start-ups, nearly 80% are new jobs, reflecting re-investment by existing plants. Communications and Machinery and Equipment activities both have an above-average proportion of start-up jobs and new jobs.

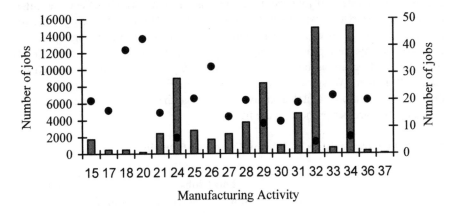

■ Number of jobs (left scale) ● Jobs / £1m investment (right scale)

Figure 6.2 Distribution of Jobs by Manufacturing Activity

Notes: NACE two-digit classification, with the activities given in the note to Figure 5.6. Activities with zero jobs not shown. The job-investment ratio for 37 is 300 and not shown.

and Plastic Products (4%) and Pulp and Paper Products (4%).

It was reported above that the larger projects are much less labour intensive, and this carries over to activities.[4] Activities with a large amount of investment promise proportionately many fewer jobs. The inverse relationship between the number of jobs and the labour intensity is apparent from Figure 6.2.[5] The four manufacturing activities that have received most jobs occupy the bottom four positions out of the eighteen activities in terms of the ratio of jobs to investment. It reflects the small number of very large, but highly capital-intensive projects in these activities (see Table 5.3 on the 28 large investment projects). It explains why the jobs are much less concentrated across projects than was the case for investment. Excluding these four activities the jobs per £1 million of investment doubles from 9 to 19 jobs.

Origin

Around 25,000 jobs originate from each of Western Europe, North America and the Far East, with only 1,400 jobs coming from elsewhere in the world. However, while Western Europe and North America are similar in terms of the proportion of jobs

---

[4] The labour-capital ratio is nine-times higher for a £5m investment compared to a £500m project. Further, these are prospective jobs, and we find in the next chapter that the larger projects are proportionately less likely to achieve their job targets.
[5] The mean investment scales of the activities are shown in Figure 5.6.

that are new, in start-ups or in manufacturing, Table 6.4 shows that there is a much higher proportion of jobs in each category that originate from the Far East. Thus, in excess of 90 per cent of jobs from the Far East are new, which reflects the higher proportion of start-ups, while nearly all these jobs are in manufacturing. The job-investment ratio is lower for Far Eastern projects, although the average number of jobs provided by these projects is higher, as they tend to be larger in scale. Projects from the Far East are associated with around 200 jobs on average, compared with about 140 jobs for Western Europe and North America. Thus, while projects from the Far East are more capital-intensive, on average they generate more jobs, and of which a much greater proportion are new jobs.

Table 6.4 Characteristics of Jobs by Country of Origin

	Total Jobs				Jobs /
	No.	New (%)	Start-up (%)	Manuf. (%)	Inv
Western Europe	27,698	40	14	79	9
North America	24,300	41	17	86	7
Far East	26,983	90	42	99	6
Rest of the World	1,337	15	6	63	35
Total	**80,318**	**57**	**24**	**87**	**9**

Note: Final column gives jobs per £1 million in investment (1995 prices), but for known cases only.

An Analysis of Variance

The preceding section considers the pattern of project jobs according to a number of characteristics, such as the time, location, activity and country of origin. However, it provides no real sense of the relative importance of these different characteristics in explaining variations in the number of project jobs. For example, is it that the projects generating a relatively large number of jobs do so because they arise from a particular source region, because they are in a certain activity or because they arrive at a particular time? Pauly and Reich (1997) argue foreign-owned plants reflect and retain the characteristics of the host country. However, an alternative view is that projects simply reflect their intrinsic physical characteristics. While we cannot address this argument directly, what we can do in the remainder of the chapter is to see if the number of project jobs reflects the intrinsic project characteristics or not.

The project characteristics are considered together in a multivariate setting using an Analysis of Variance (ANOVA) and an Analysis of Covariance (ANCOVA). ANCOVA differs from ANOVA as it includes a continuous independent variable, known as a concomitant variable, which in this case is the project investment scale. It allows us to examine if there are characteristics that determine the project job scale in addition to the scale. The two types of analysis give answers to different questions. In ANOVA the issue is whether there are certain project characteristics (e.g. year, type, location, activity, country of origin and so on) that lead to more or less jobs in projects. In ANCOVA the issue is whether there are characteristics that lead to more or less jobs in projects of a similar investment scale.[6] After having established which variables are significant, in the next section an attempt is made to determine which categories of each variable are important. Not only is the total number of project jobs examined, but so are the job type (i.e. new or safeguarded) and the project type (i.e. start-up, acquisition and so on).

The idea behind both ANOVA and ANCOVA is that they decompose the total variation of a variable (total sum of the squares) into two components: that part that is explained by the independent variables (explained sum of the squares) and the remaining part that is unexplained by the regression (residual sum of the squares). The explained sum of the squares of each variable is identified in order to determine its contribution to the total sum of the squares of the regression, and an F-statistic is calculated to examine if it makes a significant difference to the variation in the dependent variable. As such, the analyses allow statistical identification and testing of the variables to see which contribute to more or less jobs promised by the inward investors. The analyses are conducted at the project level, but both the jobs (*JOB*) and investment (*INV*) are measured in natural logarithmic form. An F-statistic is calculated for each variable under the null hypothesis that it makes no significant difference to the variation in ln *JOB*. An F-test depends on the degrees of freedom associated with each variable, so that these are also reported.

The Variables

Initially, ANOVA and ANCOVA were carried out using as independent variables all of the terms for the project characteristics and policy terms in Appendix Table 2.[7] However, the results from this, which are reported in Jones (2004), were largely meaningless. This is because a country of origin term could be significant in the analysis of variance, but due to a small number of countries that as a source of FDI are relatively unimportant. The problem is that by themselves the categories are not necessarily meaningful, so that it is better to focus on a small number of categories of interest, making use of the results obtained earlier in this chapter. In the case of

---

[6] To illustrate the difference, suppose projects from some country lead to more jobs because they are larger in scale. Then it is expected that the country of origin will be significant in the ANOVA regression, but insignificant in ANCOVA.

[7] This meant that there were 4 counties (*COUNTY*), 22 local authority districts (*TOWN*), 11 industrial sectors (*SECTOR*), 19 manufacturing activities (*MANUF*), 29 countries of origin (*ORIGIN*) and 14 project years (*YEAR*).

the *COUNTY* variable a fourfold classification by county is fine, but for the other variables the number of categories was reduced as follows:

SECTOR – two categories: manufacturing and all other sectors;

MANUF – five categories: one for each of the four main manufacturing activities (Transport Equipment, Communications, Chemicals and Machinery and Equipment) and the other for the remainder of manufacturing;

ORIGIN – four categories: North America, Western Europe, the Far East and the Rest of the World; and

YEAR – three categories: sub-periods 1985-88, 1989-93 and 1994-98.

These are reasonably self-explanatory. In the case of *YEAR* it allows us to focus on the dramatic increase in FDI from the mid-1990s and the lower number of jobs provided in projects in the mid-to-late 1980s (see Figure 6.1). In addition to these, binary variables are included for the other project characteristics (*OTH1* to *OTH6*), for the receipt of Regional Selective Assistance (*RSA*) and the involvement of the agencies (*REG* and *NAT*). The *OTH* terms act as controls, but capture some events occurring outside the study period. The *TOWN* term is omitted, as there was no easy way of using this at the sub-county level to give a small number of categories, e.g. between urban and rural areas.[8] The results are now considered, which begins with those for the total number of project jobs.

Total Project Jobs

The results for the total number of project jobs are reported in Table 6.5, both for ANOVA (Models I to III) and ANCOVA (Models IV to VI). Models I and IV form the basic results, but in order to test the robustness of the findings, the regressions are estimated with the 28 very large investment projects excluded (Models II and V), and with two-way interaction effects (Models III and Model VI). The 28 large investments are shown in Table 5.3. There are 511 projects for which the number of jobs are known, but only 350 projects for which the investment scale is also known, explaining the number of observations in the table.

The ANOVA results are reported in the first three models of Table 6.5. Model I shows that five terms account for significant variations in ln *JOB*. These are the project type (*TYPE*), sector (*SECTOR*), manufacturing activity (*MANUF*), receipt of a government grant (*RSA*) and involvement of the national agency (*NAT*). The location (*COUNTY*), origin (*ORIGIN*) and project year (*YEAR*) are insignificant, as is the term for the regional agency (*REG*). The significance of *TYPE* is perhaps not surprising given the pattern of jobs described above. Likewise, the significance of the activity terms, *SECTOR* and *MANUF*, reflect the concentration of the jobs in a few activities. The policy terms, *RSA* and *NAT*, suggest the public agencies tend to

---

[8] In any event when the *TOWN* variable is included in the full analysis it is insignificant.

Table 6.5 Analysis of Variance of Total Project Jobs

Model	df	I	II	III	IV	V	VI
			ANOVA			ANCOVA	
TYPE	3	68.8***	54.0***	13.5**	13.5***	12.2***	5.7**
COUNTY	1	7.3	6.9	4.0	2.0	2.6	2.4
SECTOR	1	18.1***	21.1***	0.04	7.8***	4.8**	0.4
MANUF	4	42.1***	23.4***	13.6**	18.5***	13.8***	8.8**
ORIGIN	3	2.6	2.9	2.6	0.4	0.3	1.7
YEAR	2	1.3	1.1	0.2	1.9	3.1	0.7
OTH1	1	2.8	1.2	0.5	0.01	0.5	0.2
OTH2	1	0.04	0.1	0.4	0.3	0.2	0.06
OTH3	1	5.5*	6.6**	5.5*	0.9	1.8	1.0
OTH4	1	0.03	0.01	0.06	0.1	0.2	0.01
OTH5	1	1.0	0.4	0.06	0.1	0.2	0.2
OTH6	1	4.3*	0.3	3.3	0.2	0.01	0.1
ln (INV)	1	-	-	-	172.9***	125.5***	162.0***
RSA	1	23.0***	17.9***	21.3***	8.1***	5.7***	14.1***
REG	1	0.5	0.4	0.1	0.3	0.7	0.2
NAT	1	7.2**	6.8**	0.3	7.0***	6.3**	3.7**
Two-way effects		No	No	Yes	No	No	Yes
TSS		981.7	841.5	981.7	586.5	456.9	586.5
R^2		0.26	0.23	0.35	0.54	0.47	0.64
F		6.68***	5.57***	3.45***	14.8***	10.1***	7.3***
n		511	484	511	350	323	350

Note: The contribution of each variable to the total sum of squares TSS of ln *JOB*. The significance of each coefficient is reported under an F-test; df = degrees of freedom, *** = significant at 1%, ** = 5% and * = 10% level. F-tests for significance of all regressors. Models I to III report the results for ANOVA and Models IV to VI for ANCOVA with the concomitant variable ln *INV*. Models I and IV give basic result, Models II and V exclude large investment projects and Models III and VI include two-way interaction terms.

be involved with the projects promising relatively more jobs, but given the agency objectives, it is again not surprising. As regards the insignificant terms it may be thought that the *COUNTY* is too crude as a variable, but when the *TOWN* term is included it is also insignificant. The insignificance of the *ORIGIN* term is expected given the even distribution of jobs across the three regions (Table 6.4).[9] Overall, Model I suggests it is the intrinsic characteristics of projects (type and activity) that are important, and that other aspects are unimportant in explaining the number of project jobs, including when a project arrives (time period), where it originates from (country of origin) and where it goes to (location).

The robustness of the result is examined in Models II and III. The first of these excludes the 28 large investments.[10] It shows that these large projects do not affect the results, possibly because the dependent variable is measured in log form. Model III repeats the estimation of Model I, but includes two-way interaction effects. It is not possible to include all interaction effects, due to computational difficulties, but only those in respect of the terms that are significant in Model I, for which there is a total of ten interaction terms. The significance of the one-way terms is weakened, related to two interaction terms: *SECTOR*RSA** and *MANUF*NAT*. The first of these suggests that RSA is associated with a larger number of jobs in projects in the manufacturing sector, while the second interaction term indicates that the national agency concentrates its efforts in some parts of manufacturing.

The second three models of Table 6.5 report the results for ANCOVA. These include the additional regressor for the natural logarithm of the project investment scale (*INV*), which is strongly significant in each case. Each model is the respective analogue of the first three models in the table. The interaction terms are included on the same basis as before, although not for the investment scale term *INV*.[11] The respective results are similar to those of Models I to III, implying that the factors that lead to more jobs are the factors that lead to more jobs in projects of a similar investment scale. That is to say, projects providing a large number of jobs tend to be labour intensive. For example, projects in receipt of a regional grant not only promise a larger number of jobs, but they are also relatively labour intensive. The regional agency term is significant at or about the 10 per cent level when interacted with each of *TYPE, SECTOR, MANUF* and *RSA*, so only in some kinds of project are these regional-agency projects more labour intensive.

New and Safeguarded Jobs

The results for the analysis of variance of new and safeguarded jobs are reported in Table 6.6. These regressions take as their dependent variable the natural logarithms of the number of new jobs (*JOBNEW*) in Models VII and VIII, and number of safeguarded jobs (*JOBSAFE*) in Models IX and X. Models VII and IX repeat the ANOVA regression of Model I in Table 6.5, while Models VIII and X repeat the ANCOVA of Model IV. Much the same results are obtained for the new jobs as

---

[9] The *ORIGIN* term is also significant where it discriminates between all 29 countries of origin, but which now reflects the fact that most countries offer relatively few jobs.

[10] In respect of these 28 projects there are only 27 observations on the number of jobs.

[11] Including the interaction effects with the investment variable, a similar pattern is found, except that the *SECTOR*INV* term is also significant.

Table 6.6 Analysis of Variance of New and Safeguarded Jobs

Model	df	New Jobs VII	New Jobs VIII	Safeguarded Jobs IX	Safeguarded Jobs X
TYPE	3 / 2	17.8***	14.0***	4.3	1.4
COUNTY	1	6.1	0.9	1.8	3.6
SECTOR	1	7.1**	3.9**	4.0*	0.6
MANUF	4	44.4***	22.9***	12.8*	6.7
ORIGIN	3	8.2*	5.7**	9.9*	6.4
YEAR	2	0.6	0.8	0.2	0.01
OTH1	1	0.6	0.01	2.5	0.02
OTH2	1	0.3	1.7	0.2	0.1
OTH3	1	6.9**	0.4	0.2	0.1
OTH4	1	1.2	0.7	3.2	5.4*
OTH5	1	0.3	0.01	2.4	4.0*
OTH6	1	0.4	2.3*	3.0	1.3
ln (INV)	1	-	162.5***	-	13.1***
RSA	1	18.0***	5.3***	0.3	0.1
REG	1	0.7	0.7	3.0	0.4
NAT	1	3.3*	5.5***	1.1	0.06
TSS		698.7	469.3	291.5	188.5
R^2		0.25	0.63	0.20	0.39
F		5.23***	18.1***	1.50**	1.94**
n		410	307	174	103

Note: Results for ANOVA (Models VII and IX) and ANCOVA (Models VIII and X) for ln *JOBNEW* and ln *JOBSAFE*. Coefficients indicate the contribution of each variable to the total sum of squares TSS. The significance of each term is reported as an F-test; df = degrees of freedom; *** = significant at 1%, ** = 5% and * = 10% level.

before, except that the supranational region of origin now has explanatory power at the 10 per cent level. However, the results for the safeguarded jobs are poor, and at the 5 per cent level nearly all the regressors are insignificant. The exception is the concomitant term, which suggests that projects with more safeguarded jobs are those with a larger investment scale. It suggests that the results for the total jobs shown in Table 6.5 are being driven by the new jobs. It is also the case when the variables are defined according to a large number of categories.

Project Type

The results from running the ANOVA regression in Model I for each of four project types are given in Table 6.7. It shows that there are differences between the project types in the characteristics of the projects associated with more jobs. Broadly, the manufacturing activity is important for all types, but in the case of start-up projects the sector is also important. For re-investment and acquisition projects the country of origin is significant, although it is not significant overall in Table 6.6. The re-investments tend to originate from the Far East and the acquisitions from North America (see Table 5.6). Finally, Table 6.7 shows that the start-ups, re-investments and joint ventures in receipt of a Government grant are associated with a larger job size, which was found for all projects in Table 6.5. However, the overall impression from Table 6.7 is that relatively few of the covariates are significant, although the number of observations can be small. When the equations were re-estimated with the variables grouped into a large number of categories, the results are also poor.

Table 6.7 Analysis of Variance by Project Type

	SU	AC	JV	RE
COUNTY	8.0	5.3	2.0	2.78
SECTOR	10.9**	3.4	0.01	0.05
MANUF	12.5*	4.6	10.2**	34.8***
ORIGIN	7.3	11.7**	5.4*	14.7***
YEAR	0.8	1.2	0.4	3.2
OTH1	0.1	1.4	1.1	0.2
OTH2	0.01	0.6	0.3	0.6
OTH3	12.9***	0.6	0.7	0.01
OTH4	0.7	0.01	-	0.3
OTH5	0.2	0.01	-	1.0
OTH6	0.2	5.4**	-	0.1
RSA	11.3**	1.5	4.9***	3.8*
REG	3.6	1.6	0.2	0.6
NAT	0.01	0.6	0.01	10.2***
TSS	353.4	130.4	29.5	383.1
R^2	0.40	0.31	0.96	0.21
F	3.82***	1.35	4.33	2.82***
n	147	88	22	254

Note: Analysis of variance of ln *JOB* by project type (*TYPE*). The degrees of freedom correspond to those of Tables 6.5 and 6.6. *** = significant at 1%, ** = 5% and * = 10% level. SU = Start-up; AC = Acquisition; JV = Joint venture; and RE = Re-investment.

By Category

The above analysis shows which variables account for significant variations in the number of project jobs, but it does not indicate which of the categories is important within each variable. It is now considered and the effects are quantified. This is achieved by re-estimating the models in the previous tables, but by including each category of each variable in a dummy-variable form. To arrive at the parsimonious results, which are presented in Table 6.8, the insignificant categories are deleted by iteration.[12] The results are given for ANOVA only, corresponding to the results in Tables 6.5 (Model I), 6.6 (Models VI and IX) and 6.7 (all models), and relate to the variables with a small number of categories.[13] There may be no direct association between these two sets of results, as a variable that is significant in the analysis of variance in Tables 6.5, 6.6 or 6.7, need not imply that any of the categories making up the variable is significant effect when considered separately. The results in Table 6.8 must be interpreted relative to the baseline project, which is a joint venture that originates from the Rest of the World, locates in Northumberland over 1985-88 and is in a manufacturing activity outside of the four main activities.[14]

The dependent variable is measured in a natural logarithmic form, i.e. ln *JOB*, so that a semi-log model is regressed. In exponential form the regressors therefore have a multiplicative effect on the number of project jobs *JOB*. For example, the result for the total jobs in the first column of Table 6.8 indicates that a project with baseline characteristics has 44 jobs, i.e. exp (3.786) = 44.1, but an acquisition that otherwise has these characteristics has 126 jobs, i.e. exp (3.786 + 1.052) = 126.2. To put it another way, an acquisition will increase the number of jobs in a baseline project by a factor of 2.86, i.e. exp (1.052) = 2.86. It is expressed as these factors that the estimates are best understood, and we now consider these in turn.

Results Corresponding to ANOVA

The first column of Table 6.8 gives the result for the total number of project jobs. The mean value of the dependent variable, ln *JOB*, is 4.173, which is equal to 65 jobs, while as mentioned above a baseline project on average involves 44 jobs. The results show that an acquisition increases this by a factor of 2.86 (= exp 1.052), and that the other characteristics associated with an above-average total number of jobs are the Transport and Communications activities (by factors of 2.29 and 2.25), the receipt of a grant (1.60) and the involvement of national agency (1.57). However,

---

[12] An alternative approach is at each iteration to delete the most insignificant category for the variable that in the analysis of the previous section had the smallest F-statistic, but this gave qualitatively similar results.

[13] The results for ANCOVA can be found in Jones and Wren (2004a).

[14] The base case for each variable is: *TYPE* – joint venture; *COUNTY* – Northumberland; *SECTOR* – manufacturing; *MANUF* – rest of manufacturing; *ORIGIN* – rest of world; and *YEAR* – 1985-88. The final four columns of Table 6.8 exclude the *TYPE* variable.

Table 6.8 Factors Contributing to Project Job Size

		ANOVA			Project Type			
		Total	New	Safe	SU	AC	JV	RE
Constant		3.786**	3.438**	5.675**	3.425**	6.518**	5.718**	5.514**
TYPE	- start-up				-	-	-	-
	- acquisition	1.052**	1.131**		-	-	-	-
	- re-investment				-	-	-	-
COUNTY	- Tyne and Wear						-1.128**	
	- County Durham	-0.242*						
SECTOR	- non-manufacturing	-0.669**	-0.374*	-0.562*	-0.964**	-1.447**		
MANUF	- Chemicals		-0.402*					
	- Machinery						-4.047**	
	- Communications	0.812**	0.914**	1.044**				
	- Transport	0.827**	0.985**				1.547**	0.975**
ORIGIN	- Western Europe							-1.798**
	- North America			0.978*				-1.634**
	- Far East			-1.223*			-1.460**	-1.840**
YEAR	- 1989-93						-1.291**	
	- 1994-98						-2.232**	
RSA		0.470**	0.411**		0.775**		2.057**	
REG					0.580*		1.124**	
NAT		0.450*						0.705**
mean of dependent variable		4.173	3.790	4.633	3.657	4.898	4.176	4.215
R^2		0.23	0.22	0.18	0.31	0.04	0.86	0.19
F		19.4	15.4	4.7	13.1	-	36.6	17.9
N		511	410	174	147	88	22	254

Note: Parsimonious results from regressing the natural log of the number of project jobs on the project characteristics expressed in dummy variable form. The dependent variable is *JOB*, except *JOBNEW* in column headed 'New' and *JOBSAFE* in column headed 'Safe'. Project characteristics are grouped into a small number of categories as shown. See text for base case. *OTH* terms are included but not shown, a dash indicates a variable was not included, while interaction terms are also not included. ** = significant 1% and * = 5% level. SU = Start-up; AC = Acquisition; JV = Joint venture; and RE = Re-investment.

projects outside of manufacturing have fewer jobs (by a factor of 0.51), as do those in County Durham (0.79). Since these are multiplicative, they indicate a large number of jobs in some projects. For example, a grant-assisted acquisition in the Communications activity, but which otherwise has the baseline characteristics, is predicted to offer 455 jobs, i.e. exp (3.786 + 1.052 + 0.812 + 0.470) = 454.9, although in practice there may be few if any of these projects.

The estimates in the second and third columns of Table 6.8 show that the mean number of new and safeguarded jobs in the baseline project are 44 and 292 jobs respectively. It suggests a much larger scale associated with projects that safeguard jobs. As before, the results for the new jobs are similar to those for the total project jobs. In the case of the results for safeguarded jobs, projects outside manufacturing are less likely to safeguard jobs, as are Far Eastern projects (by a factor of 0.29), but which is in contrast to those from North America (a factor of 2.66). The differences are large, so that compared with a project from the Far East, a project from North America will on average safeguard nine times the number of jobs.[15] Projects from Western Europe lie somewhere between these.[16]

Results Corresponding to Project Type

The last four columns of Table 6.8 report the results for the four project types. They are for the total number of project jobs and correspond to those shown in Table 6.7. There are few observations on the joint-venture projects, while the fit of the model for the acquisitions is poor, although the results are plausible. The table shows that the re-investment projects originating from the Rest of the World are much larger than re-investments from elsewhere (as reflected in the large negative coefficients on the *ORIGIN* terms), so that the results are considered for a plant originating from Western Europe (the baseline plant is otherwise the same as before, except that the type varies). Again, there are differences between the types in the number of jobs. At the mean, a baseline start-up offers 31 jobs, whereas a re-investment has 41 jobs, a joint venture has 304 jobs and an acquisition involves 677 jobs. There are other differences between the types. Start-up and acquisition projects each involve more jobs if they are in manufacturing (by factors of 2.62 and 4.25 respectively), while an acquisition offers fewer jobs in certain locations (by a factor of 0.69 in Tyne and Wear and 0.74 in County Durham), so that large acquisitions occur on the periphery of the region. Finally, RSA is associated with larger start-ups, re-investments and joint ventures (by factors of 2.17, 1.31 and 7.82), as are re-investments with which the national agency is involved (by a factor of 2.02).

---

[15] For example, an acquisition from the USA, which otherwise has baseline characteristics, will safeguard 775 jobs, whereas a similar project from Japan will safeguard just 86 jobs.

[16] The first-three regressions in Table 6.8 were repeated for ANCOVA, with ln *INV* as an additional regressor. They are given in Jones and Wren (2004a), and they are similar to the respective results in Table 6.5. They are essentially generalised regressions of (6.1), given towards the beginning of the chapter, but with the omission of the quadratic ln *INV* term and the inclusion of the dummy-variable covariates. In this case, the coefficient on ln *INV* is 0.452, against an elasticity of 0.523 found previously, again indicating that the larger investments are associated with proportionally many fewer jobs. The results for the new jobs are similar to that for total jobs, except that the manufacturing sector no longer offers extra jobs once the scale of the project is taken into account. The policy terms suggest that projects of a similar investment scale offer more new jobs when in receipt of a grant or involved with the national agency (by factors of 1.37 and 1.67 respectively).

Tests of Robustness

It is possible to test the robustness of the results, but focusing on those for the total number of project jobs shown in Table 6.8. There are three tests. First of all, two-way interaction effects are included, but between significant terms only.[17] The one-way effects were more or less unchanged, both in terms of their significant and the magnitude of the coefficients, suggesting that the results are robust to the inclusion of these. The exception was the term for the Communications activity, which was picked up by interaction terms, and captured a small number of very large projects in this activity. These are untypical and may be regarded as outliers. As a second test, the sample was divided into two roughly equal groups to test for a break in the estimated coefficients.[18] The estimates were significantly different between these two groups, and hence between smaller and larger projects.[19] The break arose from three terms – *MANUF* (Communications), *SECTOR* and *TYPE* (acquisitions) – the former reflecting the very large projects in Communications referred to above, and the other terms suggesting that the smaller manufacturing and acquisition projects have more jobs compared to the other small projects.[20]

Finally, the ANOVA equation for total jobs was re-estimated, but omitting all of the independent variables except for the *TYPE* terms. The purpose of this was to see if some project types offer more jobs than the other types without conditioning on the other project characteristics. However, generally, the estimates on the *TYPE* terms did not vary much compared with the conditional estimates in Table 6.8. The only difference was for acquisition projects, suggesting that these are associated with a larger number of jobs, but which are mainly safeguarded jobs. Overall, these suggest that our results are robust to the inclusion of interaction terms and that they apply to small and large projects alike. The only difference is for a few very large Communications projects, but which may be regarded as outliers.

Conclusions

This chapter examines the pattern of jobs associated with the inward investment projects. Generally, these are jobs that the inward investors plan to have in place within two years of the project date. In total, 80,300 prospective jobs are identified, of which just over a half are new jobs and the remainder are safeguarded, i.e. pre-

---

[17] The results are reported in Jones (2004), Table 8.12.

[18] The division was made around projects promising 50 jobs, with 234 of the 511 projects promising 50 or fewer jobs. In carrying this test an intercept dummy variable was included to allow for the different project job sizes of the two sub-samples, but left unrestricted.

[19] The test statistic is $F(8, 493) = 2.38$ against $F_{0.05}(8, 331) = 1.94$.

[20] The test was also conducted for the ANCOVA regression for the total jobs, but here there was no difference ($F(8, 331) = 1.14$), partly because the inclusion of the investment term picks up the effect of the large Communications projects.

existing the project. The chapter has three objectives: to investigate the relationship between the number of jobs and the project investment scale; to describe the pattern of jobs in terms of a number of characteristics, including the project type, the time profile, size distribution, geographical location, activity and country of origin; and to undertake an analysis of variance of the number of jobs.

On the first of these, there is a close relationship between the investment scale and the number of project jobs, although larger investment projects are associated with proportionately many fewer jobs. The implication of this is that the jobs are much less concentrated in projects than is the case for investment, with the benefit that the foreign-owned jobs are much less vulnerable to the exit of a few plants than is suggested by the analysis of investment in the previous chapter. However, if the primary purpose of attracting FDI to the regions is job creation, then an implication is that the concentration of the Government grants on large plants (apparent from Appendix Table 12) may be rather poor in this respect. In relation to the chapter's second objective, the jobs are not greatly concentrated in projects, but the projects themselves tend to have certain characteristics, leading to a heavy concentration of the jobs in certain kinds of project. This is especially true of the new jobs, with half of these originating from the Far East, half located in Tyne and Wear county and half are in just three manufacturing activities. It suggests a vulnerability of the jobs to events that adversely affect particular industries or particular source countries.

Finally, the chapter finds some systematic differences in the number of jobs in the foreign-owned projects, associated with the project type, sector, activity within manufacturing and involvement of the public agencies. However, once these are taken into account, then other factors do not influence the number of project jobs, including the origin (by broad geographical region), the location (by county or local authority district) and time period (capturing different phases of the business cycle). Further, it is much the same when the investment scale is included in the analysis, which suggests that the same factors are important even when the investment scale is held constant. The implication of this is that the project job scale neither reflects where the project came from, where it goes to, nor when it arrives, so that what is important is the intrinsic project characteristics. Once these are taken into account then the job scale of a project originating from the Far East is no different from that from anywhere else with the same set of characteristics.

Chapter 7

Plant Employment

Having described the pattern of project jobs in the preceding chapter, attention now turns to plant employment. Whereas the project jobs are those that the investors plan to have in place at some time after commencement, plant employment refers to the actual employment levels of these plants. This is known for plants at the end of the study period. The chapter has two main purposes. The first is to describe the pattern of employment in terms of the plant characteristics, i.e. location, activity, country of origin, plant age and so on, and its relationship to investment. Second, the chapter analyses the extent to which the jobs promised by the foreign investors are realised in employment, and in place some time after the investment. To some degree the pattern of employment reflects the pattern of project jobs described in Chapter 6, although the analysis is now at the plant level, while it is important to know how uniformly spread is employment. Reflecting this, most of the analysis of this chapter is concerned with the issue of job targets. It is examined whether the plants deliver on their job promises, which has implications for the results of the previous two chapters. Further, from a policy perspective, it is important to know if there are some types of plant that are more likely to deliver.

The plant employment data are known for all 337 plants at 1999, of which 55 plants exited by this time according to the definition set out in the Appendix. The chapter focuses on the surviving New Plants, i.e. commencing after 1985 and open at 1998, while the issue of survival is dealt with in Chapter 8. A focus are the start-up plants, which account for up to two-thirds of investment by New Plants in the region over 1985-98 (see Table 5.9) and 27,200 jobs (see Table 7.5 below). The start-ups are often taken as synonymous with FDI, and are of interest to the policy-maker, as they are primarily new rather than safeguarded jobs. The chapter offers new insights on the pattern of employment associated with FDI, and it presents results on the extent to which the plants actually deliver the jobs that are promised. It begins by considering the pattern of plant employment.

Pattern of Plant Employment

The Inward Investment Dataset gives details on 337 plants, and the distribution of plant employment (*EMP*) at the middle of the year 1999 is shown in Appendix Table 8. It reveals that 55 plants exited by 1999, but that the other 282 surviving plants have an employment level of 62,400 jobs, which is 7 per cent of the region's employment and a third of its manufacturing employment.[1] There is concentration of employment, with 27 plants having more than 500 employees, representing half the employment in the Inward Investment Dataset. About a third of the plants have less than 50 employees. Towards the close of Chapter 5 a distinction was made between the New and Mature Plants, where the former commenced in foreign ownership from 1985.[2] Of the 282 surviving plants, Table 7.1 below shows that 67 are Mature Plants and 215 are New Plants. Of the New Plants, 129 are start-up plants, 67 plants are acquisitions and 19 are joint ventures, where the plant type is defined by the Initial investment.

New and Mature Plants

Of the 62,400 employees at 1999, Table 7.1 shows that about two-fifths are in the Mature Plants, with nearly half of the remainder in the start-ups and much of the rest in the acquired plants. As such, the Mature Plants are much larger on average, with a mean employment size of 367 jobs against 176 jobs for the New Plants. It perhaps suggests that smaller plants entering prior to 1985 were less able to survive over the long run, pushing up the mean employment size (or maybe the New Plants have yet to grow). However, another factor is that the observations on the Mature Plants are truncated, as only re-investing plants are included in the dataset, and smaller plants are less likely to re-invest (see Chapter 8).[3] The issues do not arise for New Plants, so that Table 7.1 shows that the start-up plants are smaller than the other New Plants. They have a mean employment a size of 139 jobs, against 241 jobs for the acquisition plants and 200 jobs for the joint ventures.

The truncated nature of the data on Mature Plants should be borne in mind when making a comparison, but to lessen this problem, in the remainder of Table 7.1 percentages figures are given for employment *within* each plant type. Overall, the table shows a major reorientation of FDI since the mid-1980s compared with the earlier period. Employment in the Mature Plants is far more likely to be in the north of the region, with 70 per cent in Northumberland and Tyne and Wear, but 45 per cent for the New Plants. Virtually all the employment in Mature Plants is in manufacturing, and within this there is a much higher proportion of employment outside of the four main activities, which have been a focus for FDI since the mid-1980s (Chapter 5). Also, proportionately more employment in New Plants is from the Far East and less from North America. Finally, 90 per cent of employment in

---

[1] In addition there are Mature Plants commencing in foreign ownership prior to 1985 but not investing over 1985-98, which are not included in our dataset.

[2] The difference between these was that for New Plants there is a full record of 'significant' investments, while for Mature Plants the Initial investment (and possibly some Subsequent investments) are not observed.

[3] Another possible explanation is that the Mature Plants include the Nissan car factory, which set up in 1984, and which could be regarded as an outlier. However, excluding Nissan the mean employment size of Mature Plants is still around 300 jobs.

Table 7.1 Employment Profile of Surviving Plants

	New Plants				Mature
	SU	**AC**	**JV**	**All**	**Plants**
Total Employment	17,900	16,150	3,803	37,853	24,578
Number of Plants	129	7	19	215	7
Average Employment	139	241	200	176	367
County (%)					
Northumberland	5	8	10	7	21
Tyne & Wear	41	28	69	38	49
Durham	35	37	7	33	25
Cleveland	19	27	14	22	5
Activity (%)					
Manufacturing Sector	80	85	86	83	99
Of which:					
Chemicals	4	14	10	9	26
Machinery	12	13	8	12	6
Communication	21	16	15	18	5
Transport	23	6	42	18	24
Other	20	36	11	26	38
Origin (%)					
Western Europe	20	48	25	32	36
North America	28	35	15	30	42
Far East	52	11	60	35	20
Rest of the World	0	6	0	3	2
Age (%)					
Pre 1945	-	22	0	9	6
1946 – 59	-	19	0	8	4
1960 – 84	-	36	6	16	90
1985 – 89	59	18	57	41	-
1990 – 94	25	3	22	15	-
1995 – 98	16	1	15	10	-
Not Known	-	2	-	1	-

Notes: Surviving plants at 1999. Mature Plants commenced in foreign ownership prior to 1985. A New Plant may have set up prior to 1985 if it is a foreign acquisition or joint venture after this time. SU = Start-up; AC = Acquisition; and JV = Joint-venture plant.

Mature Plants arrived since 1960, but it is not surprising, as they are included on the basis that they undertake further 'significant' investments over 1985-98.

As regards the New Plants in Table 7.1, plant employment largely follows the pattern of project jobs described in the preceding chapter. Start-up employment is largely in Tyne and Wear and County Durham, while the employment in acquired plants is towards the south of the region. Within manufacturing, employment in the acquisitions is more broadly based, while half the start-up employment is in plants owned from the Far East. However, almost 60 per cent of start-up employment is in plants commencing in the late 1980s. It is perhaps surprising, as employment is measured at 1999 and we might expect a much smaller proportion of employment to be in plants arriving in the late 1980s. Further, the analysis of project jobs shows that most of these jobs were in projects implemented in the mid-1990s (Figure 6.1). Employment in surviving start-up plants for each of three sub-periods is shown in Table 7.2. It shows there are more of the surviving plants starting-up over 1985-89, but that they are also larger in scale on average.[4] Of course, the period 1990-94 is associated with recession, while the period 1995-98 is really only three-and-a-half years, so that the crucial difference is the average project size.[5]

Table 7.2 Employment in Surviving Start-up Plants

Period	Number of Plants	Employment Total	Average
1985-89	54	10,488	194
1990-94	37	4,496	122
1995-98	38	2,916	77
Total	**129**	**17,900**	**139**

Note: The table shows employment (*EMP*) at 1999.

It turns out that the reason that plants starting-up in the late 1980s are much larger on average is because they are more likely to re-invest, which enables them to achieve a larger scale. In the case of the New Plants, a distinction was made in Chapter 5 between the Multiple and Single Investors. A Multiple Investor carries out at least one Subsequent investment after the Initial investment, but a Single Investor does not re-invest over 1985-98. The employment size of the Multiple and Single Investors is shown in Table 7.3 for the New Plants. It reveals that the employment size of a Multiple Investor is about twice the size of a Single Investor, but that this is about three-fold for the start-up plants. It explains the different sizes

---

[4] It is the case when the non-surviving plants are included. For the sub-periods in Table 7.2 the number of start-up plants (survivors and non-survivors) are 68, 53 and 43 respectively (totaling 164 plants), and the mean employment scales at 1999 are 154, 85 and 68 jobs.

[5] This pattern occurs in all years. The average employment of the open plants starting-up in each year over 1985 to 1989 is above that for each year over 1995-98.

Table 7.3 Employment in Surviving Multiple and Single Investor New Plants

	SU	AC	JV	All
Multiple Investors				
Total Employment	12,186	7,605	2,386	22,177
Projects	56	23	8	87
Mean Employment	218	331	298	255
Single Investors				
Total Employment	5,714	8,545	1,417	15,676
Projects	73	44	11	128
Mean Employment	78	194	129	123

Note: SU = Start-up; AC = Acquisition; and JV = Joint-venture plant.

of the start-up plants in the different sub-periods, as a Multiple Investor is likely to start-up earlier in time.[6] It is because plants are in place for some period of time before they carry out a re-investment, and this is explored in the next chapter.

Employment to Investment Ratio

The relationship between the jobs and investment was explored in the previous chapter at the project level.[7] An interesting issue is whether some kinds of plant generate relatively more employment relative to the investment. This bears on the labour intensity of projects, but also on how the plants grow over time. It has implications for job-creation policies, and for which plants are Multiple or Single Investors, as it was found above that the former are up to three-times larger than the Single Investors. Of course, the investment scale is known for only 364 of the 550 projects, which means that there is a complete record of investment for 172 of the 337 plants, and for 119 of the 265 New Plants. There is not much difference in this between the Multiple and Single Investors, even though the former implement more than one project.[8]

Reflecting the nature of the data, the comparison between plant investment and employment is made in Table 7.4 in three ways. First, the employment-investment ratio is calculated for 'All Plants', which divides the plant employment by the total known investment for each plant. Second, it is calculated for 'Surviving Plants', which divides employment by total known investment, but for plants surviving to

---

[6] The proportion of the plants that are Multiple Investors decreases sharply through time as follows: 1985-88: 69%; 1989-93: 41%; 1994-96: 24% and 1997-98: 0%.

[7] It also featured in Chapter 5 when the representativeness of the known investment data was explored.

[8] In the case of the New Plants a complete record of investment is known for 40 of the 98 Multiple Investors (41 per cent), and for 79 of the 167 Single Investors (47 per cent).

Table 7.4 Employment-Investment Ratios for New Plants

	SU	AC	JV	All
'All Plants'				
Multiple Investors	4.7	11.1	23.6	6.5
Single Investors	3.1	10.7	2.5	4.9
'Surviving Plants'				
Multiple Investors	15.3	14.2	23.6	15.4
Single Investors	8.5	10.8	2.5	7.7
'Known Cases'				
Multiple Investors	2.2	4.3	3.4	2.6
Single Investors	2.6	6.4	1.2	3.3

Notes: Employment (*EMP*) is measured at 1999 and investment (*INV*) in £'millions over 1985-98 at 1995 prices. The employment-investment ratio is calculated in three ways, for which details are in text. SU = Start-up; AC = Acquisition; and JV = Joint-venture plant.

1999. Finally, the employment-investment ratio is calculated for 'Known Cases', which considers surviving plants for which there is complete record of investment over 1985-98. The third of these gives the best measure, but it can be based on a small number of observations, so that all three measures are reported.[9]

The employment-investment ratios in Table 7.4 are given for the Multiple and Single Investor New Plants. The ratios for 'All Plants' and 'Surviving Plants' are larger than for 'Known Cases' as they include plants for which employment but not all investment is known. Unfortunately, a consistent pattern does not emerge. The best measure is 'Known Cases', which suggests the employment-investment ratio is greater for the Single Investors. Indeed, the Single Investors are on average associated with employment of 3.3 jobs at 1999 for each £1 million of investment over 1985-98 (1995 prices), but which is 2.6 jobs for the Multiple Investors. Thus, the greater employment size of the Multiple Investors is because they undertake more investment, rather than because they are relatively more labour intensive.

Realisation of Project Job Scales

The above analysis suggests that the investment by the foreign-owned plants leads to a relatively small number of jobs by the end of the study period. In particular, for the preferred measure, £1 million in (proposed) investment by a start-up plant

---

[9] For the Multiple and Single Investors the number of Known Cases respectively are: start-ups (31 and 55 observations), acquisitions (8 and 17) and joint ventures (1 and 7).

over 1985-98 results in only about 3 jobs by 1999. It is of concern, as it was found previously that the start-up plants account for about half the inward investment over the period (see Table 5.7). The purpose of this section is to examine whether the plans of the investors are realised, focusing on employment. For this, employment at 1999 is compared with the number of jobs that are proposed by the plants in their projects. This has important implications, as not only does it bear on the policy of attracting foreign direct investment, but it is important to know if the jobs are long lasting and whether there are some kinds of plant with more beneficial outcomes. It also has implications for locating these plants in the areas of high unemployment, although to date there is hardly any little evidence on this issue.[10]

The remainder of this chapter examines the realisation of prospective jobs, focusing on the New Plants, for which there is a complete record of 'significant' projects. In the case of the acquisition plants the number of jobs refer to those in the acquired plant, which the agencies refer to as 'safeguarded', so that in some sense these are already 'realised', so that the analysis focuses on the start-up plants. A formal econometric analysis is undertaken, which relies on a number of different models as the understanding of the underlying relationship improves. The models are informative and each is presented. However, before this, a descriptive analysis of the data is undertaken, and possible reasons why a plant may fail to achieve its job target are considered.

Failure to Achieve Job Targets

Suppose all of the investment leading to new or safeguarded jobs is observed, then there are two principal reasons why a plant may fail to achieve all of the jobs that it promised in its projects.[11] First, a plant may over-estimate the number of jobs to be created or retained. Second, it may lose jobs through redundancy or closure. The first of these may be either deliberate or in error, while even if the plant correctly estimates the number of jobs, the second of these could be due to events that are foreseen or unexpected. Foreseen events could include capital depreciation or job loss as the product goes through its life cycle, while unforeseen events may arise from either endogenous or exogenous factors, e.g. the trade cycle.

---

[10] Stone and Peck (1996) report that the National Audit Office finds that one-third of assisted projects set-up over 1981-83 with the help of Locate in Scotland failed or had not started at all, and that a further two-fifths had yet to achieve their projected job target (as at 1990). Further, in evidence to the Welsh Affairs Committee of the House of Commons, the *Welsh Development Agency* reported that the 38 projects set up in Wales over 1985-87 provided only half the number of jobs indicated by the then *Invest in Britain Bureau*.

[11] Of course, a plant could exceed its job targets because of missing data on projects or due to additions to employment that are not counted as 'significant' investments and therefore included in the dataset. We return to these possibilities below.

In the Inward Investment Dataset the prospective number of project jobs (*JOB*) is observed in each year over 1985-98 for virtually all projects, but employment (*EMP*) is observed only at 1999. If plant employment is found to be less than the number of project jobs then this presents a problem of interpretation, with different implications. It could mean that the job target was never met or that the target was met but the jobs were later lost. An inaccurate job forecast (whether intentional or otherwise) means that the jobs were never realised, with implications for which projects are attracted, while if the jobs are realised but later lost it suggests policies to maintain and nurture the investors. In the latter case, the issue of which plants are more or less likely to lose jobs is an empirical matter, but in the former case there are several reasons why an investor may deliberately over-state the number of project jobs.

An inward investor may intentionally over-estimate the number of jobs where it is in contact with the public agencies, as it may get more favourable treatment. It could be in terms of direct financial assistance, help in finding a suitable location or even infrastructure, including roads, buildings, works to land, utilities and so on. In the case of the financial aid it was found in the previous chapter that Regional Selective Assistance (RSA) went to projects promising more jobs, although there may be reasons why these plants do not intentionally over-state the jobs. First, RSA is subject to claw-back if the job target is not met, which lessens the incentive for firms to exaggerate the number of jobs (although relatively small amounts may in fact be clawed back in practice). Second, only a third of projects receive RSA (Appendix Table 12), of which some are multiply funded, so that the problem only exists for a minority of plants. Finally, RSA is related to the number of jobs, and it is plausible it will go to the larger and more labour-intensive projects.

While there may be no incentive to over-state the number of jobs in the case of RSA the same cannot be said for those plants having involvement with the other agencies. Generally, the agencies do not give substantial direct financial support to projects, but they may benefit if the plants over-state the number of jobs. This is because the agencies report these jobs as a key output measure for the success of their operations, but with little or no attempt to determine whether the jobs actually all arrive or not, nor indeed if the projects or jobs depend on their operations.

Employment to Jobs Ratio

A summary of the plant employment (*EMP*) around the middle of the year 1999, and the proposed jobs in the project investments (*JOB*) over the study period 1985-98, is given in Table 7.5. This is for New Plants, with a breakdown by plant type. The first part of the table shows employment and project jobs from the raw data, while the second part adjusts these data to address several issues. The raw data show the New Plants promised 56,264 jobs in their projects over 1985-98, whereas their employment at 1999 is only 37,853 (i.e. about 67 per cent). It suggests only two-thirds of the jobs promised over the study period were in place at the end of the study period. However, in terms of whether plants achieve their targets or

Table 7.5 Plant Employment and Project Jobs in New Plants

	SU	AC	JV	All
Raw Data				
Employment	17,900	16,150	3,803	37,853
Project Jobs: All	27,183	24,853	4,228	56,264
Survivors	19,650	22,707	4,110	46,467
Adjusted Data*				
Employment	16,092	14,760	3,312	34,164
Project Jobs: All	25,484	20,484	2,857	48,825
Survivors	18,453	18,508	2,739	39,780
Employment / Jobs:				
All	0.63	0.72	1.16	0.70
Survivors	0.87	0.79	1.21	0.86
Multiple Investors	0.76	0.94	1.01	0.95
Single Investors	1.04	0.71	2.54	0.77

Note: Plant employment (*EMP*) at 1999 and project jobs (*JOB*) promised by plants over 1985-98. Plant survival at 1999. * Includes plants for which there is a complete record of project jobs, but excluding safeguarded jobs in Subsequent investments to avoid double counting. The employment / jobs ratios for the Multiple and Single Investors are for survivors only. SU = Start-up; AC = Acquisition; and JV = Joint-venture plant.

not, attention should be restricted to the plants that survived to 1999. In total, these plants promised 46,467 jobs, leading to the employment of 37,853 at 1999, which suggests that in fact about 80 per cent of the jobs are in place. The impression is that the plants fall someway short of their job targets.

The analysis of the raw data may give a misleading picture for two reasons. First, there are some projects for which the jobs are not known.[12] Second, there is double-counting of jobs, as safeguarded jobs in the Subsequent investments refer to jobs (new or safeguarded) that are already promised in earlier investments. In the remainder of Table 7.5 the raw data is adjusted to correct for these problems. Only plants are included for which there is a complete record of project jobs, while safeguarded jobs in Subsequent investments are not included in the project jobs. However, a similar picture is obtained. Only about 70 per cent of jobs are in place at 1999, which in the case of the survivors is 86 per cent. For all plants (i.e. survivors and non-survivors) the correlation coefficient between plant employment and project jobs for these plants is +0.59, indicating that the plants promising more

---

[12] Appendix Table 2 shows that the jobs are known for 511 of the 550 projects.

jobs have a higher employment level.[13] This is perhaps on the low side, although it increases to +0.70 when the non-survivors are excluded.

In interpreting all this, it is not clear whether the jobs were achieved in the first place and then lost, or whether the jobs never turned up in the first place. For now, we can note that the aggregate job loss rate is 14 per cent in the survivors over the whole period (i.e. 1 - 0.86). It is on the low side and perhaps suggests the targets were met, although it could well be misleading as it excludes the safeguarded jobs in the Subsequent investments, so that is a *net* job loss rate. If the safeguarded jobs in the Subsequent investments are included then the *gross* aggregate job loss rate is 31 per cent, but which again leads to ambiguity in interpreting the results.

Finally, before moving to the formal regression analysis, it can be noted that the employment-job ratios for survivors in Table 7.5 vary across the plant types. The ratio for the start-ups is similar to that for all New Plants, but it is much lower for the acquisitions. In the latter case, the jobs are mainly safeguarded jobs, but it suggests that the acquisitions are followed by redundancies. The net aggregate job loss rate for acquisitions is 21 per cent (1 - 0.79), which increases to a gross job loss rate of 43 per cent once safeguarded jobs are taken into account. For the joint ventures, the plant employment actually exceeds the number of project jobs, which arises in a few Single Investors plants, and perhaps indicates missing data on the Subsequent investments undertaken by these plants.[14] It is of concern, but the joint ventures may occur within existing plants, some of which are UK-owned, making it more difficult to track the Subsequent investments for these plants.

The last two rows of Table 7.5 give the employment-job ratios separately for the Multiple and Single Investors, but for surviving plants only. In the case of the start-ups it shows a much higher ratio for the Single Investors (at around unity), which is the pattern found for the employment-investment ratios in the previous section. In fact, we show that it is related to the size of the plants, with larger plants less able to reach their targets, but which are mainly Multiple Investors.

Regression Analysis of Job Targets

A more thorough-going statistical analysis of the relationship between the number of jobs promised by the inward investors in their projects and the level of plant employment at 1999 is now undertaken. Since plant employment is known only at 1999, then crucial to this is a model to structure the analysis. The examination is for surviving New Plants only, focusing on the start-ups. A number of approaches are used, each shedding light on the relationship between employment and jobs,

---

[13] It reduces to +0.48 when only the jobs in the Initial investment are included, which indicates that the larger plants on entry also tend to employ more.

[14] The joint ventures are not the focus of our analysis, while the gross job loss rate for these over the whole period is correctly signed, and perhaps reasonable at 11 per cent.

and each a development of the preceding model. Initially, it is supposed the jobs accrue and plant employment depreciates smoothly at constant rates over time. Subsequently, distributed-lag and log-linear models are used.

Model of Constant Job Addition and Loss

The relationship between plant employment and project jobs is modelled under the assumption that firms do not experience unexpected events, so that employment changes smoothly over time, with project jobs adding to and being lost at constant rates over time, reflecting physical adjustment possibilities and the technical life of capital respectively. This means that any shortfall in plant employment is because firms fail to reach their targets, and since there are no unexpected events it suggests that the plants must deliberately over-state the number of project jobs.

The relationship between plant employment and project jobs is specified as a partial adjustment mechanism, in which employment depends on the planned or desired level of project jobs. This allows a constant adjustment parameter and a constant depreciation rate to be estimated, where the former tells us whether the firm reaches its job target. It imposes a geometric lag on the coefficients, although a less restricted version of this model is later estimated. For plant i the relationship between the change in plant employment y over the period t -1 to t, and the desired or planned number of project jobs x is as follows:

$$y_{it} - y_{it-1} = \lambda x_{it} - \delta y_{it-1} \qquad (7.1)$$

where λ $(0 < \lambda < 1)$ is the adjustment parameter, measuring the extent to which the project jobs are realised over the unit period, and δ is the constant job depreciation rate. With the data to hand, the partial-adjustment equation cannot be estimated directly, as plant employment is observed for a single year only, but by repeated substitution of (7.1) into itself, lagged one period at each iteration (the inverse Koyck transformation), then:

$$y_{it} = \lambda [x_{it} + (1 - \delta) x_{it-1} + (1 - \delta)^2 x_{it-2} + \dots + (1 - \delta)^k x_{it-k} + \dots] \qquad (7.2)$$

This includes plant employment y at period t only. An apparent difficulty with (7.2) is that only a fraction λ of jobs planned at any time $t - k$ appear by time t, so that the number of project jobs never seem to be fully implemented, but in fact it is not so. The number of project jobs x_{it} is revised in each period to take account of the number of jobs promised in previous periods that have not been implemented up to that time. It can be seen by decomposing x_{it} as follows:

$$x_{it} = y_{it}^* - y_{it-1} + \delta y_{it-1} \qquad (7.3)$$

where y_{it}^* denotes planned plant employment at time t, so that $y_{it}^* - y_{it-1}$ are the number of 'new' jobs and δy_{it-1} are the 'safeguarded' jobs that would otherwise be lost. Substituting (7.3) into (7.1) and proceeding as before gives the pattern of lagged coefficients on y_{it}^* (rather than x_{it}) as λ, $\lambda(1 - \lambda)(1 - \delta)$, $\lambda(1 - \lambda)^2(1 - \delta)$, ... Ignoring depreciation for the moment, so setting $\delta = 0$, planned employment levels are always fully implemented, since $\lambda + \lambda(1 - \lambda) + \lambda(1 - \lambda)^2 + \ldots = 1$. In our case, the plants plan to have the project jobs in place within two years, so that letting t denote years then $\lambda + \lambda(1 - \lambda) \sim 1$, which gives $\lambda \sim 1$. An estimate of λ close to unity therefore tells us that the two-year job target has been realised.

To proceed to an estimating equation a first-order approximation is taken of (7.2). Since δ is small, it is assumed that δ^2 and all higher powers are zero, so that geometric depreciation is approximated by straight-line depreciation. Letting $t = \tau$ denote the time at which employment is observed, then (7.2) can be rewritten with an error term as follows:

$$y_{i\tau} = \alpha z_{i\tau} - \beta d_{i\tau} + u_{i\tau} \qquad (7.4)$$

where $z_{i\tau} = x_{i\tau} + x_{i\tau-1} + x_{i\tau-2} + \ldots + x_{i\tau-k}$, $d_{i\tau} = x_{i\tau-1} + 2 x_{i\tau-2} + \ldots + k x_{i\tau-k}$, $\alpha = \lambda$, $\beta = \delta\lambda$ and $u_{i\tau}$ is the error term. The parameters to be estimated are α and β, from which λ and δ can be unscrambled. If the job targets are realised then a value of λ close to unity is expected. In addition, δ should be small and positive. Equation (7.4) is regressed across plants i, where employment $y_{i\tau} = EMP_{i\tau}$ is measured at $\tau = 1999$ and project jobs x_{it} are measured for each plant over the period 1985-98, so that $x_{it} = 0$ and $k = 13$. According to (7.3), safeguarded jobs are included in the expression for the number of project jobs, so that $x_{it} = JOBNEW_{it} + JOBSAFE_{it}$.

In estimating (7.4) there are two issues. First, an error term is added, but this is not problematic, as (7.4) is estimated across plants using cross-sectional data, and for the Initial investments x_t are calculated for different cohorts of plants starting-up over time.[15] Second, in any year, coefficients on the Initial investments relate to the same vintage of plant (i.e. plants starting in that year), whereas those on the Subsequent investments relate to different vintages of plant. The model assumes that the coefficients on these are the same, but there is evidence that plant age is important in determining a firm's performance (Evans, 1987), which suggests that the coefficients should be allowed to vary between the two kinds of investment.

The ratio of the coefficients on $z_{i\tau}$ and $d_{i\tau}$ give the estimated value of δ, and the plausibility of this and the significance of the estimated coefficient on the $d_{i\tau}$ term determine whether the constant rate of depreciation can be accepted. Further, as a test of (7.4) it should be found that the estimated coefficient on $z_{i\tau}$ is the same for all the x_{it} terms and that a constant term is insignificant when included.

---

[15] Issues concerning autocorrelation arise when estimating distributed lag models with time-series data, but it is usually assumed that the error on (7.2) is white noise, while first-order autocorrelation is induced in (7.1) by the Koyck transformation. If an assumed white-noise error term ε_{it} is added to (7.1) it implies that the error term on (7.4) is of the form $u_{it} = \varepsilon_{it} + \lambda \varepsilon_{it-1} + \lambda^2 \varepsilon_{it-2} + \ldots$, but given that the dependent variable y_{it} is observed for only one year then not even first-order autocorrelation can be investigated.

Table 7.6 Results for Start-ups with Constant Job Loss Rate

Model	Estimated Equation	n	R^2
I	$y_t = 30.27 + 0.353\ z_t + 0.052\ d_t$ (1.28) (1.22) (1.03)	113	0.58
II	$y_t = 1.79 + 4.598\ z_t^1 + 1.183\ z_t^2 - 0.349\ d_t^1 - 0.189\ d_t^2$ (0.11) (2.67) (4.78) (2.14) (3.17)	113	0.78
III	$y_t = 25.91 + 0.526\ z_t^I + 1.465\ z_t^S - 0.033\ d_t^I - 0.006\ d_t^S$ (1.71) (3.15) (1.88) (0.86) (0.04)	113	0.74
IV	$y_t = 15.42 + 1.994\ z_t^{1I} + 1.004\ z_t^{2I} + 12.60\ z_t^{1S} + 1.437\ z_t^{2S}$ (1.48) (1.66) (6.45) (2.98) (1.83)	113	0.84
	$-\ 0.143\ d_t^{1I} - 0.159\ d_t^{2I} - 1.340\ d_t^{1S} - 0.148\ d_t^{2S}$ (1.14) (4.08) (2.65) (0.81)		

Note: Results from estimating (7.4). Model I is basic equation, and Models II to IV enter the z_t and d_t terms in spline form, where 1 = 1985-91, 2 = 1992-98, I = Initial investment and S = Subsequent investment. Parentheses report t-ratios with robust standard errors.

The results from regressing (7.4) for surviving start-up plants are given in Table 7.6.[16] Model I is regressed across all start-up plants for the period 1985-98, but a number of different versions of (7.4) are estimated, which include the $z_{i\tau}$ and $d_{i\tau}$ terms in spline form for different sub-periods, and separately for the Initial and Subsequent investments. In the case of Model I the result is not good, as while the coefficient on $z_{i\tau}$ is in the admissible range and insignificant, and the constant term is insignificant (omitting it does not alter the results), the coefficient on $d_{i\tau}$ implies a depreciation rate that is wrongly signed but insignificantly so. An F-test for the constancy of the coefficients on the x_{it} terms making-up $z_{i\tau}$ is also strongly rejected by the data (F(13, 97) = 18.30; $F_{0.01}$(13, 97) = 2.40). Hence, Model I suggests that (7.4) does not provide a good description of the data.

As an attempt to improve on this the sample was divided into two sub-periods of equal duration (1 = 1985-91 and 2 = 1992-98), and the $z_{i\tau}$ and $d_{i\tau}$ terms were entered in spline form. The result is Model II, which shows an improved fit of the model. The estimates on $d_{i\tau}$ are now significant and negative, and the estimated depreciation rates are 7.5 and 16 per cent for the two sub-periods. The coefficients on the $z_{i\tau}$ terms give estimates of the adjustment parameter λ in (7.1), measuring the extent to which the project jobs are realised over the first year. For the period 1992-98 it is not significantly different from unity, but for 1985-91 it is outside the admissible range, implying an implausibly large effect. An effort was made to

---

[16] There are 164 start-up plants, of which 35 closed by 1999, and the jobs in the Initial project are not observed for a further 16 plants, so (7.4) is regressed with 113 observations.

separate out the Initial investments (I) from the Subsequent investments (S), but the result of this, which is given as Model III in Table 7.6, is again unsatisfactory. In this case, the estimates of the $d_{i\tau}$ terms are insignificant. Finally, both the period and the type of investment were allowed to vary, and this is reported as Model IV. Again, the result is poor, as for the Subsequent investments in the second sub-period there was a very large estimated coefficient on the $z_{i\tau}$ term.[17]

In conclusion, a satisfactory result is obtained for the model for the period 1992-98 only, when economic conditions were stable, and the partial adjustment model seems to perform well. However, in general, the model is unsatisfactory. The term for the constant depreciation ($d_{i\tau}$) is often insignificant and wrongly signed, while the temporal constancy of the estimated coefficients on the x_{it} terms (making-up the $z_{i\tau}$ term) is strongly rejected. The possibility that neither the adjustment parameter nor the depreciation rate is constant over time is now allowed for.

General Distributed-Lag Model

The model developed in the previous section supposes that events are foreseen, so that jobs accrue and plant employment depreciates smoothly and at constant rates over time. However, it is generally not supported by the data. Obviously, events that are neither foreseen nor anticipated by the firm are a possible explanation for this. When viewed retrospectively, these unexpected events lead firms to make mistakes in their job projections, leading to redundancies that are not related to the technical life of capital or a product. There are reasons to believe 'mistakes' are important, as the study period is characterised by a sharp and largely unexpected downturn in the early 1990s, while Sterling's expulsion from the Exchange Rate Mechanism in 1992 may also be a factor. Indeed, it may be no coincidence that the best estimates for the partial adjustment model were obtained for the period 1992-98 when there were relatively stable economic conditions.

A distributed-lag model is now considered, allowing for a variable response pattern of plant employment to project jobs over time. In effect, the relationship between plant employment and project jobs is separately estimated for each year. In any year the Initial and Subsequent investments relate to different vintages of plant, and there is the possibility that the coefficients on these vary due to the plant age. To control for this, the analysis focuses on the coefficients obtained for jobs in the Initial investments of the same vintage. Jobs promised in the Subsequent investments relate to different vintages of plant, and are included as controls.

---

[17] Some other estimations of (7.4) were undertaken for different sub-samples of plant (not shown), but these proved unsatisfactory. It included regressing (7.4) for the acquisition plants, for all New Plants and for all plants, including the Mature Plants. These are given in Jones and Wren (2004b).

A general distributed-lag model is estimated of the following form:

$$y_{i\tau} = \alpha + \beta_1 x_{i\tau\text{-}1} + \beta_2 x_{i\tau\text{-}2} + \ldots + \beta_k x_{i\tau\text{-}k} + u_{i\tau} \qquad (7.5)$$

As before, $y_{i\tau}$ is plant employment (*EMP*) measured at $\tau = 1999$ and project jobs x_{it} are measured in each year over 1985-98 (i.e. $k = 13$). Equation (7.4) is a restricted version of (7.5) in which $\beta_t = \lambda (1 - \delta t)$ and $\alpha = 0$. Equation (7.5) is regressed across start-up plants *i*. To allow for a different estimated effect between the jobs promised in the Initial investments (*I*) and in the Subsequent investments (*S*) the x_{it} are measured as:

$$x_{it} = JOB_{it}{}^I + \gamma_t JOBNEW_{it}{}^S \qquad (7.6)$$

where the γ_t are parameters. The Initial investments include all project jobs, whether new or safeguarded, whereas the Subse uent investments include only new jobs. This is to avoid the double counting of project jobs, referred to above.[18] The coefficients on the job terms for the Initial investments $JOB_{it}{}^I$ are of interest, so that it is the β_t's that are reported, while those on $JOBNEW_{it}{}^S$ are controls and are not reported. A value of β_t less than unity means that the number of project jobs in the Initial investment were either over-estimated by the firm or that the jobs were later lost, or both of these. The constant term captures the extent to which project jobs are not reflected in plant employment across all plants.

An advantage of estimating a distributed lag model in (7.5) cross-sectionally, rather than by time series, is that there are potentially many more observations and the issue of multicollinearity does not arise. In fact, there are 113 observations on start-up plants over 1985-98, but this means that an estimate of β_t at any time *t* in (7.5) can be based on a small number of observations on the x_{it}, and will therefore be sensitive to the performance of individual plants. Where this occurs it is not regarded as an outlier, so that rather than dummying out these observations in an *ad hoc* manner, they are kept in the analysis and the years are later aggregated into sub-periods, which dilutes their effect. The number of observations on each x_{it} is shown in Table 7.7, which reports the results from estimating (7.5) with (7.6).

The estimated coefficients on the β_t's from the basic estimation are reported as Model I in Table 7.7. This seems to perform well, with nine of the fourteen β_t's significant. A pattern is discernable, with coefficients that are generally less than unity over the periods 1986-88 and 1994-96, but coefficients greater or equal to unity over 1989-93 and 1997-98. Given this, the JOB^I terms were grouped together over time to form the four sub-periods, so that the estimates of the β_t's are each based on a larger number of observations, and shown as Model II. When taken together the estimates on these four groups were significantly different from one

---

[18] The safeguarded jobs in the Subsequent investments refer to jobs that have already been promised, and which will therefore not lead to a net increase in plant employment. It differs from (7.4), which makes explicit allowance for the jobs that are lost through depreciation.

Table 7.7 Distributed Lag Results for Start-up Plants

Coeff.	No. of plants	Model I	Model II	Model III	Model IV
β_{98}	6	2.690	1.017**	2.961	1.051**
β_{97}	11	0.984**		1.019**	
β_{96}	9	0.509**	0.354**	0.438**	0.354**
β_{95}	8	0.264		0.398**	
β_{94}	8	0.356**		0.356**	
β_{93}	4	1.431*	1.056**	1.919**	1.205**
β_{92}	4	0.077**		0.116**	
β_{91}	5	1.010*		1.478**	
β_{90}	12	1.016*		1.049**	
β_{89}	14	1.196		1.704**	
β_{88}	12	0.621**	0.695**	0.700**	2.525*
β_{87}	7	0.989		4.453**	
β_{86}	7	0.112		1.049**	
β_{85}	6	1.116**		3.455**	
α		18.20*	21.65**	3.81	9.91
n	113	113	113	69	69
R^2	-	0.929	0.920	0.944	0.866

Note: Estimates from regressing (7.5) with (7.6). Dependent variable is plant employment at 1999 (*EMP*) and independent variables are number of project jobs (x_i). The β_i report the estimated coefficients for Initial investments only. Models III and IV are for the Single Investors only. Models II and IV group years into sub-periods: 1985-88, 1989-93, 1994-96 and 1997-98. Robust standard errors, where ** = significant 1% and * = 5% level.

another ($F(3, 95) = 11.57$; $F_{0.01}(3,95) = 4.05$), but not significantly different from the estimates in Model I ($F(10, 95) = 1.12$; $F_{0.05}(10,95) = 1.95$).[19] The estimates for the periods 1989-93 and 1997-98 are not significantly different from unity, while those for 1985-88 and 1994-96 are less than unity at the 1 per cent level.

Models I and II include jobs in the Subsequent investments as controls, but as a check Models I and II were re-estimated for the Single Investor start-up plants only, which do not have Subsequent investments. These are reported as Models III and IV in Table 7.7. A drawback is that they are based on a much smaller number of observations, but nonetheless they are interesting. They show a similarity with the respective estimates in Models I and II, but that this is less good the earlier on

---

[19] In constructing the term for the sub-period 1989-93, four observations for the year 1992 had to be dummied out. It was not related to any obvious single outlier observation, and it may be related to the crisis surrounding the Exchange Rate Mechanism of September 1992.

in time is the Initial investment. In particular, when comparing Models II and IV there is slightly higher estimated coefficient for the Single Investors over 1989-93 and a much higher estimate over 1985-88. It is consistent with the above finding that the ratio of employment to project jobs is higher for the Single Investor start-ups (see Table 7.5), but why should this be so?

As a first point, it was previously noted that the Multiple Investors start-up much earlier in time than the Single Investors, but it cannot explain the difference between the two sets of estimates in Table 7.7, as for each sub-period the start-up date has effectively been held constant. As a second point, apart from 1994-96, the estimated coefficients for the Single Investors are greater than unity (although none is significantly so). It perhaps suggests missing data on the Subsequent investments by the Single Investors, although the constant term that is picking up that part of employment that is not explained by the known project jobs is insignificant. It is possible that every single addition to plant employment is not captured, as the data include those jobs associated with 'significant' investments, and they exclude the routine recruitment activities and smaller additions to plant employment.[20] Again, it does not really explain the two sets of estimates in Table 7.7.

The reason the discrepancy arises between the two sets of estimates in Table 7.7 is because the Multiple Investor start-up plants are much larger in size. At the mean, Table 7.3 shows that they are three-times larger in employment terms than Single Investors. As we see, larger plants are less able to achieve their job targets, and this becomes more important as we go back through time, as there is a greater preponderance of Multiple Investors. Conversely, the later in time that a plant is observed the more likely it is to be a Single Investor, and the censoring of the data means it is less likely to be observed to re-invest.

The t-tests reported in Table 7.7 are based on robust standard errors, so that the estimates of the β_i are efficient as well as unbiased. However, the results for Models III and IV make us wonder if the distributed-lag model is appropriate. While the reported standard errors are robust, OLS estimation of (7.5) with (7.6) will give greater weight to the large plants, which have larger errors. Of course, it could be argued that this is perfectly satisfactory, as the failure of the larger plants to satisfy their targets has much greater importance. However, equally, it could be argued that this implicit weighting procedure is arbitrary and that the plants should have equal weight. Reflecting this, in the next section the data are unweighted, but a non-linear relationship is estimated that allows for the possibility that the smaller plants are better able to satisfy their job targets. It also enables the characteristics of the plants that over-estimate the number of project jobs to be examined.

---

[20] It could be argued that there are errors in variables, as the Subsequent investments are not picking up all of the jobs promised by the firms. However, the known project jobs are not measured with error, it is just that they are incomplete, and this is picked up the error term.

Log-Linear Model

Using the same notation as before, the log-linear model is specified as:

$$\ln y_{i\tau} = \alpha + \beta_1 \ln x_{i\tau\text{-}1} + \beta_2 \ln x_{i\tau\text{-}2} + \ldots + \beta_k \ln x_{i\tau\text{-}k} + u_{i\tau} \qquad (7.7)$$

For any x_{it} the deterministic part of (7.7) can be written as:

$$\ln (y_{i\tau} / x_{it}) = \alpha + (\beta_t - 1) \ln x_{it} \qquad (7.8)$$

so that an estimated value for β_t that is not significantly different from unity implies that the ratio of employment to project jobs $(y_{i\tau} / x_{it})$ is independent of the initial project size (x_{it}), and in particular it is equal to exp α. However, a value for β_t that is significantly smaller than unity implies that $y_{i\tau} / x_{it}$ is negatively related to x_{it}, so that the employment to the project jobs ratio is smaller the larger are the number of jobs promised. The advantage of (7.7) is that the employment-job ratio varies with the initial project size. However, a difficulty is that the log-linear form means the project jobs are no longer additive, and it is no longer possible to estimate the coefficients on the Subsequent investments separately from those on the Initial investments. Thus, the project jobs must be organised on a plant basis, and this is done by adding the jobs in the Subsequent investments back through time to those of the Initial investment, so that:

$$x_{it} = JOB_{it}^I + \Sigma_{j\,=\,t} \; JOBNEW_{ij}^S \qquad (7.9)$$

This embodies two restrictions. First, $\gamma_i = 1$ in (7.6) for all t, so that the same coefficient is estimated for Initial and Subsequent investments. Second, the jobs are organised on a plant basis by the vintage of the plant, so that the β_t in (7.7) pick up the employment effect of both kinds of investment, i.e. Initial and Subsequent.[21]

The analysis proceeds in several stages. First, (7.7) is regressed with (7.9) to examine if the estimated coefficients on α and β_i in (7.7) vary between the four sub-periods identified above. Second, an analysis of covariance is undertaken to see what factors explain variations in the ratio of plant employment to project jobs. Finally, the characteristics are examined of the plants that are more or less likely to reach/sustain their job targets. While the results from all three of the exercises are

---

[21] To gain some idea of the effect of these restrictions, (7.5) was re-estimated for the start-up plants but with x_{it} given by (7.9) rather than (7.6). The results, which are reported in Jones and Wren (2004b), are similar to the respective results in Models I and II of Table 7.7. While attempts to test the two restrictions proved inconclusive (see Jones and Wren, 2004b), the similarity of the estimates leads us to believe that the restrictions are not a serious issue. The alternative is at each time t the coefficient on the Subsequent investments is estimated along with the Initial investments undertaken by all other plants at this time, but this makes no recognition of the log-linear specification. The approach adopted is reasonable, as no simple pattern has been found in the coefficients related to time.

discussed, in order to focus on the main points, only the regression results for the last of these exercises are formally presented.[22]

First, (7.7) and (7.9) were estimated with the α and β_t allowed to vary across the four sub-periods, by including intercept dummies and the x_{it} terms in spline form. Compared with the base period of 1985-88, a significantly different estimate was found only for the period 1994-96, where a smaller estimate is obtained. This means that plants setting-up over 1994-96 were less able to reach their job targets. The differences found for the other sub-periods may be compositional effects, for example, arising from the number of small and large plants. As an explanation for the weaker effect over 1994-96, Chapter 5 found that this period was characterised by some extremely large investments from Germany, Japan and Korea. Indeed, 43 per cent of known investment over 1985-98 occurred in these three years. These plants may be more prone to exaggeration and/or the agencies were more inclined to believe these job targets, but either way the plants were significantly less able to deliver the jobs. In general, the employment-job ratio was found to vary inversely with the number of jobs promised, i.e. $y_{i\tau} / x_{it}$ depends negatively on x_{it}. However, to check that it is the number of project jobs that is important, rather than whether a plant is a Single or Multiple Investor, dummies were placed on the intercept and slope terms for these two kinds of plant. As a group they were insignificant, which indicates that it is the total project job size that matters.[23]

The second of the three exercises is an analysis of covariance of the ratio of the plant employment to project jobs, expressed in log form, i.e. $\ln (y_{i\tau} / x_{it})$. The purpose of this is to see what plant characteristics explain variations in this ratio. In effect, it involves regressing a model of the following form:

$$\ln (y_{i\tau} / x_{it}) = \alpha + (\beta - 1) \ln x_{it} + CHAR_{it} + u_{i\tau} \quad (7.10)$$

where *CHAR* $\equiv$ *YEAR, TYPE, COUNTY, SECTOR, MANUF, ORIGIN, RSA, REG, NAT, MULT, OTH1,..., OTH6*. These variables are similar to those used in the previous chapter for the analysis of variance of project jobs, except that they are measured at the plant level according to the Initial investment project. They are defined according to a small number of categories. A difference is that *YEAR* now distinguishes between four sub-periods, 1985-88, 1989-93, 1994-96 and 1997-98, while *MULT* takes a value of unity for the Multiple Investors. The concomitant variable is the natural log of project jobs, $\ln x_{it}$, which is measured according to (7.9), and which allows for the effect of the project job size.

The results show that relatively few of the variables explain variations in the ratio of plant employment to project jobs, $\ln (y_{i\tau} / x_{it})$. In fact the only variables to be consistently significant in our regressions are the *YEAR, RSA* and concomitant term, where the latter accounted for about 10 per cent of the variation in the ratio

---

[22] The other results are given in Jones and Wren (2004b).

[23] The test statistic is $F(5, 103) = 0.14$.

of employment to project jobs. When the estimation was made just for the New Plants the plant type (*TYPE*) was also significant.

The third and final exercise is to estimate (7.10) with (7.9), but now including as independent variables each category of each variable in *CHAR* in a binary form. The results are reported in parsimonious form in Table 7.8.[24] These are considered relative to a baseline plant, which is a joint venture in   orthumberland, starting over 1985 88, operating in the   est of   anufacturing outside of the four main activities, and originating from the   est of the   orld but outside   orth   merica,   estern   urope and the   ar   ast.   odel I of Table 7.8 gives the result for all   ew   lants, and shows that compared to the baseline plant, the categories that lead to a smaller employment to project jobs ratio are start up plants, Initial investments over 1994 96 or plants with an involvement with the national investment agency.

Table 7.8 Log-Linear Results of Employment to Project Jobs Ratio

Variable	Model I	Model II	Model III	Model IV	Model V
Constant	1.603***	0.668***	0.761***	2.166***	1.549*
TYPE - Start-up	-0.669***	-	-	-1.083***	0.313*
TYPE - Acquisition	-0.364	-	-	-0.697**	0.410**
MANUF - Transport	0.452**	0.367*	0.218	0.417	0.446**
YEAR - 1989-93	-0.198	-0.132	-0.264	-0.211	-0.105*
YEAR - 1994-96	-0.431**	-0.530**	-0.688**	-0.394	0.534**
YEAR - 1997-98	0.124	-0.001	-0.047	0.255	-0.235
RSA	0.355**	0.196*	0.316*	0.505**	0.358*
NAT	-0.421**	-0.239*	-0.328*	-0.668**	0.113
$\ln x_{it}$	-0.268***	-0.184***	-0.175**	-0.346***	-0.398***
R^2	0.23	0.18	0.20	0.29	0.20
F	4.81***	3.08***	2.91**	3.36***	2.15**
n	193	113	69	117	76

Note: Parsimonious results from estimating (7.10) at plant level. The dependent variable is the log of the ratio of plant employment at 1999 to the total number of project jobs, $\ln (y_{it} / x_{it})$, where $y_{it} = EMP$ and x_i is given by (7.9). Robust standard errors, where *** = significant at the 1, ** = 5 and * = 10% level. Model I reports the results for all New Plants, Model II for start-up plants and Model III for Single Investor start-ups. Models IV and V re-estimate Model I for small ($x_i \leq 100$) and large New Plants ($x_i > 100$). *OTH* variables are included, but generally insignificant and not reported.

---

[24] Insignificant terms were deleted sequentially according to the variables that are least significant in the analysis of covariance.

The period 1989-93 also displays a weaker effect, but only at the 10 per cent level. Plants with a higher employment to project jobs ratio are those in the Transport activity or in receipt of RSA. The *MULT* term is insignificant, indicating that the same relationship holds for both Multiple and Single Investors. Models II and III repeat the estimation, but for the start-up plants and for Single Investor start-ups respectively, but again with similar results.

Finally, Models IV and V repeat the estimation of Model I for small New Plants (with total project jobs x_{it} of less than 100 jobs) and large New Plants (other plants) respectively. Some coefficients now change sign between these two groups of plant, although the coefficient on the ln x_{it} term is remarkably stable. It shows that the weaker employment to jobs ratio over 1994-96 and the stronger effect in the Transport activity occur in the large plants, while the poorer employment to jobs for plants involved with the national agency occurs in the small plants. RSA has a stronger effect on the employment-job ratio in both size classes.

Interpretation of the Regression Results

Using the results in Table 7.8 the plant employment to project jobs ratios ($y_{i\tau} / x_{it}$) are evaluated in Table 7.9 for different job sizes of plant (x_{it}). Employment ($y_{i\tau}$) is measured at 1999 and the project jobs (x_{it}) are those jobs promised over 1985-98 but summed back through time to the date of the Initial investment. The ratios are for start-up plants surviving to 1999. They are calculated at the mean value of the logarithm of the total project jobs (ln x_{it}), and plus or minus one or two standard deviations, which means they are evaluated at five project job scales: 2, 11, 53, 254 and 1230 jobs. They are based on Model I in Table 7.8, which was estimated for all New Plants and hence the largest number of observations. It was re-estimated with a robust estimator, while for the purpose of comparison the employment-job ratios were also evaluated for Model II, which is estimated for start-up plants only.[25]

When calculated at the mean employment-job ratio, Table 7.9 shows that a baseline plant broadly achieves its job target, with ratios of between 90 and 94 per cent. These are for surviving plants, but allowing for the fact that some plants may have promised the jobs as far back as 1985 then they strongly suggest that the investors broadly put the jobs in place. However, when calculated away from the mean different implications follow. Whereas the smaller firms overshoot their job targets, possibly indicating additions to plant employment in projects that are not viewed as 'significant', the larger plants fall someway short. For example, a plant promising a total of 254 jobs will have employment of around 147 to 180 jobs at 1999 (i.e. 58 to 71 per cent), while a plant promising 1230 jobs will have only between 455 and 652 of the jobs in place, i.e. 37 to 53 per cent. It suggests that the

---

[25] The robust estimator works by weighting the observations by the absolute values of the residuals. It is the RREG routine in *STATA*.

Table 7.9 Evaluation of Employment to Job Ratio for Start-up Plants

Variable	Mean −2 s.d.	Mean −1 s.d.	Mean	Mean +1 s.d.	Mean +2 s.d.
Project Job Size (x_{it})	2	11	53	254	1,230
Employment-Job Ratio ($y_{i\tau} / x_{it}$)					
Model I	2.20	1.41	0.90	0.58	0.37
Model I (robust)	1.76	1.28	0.94	0.68	0.50
Model II	1.68	1.26	0.94	0.71	0.53
Model I:					
$RSA = 1$	3.12	1.99	1.28	0.82	0.52
$NAT = 1$	1.54	0.99	0.63	0.40	0.26
YEAR: 1994-96 = 1	1.36	0.87	0.55	0.36	0.23

Note: Evaluation of ratio of employment ($y_{i\tau}$) to total project jobs (x_{it}), based on the results reported for Models I and II in Table 7.8. It also presents the results for Model I under a robust estimator. The main part evaluates the ratio for a baseline plant, while the subsequent part examines the ratio for a plant receiving RSA ($RSA = 1$), having involvement with the national inward investment agency ($NAT = 1$) or initially investing over 1994-96. Each ratio is calculated at the mean value of the natural logarithm of the total project jobs (ln x_{it}), and at plus or minus one and two standard deviations (s.d.).

extremely large plants deliver only half the jobs promised after a period of time, although the number of these very large plants is relatively small.[26]

In interpreting the results, the possibility is that the larger plants achieve their job targets, but then lose employment prior to 1999. It is not possible to examine this directly as the plant employment is measured for the year 1999 only. However, it is feasible to examine the employment-job ratio for different time durations up to 1999, i.e. for the periods 1998-99, 1997-99, 1996-99 and so on. Thus, Model I in Table 7.8 was re-estimated, but with intercept dummy variables for each year over 1985-98 included in place of YEAR terms. The employment-job ratio evaluated at the mean for all start-up plants, but averaged over 2 or 3-year periods, are: 1997-98: 0.86; 1994-96: 0.56; 1991-93: 0.75; 1988-90: 0.94; and 1985-87: 1.04. Even allowing for the smaller coefficient over 1994-96, these do not suggest a build-up of employment followed by job loss. Indeed, if anything the higher employment-job ratios are obtained for the longer durations. The conclusion is that the larger plants failed to reach their job targets.

The employment-job ratios are also calculated for certain categories of plant in Table 7.9. The ratios are higher for plants receiving RSA, but lower for the plants involved with either the national investment agency or starting-up over 1994-96. At the mean, they suggest a plant promising around 50 jobs will have employment

---

[26] Only nine projects promised more than 1,000 jobs.

equal to 128 per cent of these jobs if in receipt of RSA, but only 63 and 55 per cent if involved with the agency or initially investing over 1994-96 respectively. The employment-job ratio is also higher for larger plants receiving RSA, so that a plant promising 254 jobs will have 82 per cent of jobs in place (compared with 58 per cent for a non-assisted plant), and a plant promising 1,230 jobs will have 52 per cent in place (compared with 37 per cent). Thus, larger plants receiving RSA seem more able to reach their job targets, although they still fall short. The grant claw-back condition may make the investors more realistic in their job claims, but this cannot be said for the inward investment agency, where there may be exaggeration. The result for 1994-96 has previously been commented upon.

While the results generally suggest that the smaller plants are more likely to achieve their targets, these plants are of much less significance compared to larger plants. This can be seen by examining the employment-job ratio at plus or minus one standard deviation from the mean. At one standard deviation below the mean, Table 7.9 shows that a baseline plant promising around 11 jobs will deliver about 13 jobs by the end of the study period, while at one standard deviation above the mean a plant promising around 250 jobs will deliver somewhere in the region of 160 jobs. It suggests for every one large plant there will need to be thirty smaller plants in order that the job target is met in aggregate.

Finally, it is worth briefly considering potential problems with the analysis. First, in the project job term, x_{it}, the jobs promised over 1985-98 are summed back through time to the date of the Initial investment, so that no allowance is made for the timing of the Subsequent investments. However, it was argued that including the project jobs by the plant vintage does not materially affect the results. Further, the year dummies did not support a declining effect with time, while a time trend when added to Model I in Table 7.9 is also insignificant (t-ratio of 0.75). Second, the distributed lag model is sensitive to the performance of individual plants, but owing to a small number of observations. However, the robust estimation of Model I in Table 7.9 suggests that outliers are not a problem in this case. Further, the normality of the residuals in Model I is accepted.[27]

Conclusions

The chapter has two main purposes: to describe the pattern of employment in terms of the plant characteristics; and to if whether the jobs promised by the inward investors are actually achieved. Both of these objectives lead to important policy conclusions. In relation to the first purpose, it is found that there are important differences between the New and Mature Plants – the latter commencing in foreign ownership prior to 1985 – but possibly related to the truncated nature of the data. It is because only those Mature Plants carrying out a 'significant' investment over 1985-98 are observed. Perhaps reflecting this, the Mature Plants tend to be much

---

[27] This is a Jarque-Bera test statistic of 209.7 against a critical value of just $\chi^2_{0.01} = 9.2$.

larger in scale, but there are other differences, as the earlier investment is more broadly based in terms of activity and more likely to be from the US. In the case of New Plants there is a strong concentration of employment – four-fifths is in four manufacturing activities and over half is in plants from the Far East – suggesting that it is vulnerable to adverse events that affect particular activities or countries. The analysis points to the importance of the start-up plants that multiply invest. On average, a Multiple Investor is three times the employment size a Single Investor, even though the jobs to investment ratio is much the same. However, it takes some time for a plant to re-invest and grow, so that even though most jobs arise from projects implemented in the 1990s, sixty per cent of start-up employment at 1999 is in the New Plants that started prior to 1990.

The other purpose of the chapter is to examine the extent to which the jobs promised by the investors over 1985-99 are realised in plant employment at 1999. This examination was carried out for surviving New Plants, again focusing on the start-ups. At the mean logarithmic size it was found that about 90 to 94 per cent of the promised jobs are reflected in plant employment at 1999. However, the mean log job size is small, and of much greater concern is that the larger plants fail to achieve their targets and can fall a long way short. A plant promising 250 jobs has employment of only 150 at 1999, while a plant promising 1250 jobs has half this number of jobs in place. The receipt of a Government grant substantially improves on this, no doubt because the subsidy is made contingent on the plants delivering the jobs, but plants involved with the investment agency have poorer results, as do the very large plants starting-up in the mid-1990s, when optimism regarding the contribution of these foreign-owned plants may have been excessive.

Obviously, given the nature of the data, a key question is whether the larger plants achieved their job targets but then lost jobs by 1999, or whether they failed to achieve their job targets in the first place. In fact, the evidence presented in the chapter supports the latter explanation. A possible reason for this is that the plants were mistaken in their job projections, and the recession of the early 1990s is an event that could have led firms to over-estimate the number of jobs. However, the remainder of the decade was characterised by stable economic conditions, and the problem persisted. Thus, it seems that the jobs were deliberately exaggerated, and there are a number of reasons to believe this. First, plants may get better treatment from the investment agencies in terms of help with land, premises and other forms of support. Second, the agencies themselves may benefit from an over-statement of the number of jobs, as it may increase their grant-in-aid from the central sources. Overall, it not only suggests that healthy skepticism should be exercised by the agencies in dealing with these prospective investors, but that a similar skepticism should be exercised in relation to the job claims of the agencies themselves.

Chapter 8

Survival

For the purpose of economic development, Hudson (1998) notes that there are three important characteristics of foreign-owned plants; the quantity, quality and permanence of employment provided by the plants. Having described the pattern of project jobs and plant employment in the preceding two chapters, this chapter focuses on the issue of plant survival. From the discussion of Chapter 4 it is well known that the success in attracting FDI to the regions is blighted by the relatively high failure rate of these plants (McCloughan and Stone, 1998; Gorg and Strobl, 2003). It poses a dilemma for the policymaker, as the FDI plants are often located in high unemployment areas (Head et al, 1995; Friedman et al, 1992), attracted by generous location packages that are available both in the UK and elsewhere (Wren, 2005a; Crozet et al, 2004). The issue is not trivial, as in the North-East region about a fifth of FDI plants arriving since the mid-1980s closed within a decade or so, taking with them more than 10,000 jobs (Jones and Wren, 2004c), and there is a similar pattern in other UK peripheral regions (see Stone and Peck, 1996).

As a way out of this dilemma, and as an attempt to forestall exit, agencies try to 'embed' foreign-owned plants in the local economy. This is defined in terms of the depth and quality of the relationships that exist between the inward investors and local organisations, and the extent to which these provide opportunities for economic development (see Phelps and MacKinnon, 2000). This was discussed in Chapter 4, with Phelps et al (2003) identifying forms of plant 'embeddedness' that are amenable to testing, of which one is re-investment. Of interest, is whether re-investment signals or imparts some benefit to the plant, leading to longer survival time durations. If re-investment is associated with longer durations, then it offers a policy handle by which to root these plants in the local economy. Further, re-investing plants provide most of the investment and employment.[1]

The purpose of this chapter is twofold. First, it is to examine the issue of plant survival, to get a handle on plant lifetimes and to see if there are characteristics associated with longer survival durations. Second, it is to investigate the issue of plant re-investment, and to see whether a Subsequent investment is qualitatively different to an Initial investment, leading to longer survival time durations. In both cases the focus is on new entrant foreign-owned plants (i.e. the New Plants), and in particular the start-ups. These have greatest policy interest in terms of job losses.

---

[1] Re-investment accounts for about 60 per cent of the known investment by start-up plants (Table 5.8), and in employment terms a Multiple Investor start-up plant is three-times the size of a Single Investor start-up (Table 7.3).

The analysis is conducted at the plant level, and a variety of approaches are used, including logit models to analyse the probability of re-investment, and duration models to examine the time duration to re-investment and plant exit.

Characteristics of Exiting Plants

Of the total of 337 plants in the Inward Investment Dataset, 55 (16 per cent) exited by the year 2000.[2] Excluding the Mature Plants (i.e. plants commencing in foreign ownership prior to 1985), then 50 of the 265 New Plants exited (19 per cent). Table 8.1 gives details of the plant exits for the different types of New Plant. The exit rate is higher for start-up plants than for other New Plants, which is perhaps surprising, as an acquisition may be undertaken for the purpose of closing down a

Table 8.1 Plant Exits

	SU	AC	JV	All
Plants				
No. of Plants	164	79	22	265
Exits	35	12	3	50
% Exits	21%	15%	14%	19%
Project Jobs				
All Plants	27,183	24,853	4,228	56,264
Plant Exits	7,533	2,146	118	9,797
% Jobs Lost	28%	9%	1%	17%
Large Plants				
% Plant Exits	20%	11%	11%	15%
Jobs Lost	6,916	1,986	73	8,975
% Jobs Lost	28%	8%	2%	17%
Small Plants				
% Plant Exits	26%	29%	18%	25%
Jobs Lost	617	160	45	822
% Jobs Lost	23%	14%	13%	19%

Notes: Plant survival / exit defined by SURV variable in Appendix Table 2. Project jobs are new and safeguarded jobs promised by plants over 1985-98. Small plants promise less than or equal to 50 jobs in the Initial Investment, and Large plants promise more than 50 jobs. SU = start-up; AC = acquisition; JV = joint venture; and All = all New Plants.

competitor (see Chapter 1). The jobs in Table 8.1 are those that are promised by the plants over 1985-98 prior to closure, but not all of the jobs will necessarily be

---

[2] The definition of plant exit is given in the Appendix. Plant survival to the year 2000 is coded by the *SURV* variable in Appendix Table 2.

delivered, especially in the case of the larger plants.[3] It reveals the importance of the start-up plants. Of the nearly 10,000 (prospective) jobs lost through exit, about three-quarters are in the start-ups, representing around a quarter of the total jobs promised by these plants. The remainder of Table 8.1 gives a breakdown between Large and Small plants, where the former promise more than 50 jobs in their Initial investment.[4] Perhaps not surprisingly virtually all of the jobs lost through exit are in the Large plants, so that closure is really about the larger start-up plants.

The nature of the job losses in the exiting start-up plants is explored in Table 8.2. In jobs terms, it suggests that the characteristics of the exited plants reflect the entry pattern, so that the plant and job losses occur in certain areas and activities, and is heavily concentrated. Thus, of the 7,533 (prospective) job losses, 58 per cent are in Tyne and Wear, 93 per cent are in manufacturing, of which 69 per cent are in the Communications activity, and 54 per cent are in plants originating from the Far East. Further, it was noted in Chapter 7 that most of the employment in start-up plants relates to plants setting-up in the late 1980s (see Table 7.2). This is reflected in the pattern of job loss, with just over half the jobs being lost in plants that established themselves in the late 1980s. The implication is that while plant closure is heavily concentrated by certain kinds of plant, exit is in fact a general phenomenon that really just reflects the pattern of entry.

Plant Survival

The review in Chapter 4 found that foreign-owned plants have higher failure rates. As an explanation for this, researchers focus on the fact that they are often part of multi-plant enterprises, but it appeared that the foreign-owned plants have higher exit rates even when the ownership structure and the plant size are held constant. The issue of exit is now explored using our dataset.

Modelling Plant Survival and Exit

Firm survival is analysed using duration analysis. It can handle censoring, which is a feature of the data. In particular, the New Plants are observed commencing in foreign ownership over 1985-98 but it is only known if they survived to the year 2000 or not. For plants surviving to this year the actual lifetime is not observed, as it is not known for how much longer the plant would have survived. This kind of data censoring is encountered in other studies (e.g. McCloughan and Stone, 1998), and it is handled through the specification of the likelihood function. However, the data is subject to another kind of censoring, as for plants that do not survive to

---

[3] The jobs are known for 34 of the 35 exited start-up plants. The missing case is a US plant outside of the manufacturing sector setting-up in County Durham in the late 1980s.

[4] This employment level roughly accords to the median size of start-up plants.

Table 8.2 Jobs Lost in Exited Start-up Plants

	Jobs Lost	Plants Closed
Total	7,533	34
County		
Northumberland	259	2
Tyne and Wear	4,416	17
Durham	2,148	7
Cleveland	710	8
Sector		
Manufacturing	6,974	18
of which:		
(Chemicals)	(500)	(1)
(Machinery)	(804)	(2)
(Communication)	(4,828)	(6)
(Transport)	(505)	(2)
(Other)	(337)	(7)
Wholesale and Retail Trade	67	7
Real Estate, Renting and Business	142	5
Other	350	4
Country of Origin		
Western Europe	2,117	12
North America	1,328	11
Far East	4,077	10
Rest of the World	11	1
Age		
1985 – 1989	4,191	13
1990 – 1994	1,477	16
1994 – 1998	1,865	5

Note: Job details known for 34 of the 35 exited start-up plants. Missing case is a US plant outside the manufacturing sector setting up in County Durham in the late 1980s.

the year 2000 the lifetime is also not observed. This is more unusual, but it is encountered elsewhere (e.g. Cressy, 1996), and like the first kind of censoring it is handled through the specification of the likelihood function.

To model the survival time duration, a subscript i denotes the plant, and, in general, the following notation is used. The actual time duration of a plant in the absence of censoring is denoted by T_i, i.e. the time between the date of start-up (time origin) and the time of exit, while L_i denotes the period of observation on the plant. The observed duration of a plant is $t_i = \min (T_i, L_i)$, and the probability density function of these durations is denoted $f(t_i)$. The survival function is denoted $S(L_i)$, which is the probability that a plant has a duration greater than L_i (hence $S(L_i) = 1 - F(L_i)$ where F is the cumulative frequency distribution of f). An indicator variable δ_i is defined by $\delta_i = 1$ if $T_i \leq L_i$ and $\delta_i = 0$ if $T_i > L_i$. When $\delta_i = 1$ the plant does not survive to the year 2000 and $1 - S(L_i)$ is observed, but when $\delta_i = 0$ the plant survives and $S(L_i)$ is observed. Under the assumption that the pairs (t_i, δ_i) are independently and identically distributed, the likelihood function L is (see Lawless, 1982):

$$L = \prod_i [1 - S(t_i)]^{\delta_i} S(t_i)^{1 - \delta_i} \qquad (8.1)$$

The survival function $S(t_i)$ is the probability that a plant i survives to time t, while the hazard rate $h(t_i)$ is the probability that a plant exits at time t given survival to that time. These are related, as $h(t_i)$ equals $f(t_i) / S(t_i)$. Taking the log of (8.1), the log-likelihood function (dropping i subscripts) is:

$$\log L = \Sigma \{\delta \log [1 - S(t)] + (1 - \delta) \log S(t)\} \qquad (8.2)$$

Once $S(t)$ is determined, so is $h(t)$, which is the conditional probability of exit. It requires a functional form to be given to the survival function $S(t)$, and in what follows (8.2) is estimated using each of the Weibull, log-logistic and lognormal functions. They are described in McCloughan and Stone (1996), where they are graphed for different parameter values. A brief description of these is now given.

The Weibull hazard and survival functions are:

$$h(t) = \lambda \alpha (\lambda t)^{\alpha - 1} \qquad S(t) = \exp [-(\lambda t)^{\alpha}] \qquad (8.3)$$

where t is the observed duration, λ is a term on which more is said below and α is the shape parameter. The Weibull distribution embodies monotonic behaviour in the hazard rate, which is captured by the shape parameter. When $\alpha > [<] 1$ there is positive [negative] duration dependence as the hazard rate increases [decreases] with the period from the time origin, i.e. the probability that a firm exits increases [decreases] the longer [shorter] is the period of time from the date of the Initial investment. This is also known as an increasing [decreasing] failure rate. The exponential distribution is a special case of the Weibull, which is when $\alpha = 1$, and it gives a constant hazard rate $h(t) = \lambda$ that is independent of time. The inclusion of covariates in the Weibull model is straightforward, although interpretation is less easy (see Greene, 2003, Chapter 20), and it is achieved by setting:

$$\lambda \equiv \exp (-\beta x), \qquad (8.4)$$

where x is a vector of covariates with associated coefficients β. As with the other models presented here, the covariates do not bear on the issue of duration dependence, but rather it is equivalent to changing the units of measurement on the time axis, so these models are sometimes called 'accelerated failure time' models.

The lognormal is the distribution of a variate whose natural logarithm obeys the normal law of probability, i.e. the natural logarithm of the observed duration follows a normal distribution. The hazard function is:

$$h(t) = \phi(z) / \sigma t (1 - \Phi(z)) \tag{8.5}$$

where ϕ and Φ are the probability density function and cumulative distribution function of the normal distribution $N(0, 1)$ respectively, and $z = (\ln t - \mu) / \sigma$ is the standard normal equivalent of $\ln t$. It is parameterised by setting $\mu = \beta x$. It can be shown that $h(t) = 0$ at $t = 0$, but $h(t)$ reaches a maximum before approaching zero as t tends to infinity, so that it implies a pattern of increasing and then decreasing failure rate. The standard deviation σ is estimated as an ancillary parameter.

The log-logistic is the distribution of a variate whose natural logarithm follows the logisitic distribution, i.e. the natural logarithm of the observed duration is a logistic distribution. The log-logistic hazard function is:

$$h(t) = (\lambda \kappa) (\lambda t)^{\kappa - 1} / [1 + (\lambda t)^{\kappa}] \tag{8.6}$$

where κ is a shape parameter. It is parameterised by setting $\lambda \equiv \exp(-\beta x)$, as in (8.4). It is more general than the lognormal distribution, as it allows for an increasing but then decreasing failure rate when $\kappa > 1$, but a monotonic decreasing failure rate when $\kappa \leq 1$. In this sense, it is also more general than the Weibull, but it does not allow for a monotonic increasing failure rate, so that the longer the period of time that a plant is observed the smaller is the probability of plant exit. However, unlike the Weibull distribution, the lognormal and log-logistic functions allow for non-monotonic behaviour in the hazard rate. These tend to yield similar results, but the log-logistic allows for a monotonically declining failure rate.

In dealing with the different survival functions there are two issues: how to compare the competing models and how to interpret the obtained coefficients. On the first of these, there are two ways to compare the distributions. One is to see how well the data conform to the assumptions underlying a model, possibly using non-parametric or semi-parametric methods. The second is to estimate (8.2) with each distribution and see how well they perform. In relation to the interpretation of the coefficients this is achieved by examining the effect of the covariates on the median duration M. The median duration is obtained from the survival function by setting $S(M) = 0.5$. Solving this for the Weibull distribution gives $M = (1 / \lambda) (\ln 2)^{1/\alpha}$, while for the other two distributions it is $M = 1 / \lambda$.

Estimation Approach

To determine the appropriate form of the survival function, the hazard functions were plotted for start-up plants for each of the competing distributions (reported in

Jones, 2004d). Each plot implies positive duration dependence, and the probability of exit increases monotonically with the period over which the plant is observed. They gave a similar pattern, with a very low probability of exit for the first 4 or 5 years that rises to about 10 per cent after 10 years and to 15 per cent after 14 years. A problem with the Weibull distribution was that the estimated shape parameter, i.e. α in (8.3), was significantly greater than 2, which is implausible, implying that the probability of exit increases at an increasing rate with the duration. The other two functions implied an increasing and then decreasing failure rate, which is more plausible, and since there is little to choose between them, then the log-logistic function is preferred for reason of simplicity.

In estimating the survival function, we include as independent variables terms for the plant and project characteristics. The purpose of these is to examine which kinds of plant are more likely to survive or exit. However, in order to get a handle on the overall failure rate, the covariates are excluded, except for the constant term and shape parameter. It is not an issue, as we have data for the population of all new foreign-owned plants in the study area. The included variables are basically those used in Chapters 6 and 7, with the Initial investment is used to determine the plant characteristics.[5] They are grouped into a small number of categories and in a dummy variable form, as set out in Chapter 6: *TYPE, SECTOR, MANUF, ORIGIN* and *OTH1* to *OTH6* (see Appendix Table 2). In place of the *COUNTY* term, an *URBAN* term is included, which takes a value of unity if the plant is located in the metropolitan counties of Tyne and Wear or Cleveland, but which otherwise is zero. The policy terms, *RSA, REG* and *NAT*, are also included.

Some other terms are included to pick-up particular effects, and each of these is measured continuously. The *AGE* term is included to capture the plant age in years (Appendix Table 2). It is the difference between the establishment of the production unit (*ESTDATE*) and the year of the Initial investment (*YEAR*), i.e. $AGE \equiv YEAR - ESTDATE$, where *YEAR* relates to the Initial investment. For a start-up plant, *AGE* is zero, but non-zero for an acquisition. Second, the growth rate of UK Gross Domestic Product, *GDP*, is included for the calendar quarter in which the plant commits to an Initial investment. The *GDP* term is measured as a percentage, and picks up the possibility that the timing of entry affects the survival prospects. Finally, a *SIZE* term is included to pick-up the scale of the plant, as there is good evidence that the plant size affects the survival of new plants (see Chapter 4). It is measured by the number of jobs in the Initial investment, so that $SIZE \equiv JOB$. Employment is used as a measure of initial size, and Hart (2000) notes that it is correlated with other measures of size (see Figure 5.1).

The *AGE* and *SIZE* terms are not known for every plant (see Appendix Table 2), so the inclusion of these affects the number of observations in the regressions.[6]

---

[5] For example, *RSA* takes a value of unity for plants that receive RSA in their Initial investment, but otherwise it is zero.

[6] In fact, *AGE* is not known only where the *SIZE* is also not known. *SIZE* is preferred, as the investment scale *INV* is known for only two-thirds of projects.

In total, the jobs are known for 511 of the 550 projects, but for the New Plants this means that the number of jobs in the Initial investment is not known for 29 of the 265 New Plants plants, giving 236 observations. Likewise, for the start-up plants, *SIZE* is not known for 17 of the 164 plants, giving 147 observations. The results are considered relative to a baseline plant, which is the same as that used in the preceding chapters; i.e. a joint venture in Northumberland, operating in the Rest of Manufacturing outside the four main activities and from the Rest of the World.

Estimation Results

The result from maximising (8.2) with the log-logistic survival function is shown in Table 8.3. The first column of this table gives the estimates for the New Plants, and the other columns give the results for the start-up plants, with a breakdown between the Small and Large start-ups. As before, the Large plants promise more than 50 jobs in their Initial project. As regards the estimation for the New Plants in Table 8.3, the coefficients on the *TYPE* terms indicate no significant difference in the pattern of exit between the types (start-ups, acquisitions and joint ventures). It is backed-up by the similar exit rates calculated from the raw data for the plant types in Table 8.1, while the results for the start-up plants in Table 8.3 are similar to that for all New Plants. There is much greater variation in the results for Small and Large start-ups, but there is a smaller number of observations.

The estimates of the shape parameter κ in Table 8.3 are significantly greater than unity in each case, implying an increasing and then decreasing hazard rate. This means that the probably of plant exit (given that the plant has survived to that time) at first increases with the observed duration, but then decreases, which seems plausible. It is supported by the plots of the hazard rates. For start-ups the results suggest longer survival durations for the plants receiving support from the national agency, but shorter durations for those plants involved with the regional agency or larger on entry. For Small and Large start-ups there are interesting results. First, the estimated constant term is similar between the two groups, which is consistent with the similar exit rates found for these plants in Table 8.1. Second, the estimate of the shape parameter κ is extremely large for the Large start-ups, which suggests that the hazard rate increases dramatically after a certain time period. Third, the coefficient on *SIZE* is insignificant for Small plants, but significant and negative for Large plants, so the very large plants on entry have the higher exit rates.[7]

The survival time durations (in years) and rates (as probabilities) are calculated in Table 8.4, based on a re-estimation of the equation for start-up plants in Table 8.3. This re-estimation includes *SIZE* and constant terms only, so that the survival figures reflect the distribution of all plants. This is more representative than for a baseline plant, given that the dataset includes the population of all foreign-owned start-up plants in the region. The survival estimates are calculated for the median

---

[7] The *SIZE* term was experimented with by including it in a quadratic form, but it performed poorly. The inclusion of the *SIZE* term in log form did not much improve on this.

Table 8.3 Results for Plant Survival

		New Plants	Start-up Plants		
			All	Small	Large
TYPE	Start-ups	-0.01	-	-	-
TYPE	Acquisitions	-0.16	-	-	-
URBAN		0.04	-0.04	-0.12	-0.02
SECTOR		-0.33**	-0.28	-0.38	0.24***
MANUF	Chemicals	-0.02	0.02	3.40**	-0.18**
MANUF	Machinery	0.19	0.15	3.19**	0.16
MANUF	Communications	-0.31*	-0.21*	3.34**	-0.24***
MANUF	Transport	0.19	0.16	-0.13	0.10*
ORIGIN	North America	-0.16	-0.07	-0.25	-0.30**
ORIGIN	Western Europe	0.03	0.11	-0.02	-
ORIGIN	Far East	0.01	0.13	0.14	0.10**
AGE		-0.01	-	-	-
SIZE $(\times 10^{-3})$		-0.05	-0.29***	1.65	-0.31***
RSA		0.11	0.14	0.29	-0.05
REG		-0.37***	-0.46***	-0.34*	-0.41***
NAT		3.54***	2.70***	3.46**	-0.86
GDP		-0.02	-0.01	-0.04	0.01
Constant		2.71***	2.62***	2.80***	2.64***
Shape parameter (κ)		4.27***	5.68***	4.91***	55.18***
N		236	147	86	61
Pseudo R^2		0.32	0.34	0.43	0.28
LogL		-64.6	-35.8	-24.7	20.22

Note: ML estimation of (8.2) with log-logistic distribution for surviving and exiting plants. Variables described in Appendix Table 2. Project variables are measured for the Initial investment. Small = plants with less than 50 jobs in the Initial investment and Large = all other plants. No Large start-up plants originate from Rest of the World. The OTH terms are included but not reported. The shape parameter is significantly greater then unity in each case. Robust standard errors. *** = significant at the 1, ** = 5 and * = 10% level.

plant. Overall, a start-up plant survives for around 14 years, and which decreases only marginally to 13 years for the very large plants. As regards survival rates, the estimates for κ in Table 8.3 indicate high hazard rates around the median survival duration. Thus, for the smaller plants two-thirds exist after 10 years, but only one-third after 15 years, whereas for larger plants the respective figures are three-quarters and one-quarter. Hence, while plants survive for a reasonable period of time, the survival rate diminishes sharply around the time of the median duration.

Table 8.4 Median Survival Durations and Rates for Start-up Plants

SIZE =	**All**	**10**	**50**	**100**	**250**	**500**
Median duration	14.1	14.2	14.1	14.0	13.6	12.9
Survival rates:						
t = 5 years	0.97	0.93	0.99	1.00	1.00	1.00
t = 10 years	0.76	0.64	0.91	0.91	0.87	0.76
t = 15 years	0.46	0.35	0.47	0.49	0.38	0.27
t = 20 years	0.26	0.19	0.14	0.15	0.10	0.07
Number of plants	147	40	46	21	23	17

Notes: Evaluation of median survival duration (in years) and rates (in probabilities) based on re-estimation of start-up equation in Table 8.3 with *SIZE* and constant term only. Median duration is exp βx and the survival rate is $S(t) = 1 / \{1 + (t / \exp \beta x)^{\kappa}\}$. Final row gives the number of plants in each size category, i.e. 40 in the range 1-10, 46 in 11-50 and so on. A few plants with more than 500 jobs are included in final size category.

The results for plant survival find support elsewhere in the literature (see Chapter 4). An increasing and decreasing hazard rate is found for all new entrants by Audretsch and Mahmood (1994) and for new small entrant plants by Holmes *et al* (2003). Using a parametric analysis, McCloughan and Stone (1998) find a hazard rate for foreign MNE subsidiary start-ups that peaks at 12 years, which is similar to that found here. However, a major difference between our results and those generally obtained elsewhere is that we find a negative relationship between size on entry and survival. In fact, it accords with that of Harris and Hassaszadeh (2002), and supports the notion that the large plants are 'footloose', although the number of the very large plants is small (see Table 8.4). Finally, McCloughan and Stone (1998) obtain shorter survival time durations for plants that commence by acquisition rather than by start-up, although here there is no difference.

Plant Re-investment

In response to the relatively high exit rates, the economic development agencies try to 'embed' foreign-owned plants in the regional economy. This was discussed in Chapter 4, where it was noted that one form of plant 'embeddedness' is plant re-investment. Re-investment implies a larger plant scale – it accounts for about 60 per cent of the known investment by start-up plants (Table 5.8), and a Multiple Investor start-up plant is three-times the size of a Single Investor in employment terms (Table 7.3) – but an interesting issue is whether it strengthens a plant and leads to longer survival time durations.

There are several reasons why a re-investment project may be different to an initial investment. First, re-investment may add functions that are associated with other features of 'embeddedness', e.g. research and development. This is capital deepening, but it may capital-widen and by promoting a larger scale make a plant more able to withstand random shocks in its input and output markets. Second, it may 'signal' the greater strength of the plant itself. In the case of a multi-plant enterprise it may indicate a commitment of the parent to sustain its operation after entry or of a plant to compete and win investment from the parent (Young *et al*, 1994). These suggest that re-investment imparts or signals a greater quality of the re-investing plants. However, contrary to this, re-investment could indicate a lack of commitment by the firm, with the plant choosing to stage its investment over time. A re-investment may even be inferior as it tends to be undertaken by older plants with more mature products. Evans (1987) finds that exit decreases with firm age, while Dunne *et al* (1989) find that plants that expand beyond their initial size do not appear to have better survival prospects. It suggests the issue of whether plant re-investment is qualitatively superior is an empirical matter.

The real options approach to investment (Dixit and Pindyck, 1994) suggests that there are a number of alternatives facing a firm, whether trading or not, comprising the option to wait to invest, to reactivate, temporarily suspend, switch use, abandon or expand, where the latter may be classified as a re-investment.[8] In the case of FDI, an incumbent has essentially three options: wait, re-invest or exit, while a potential entrant has the option to wait or invest. If markets are efficient it is reasonable that the returns from these options will be equal, and that the survival prospects will be similar across different investments, in which case there is no scope to 'embed' plants through re-investment. Proxying the investment return by the plant survival, re-investment can therefore be used to examine if investment markets are efficient. Of course, a re-investment may make no difference, as a firm's survival prospects are largely determined by random shocks, which are felt across all plants, whether re-investing or not. This is examined below, but before this the probability of plant re-investment is analysed.

The Probability of Re-investment

The analysis is for New Plants that carry out at least one further investment project after the investment by which they commence in foreign ownership. Specifically, they are Multiple Investors that implement a Subsequent investment after the

---

[8] One of the principal findings of options theory is that where there is stochastic uncertainty and investment is costly, then there is a value to waiting. Options theory is difficult to test empirically, partly because it is complex, but also because the option value depends on a number of features, including the way in which information arrives, the duration of option rights, the importance of first-mover advantages and the growth of the underlying project value (Driver and Wood, 2005).

Initial investment. The analysis is for the surviving plants, so that re-investment is not foreclosed by exit.[9] There is data censoring, as re-investment is not observed after 1998, even for surviving plants. The re-investment probability is examined using linear probability and logit models. These are not ideal, because of the data censoring, but in the next section a duration analysis is undertaken.

The probability that a plant re-invests is the probability that a plant invests given that it has already invested. It is the conditional probability, $P(SI \mid II)$, where SI = Subsequent investment and II = Initial investment. By Bayes Rule it is:

$$P(SI \cap II) / P(II) \qquad\qquad (8.7)$$

The numerator of (8.7) is the probability that a plant both carries out an Initial and a Subsequent investment, which is the probability that it is a Multiple Investor, i.e. $P(SI \cap II) = P(MI)$, where MI = Multiple Investor. It means (8.7) is:

$$P(MI) / P(II) \qquad\qquad (8.8)$$

The probability that a plant re-invests is the probability that it is a Multiple Investor weighted by the probability that it has undertaken an Initial investment. In our analysis the dependent variable is *MULT* (see Appendix Table 2), which takes a value of unity if the plant is a Multiple Investor by the end of the study period, but otherwise is zero. However, (the probability that a plant carries out an Initial investment is also relevant, i.e. $P(II)$. This is not observed directly, as the population of all plants from which the Initial investments are drawn is not known, but it is addressed as follows. It is assumed that the number of potential investors to the region is constant in any year, so $P(II)$ is proxied by the number of Initial investments in each year relative to those occurring in the study period as a whole. For the linear probability model a simple weighting procedure is adopted.[10] For the logit model an 'offset' is used so that based on (8.8) the logit model is:

$$P(MI) / P(II) \;=\; \exp{(\beta x)} / \{1 + \exp{(\beta x)}\} \qquad\qquad (8.9)$$

where x is a vector of explanatory variables with coefficients β. In each year t, $P(II)$ is a constant, and in exponential form it is $P(II) = \exp(y_t)$, which gives:

$$P(MI) \;=\; \exp{(\beta x - y_t)} / \{1 + \exp{(\beta x)}\} \qquad\qquad (8.10)$$

---

[9] As such, exit does not directly influence whether a plant is observed to be a Single or Multiple Investor, although the prospect of exit or the factors leading to exit may still have an influence on the decision to re-invest.

[10] There are data on 113 start-ups, of which there are six Initial investments in 1985, giving a weight of 6 / 113 = 0.053 for 1985, and so on.

where y_t is the offset. It is calculated for each year, and has a coefficient fixed at unity. The logit model is estimated using the routine for an offset in *STATA*.

Having carried out the weighting procedure, the date of the Initial investment is relevant in both the linear probability and logit models. This is because the earlier in time is the Initial investment the longer is the duration over which the plant is observed, and, other things equal, the greater is the probability of re-investment. For this reason, time dummies are also included in the analysis.

The independent variables are much the same as those included in the analysis of survival, except that the *NAT* term is excluded, as these plants are all Multiple Investors.[11] Likewise, plants originating from the Rest of the World are all Single Investors and this term is omitted, as is the *OTH6* (plants re-opening after 1998) for which there are no observations on surviving New Plants. As regards the *SIZE* term, the relationship with re-investment is complicated, as it could be that larger plants have no need to re-invest, but conversely that the larger plants have greater capacity to raise funds and hence re-invest. It is explored below. The analysis is for surviving plants, so the number of observations is smaller than before, while missing cases on *SIZE* means there are 191 observations.[12]

The Linear Probability Model

A robust estimator is used, as while the linear probability model is relatively easy to interpret, it may induce heteroskedasticity in the error term. The results for this model are given in Table 8.5. The table gives the estimated coefficients for New Plants and start-up plants, both according to whether either a time trend or yearly time dummies are included. There is little to choose between these two sets of estimates, although the results with the time dummies give a slightly better fit to the data. Overall, only a small number of the coefficients are significant. For the New Plants, there is a significantly higher probability of re-investment for plants in the transport activity, which includes motor-vehicle manufacture. The same follows for plants in receipt of a Government grant in their Initial project (*RSA*) and those commencing in more buoyant economic times (*GDP*). Other plants with a higher probability of re-investment are those that have other plants in the region with the same owner (*OTH1*) or are taken-over after the end of the study period, either by a foreign-owned firm (*OTH4*) or UK-owned firm (*OTH5*). The results for start-up plants are similar to those for New Plants, but overall the results are disappointing. One possible reason for this is that the linear probability model is giving far too simplistic an explanation, so that a logit model may be preferred.

---

[11] It predicts the dependent variable with perfect success.

[12] Of which 113 plants are start-ups, 63 are acquisitions and 15 are joint ventures.

Table 8.5 Results for the Linear Probability Model

		New Plants		Start-ups	
TYPE	Start-ups	-0.03	-0.05	-	-
TYPE	Acquisitions	0.08	0.07	-	-
URBAN		-0.07	-0.06	-0.05	-0.02
SECTOR		-0.07	-0.04	-0.03	-0.01
MANUF	Chemicals	0.08	0.12	0.35*	0.39**
MANUF	Machinery	0.01	0.02	0.14	0.14
MANUF	Communications	0.01	0.05	0.12	0.16
MANUF	Transport	0.26**	0.28**	0.18	0.19*
ORIGIN	North America	-0.09	-0.06	0.01	0.06
ORIGIN	Far East	0.07	0.08	0.12*	0.11*
OTH1		0.17	0.17*	0.28**	0.26**
OTH2		0.02	-0.09	-0.17	-0.19
OTH3		0.16	0.129	0.12	0.11
OTH4		0.34**	0.35**	0.18	0.25
OTH5		0.26*	0.29	0.13	0.10
AGE		-0.01	-0.01	-	-
SIZE (x 10^3)		-0.08	-0.07	-0.13	-0.11
RSA		0.13*	0.12	0.22*	0.19*
REG		-0.01	0.02	-0.10	-0.05
GDP		0.08**	0.04*	-0.01	0.02
Constant		-0.20	-0.13	0.03	0.27**
Year dummies		Yes	no	yes	no
Time trend		-	0.05**	-	0.05**
R^2		0.66	0.63	0.72	0.69
N		191	191	113	113
F		15.14**	16.94**	29.25**	26.16**

Note: OLS estimation, with weighting of variables. Robust standard errors. *NAT, ORIGIN* (Rest of the World) and *OTH6* omitted. ** = significant at the 5 and * = 10 % level.

The Logit Model

The results for the logit model for the New Plants and start-ups are given in Table 8.6. The table shows the estimated coefficients and marginal effects at the variable means, where the latter are expressed in percentage terms. They allow for a non-linear effect related to the plant size on entry. In the case of the New Plants, the regression makes a correct prediction in 83% of cases (i.e. whether a plant is a Multiple Investor or not), which is 87% for the start-ups. Indeed, the predicted probability that a New Plant is a re-investor is 0.39 when calculated at the variable

Table 8.6 Logit Results for the Re-investment Probability

		New Plants		Start-ups	
		Coeff.	$\partial P / \partial \beta$	Coeff.	$\partial P / \partial \beta$
TYPE	Start-ups	-0.01	-0.92	-	-
TYPE	Acquisitions	0.24	0.61	-	-
URBAN		-0.89*	-9.25	-1.44*	-11.56
SECTOR		-0.53	-4.21	-1.93*	-10.65
MANUF	Chemicals	0.95	9.39	5.94**	90.52
MANUF	Machinery	0.56	4.03	3.09	50.82
MANUF	Communications	0.84	11.62	3.04*	48.53
MANUF	Transport	1.14*	16.01	1.87	20.45
ORIGIN	North America	-1.21*	-9.84	-2.34	-11.08
ORIGIN	Far East	0.81	7.10	1.65*	14.89
OTH1		1.18*	14.15	7.38**	94.64
OTH2		-0.70	-5.46	-2.95*	-7.48
OTH3		0.85	7.94	4.95*	83.89
OTH4		4.00**	75.68	-	-
OTH5		3.36**	58.59	0.25	0.47
AGE		-0.06**	-0.44	-	-
SIZE (x 10^{-3})		18.03**	158.91	20.86	143.51
$SIZE^2$ (x 10^{-6})		-25.50**	-229.00	-25.50	-174.00
RSA		1.32**	13.10	4.04**	48.44
REG		-1.16*	-9.03	-2.31	-10.30
GDP		-0.46	-1.43	-0.72	-8.26
Constant		-1.50		-2.98**	
N		191		113	
LogL		-67.83		-28.88	
Pseudo R^2		0.48		0.58	
Wald (χ^2)		75.87**		45.57**	

Note: ML estimation of logit model for New Plants and start-ups with offsets. Time dummies included but not shown. *NAT, ORIGIN* (Rest of the World) and *OTH6* excluded. $\partial P / \partial \beta$ is marginal effect times 100, calculated at variable means, but from 0 to 1 for discrete variables. Robust standard errors. ** = significant at the 5, * = 10% level.

means, which is close to the actual probability of 0.40.[13] Overall, the results are preferred to that for the linear probability model. The estimates for all New Plants

---

[13] It differs to the 0.37 reported in Appendix Table 2, but for open and closed plants.

are similar to those for the linear model, with the significance of the motor vehicle and RSA terms, but, in addition, the re-investment probability decreases if the plant is in an urban area, originates from North America, is older or involved with the regional agency. When entered by itself, the scale (*SIZE*) is insignificant, but when included as a quadratic it is significant, implying that the probability of re-investing increases up to an initial plant size of about 350 jobs, but then decreases. Possible reasons for this were considered above. The New Plant results suggest there is no significant difference between the start-up and acquisition plants, but when the *AGE* term is excluded (which is zero for start-ups), the acquisition plants are significantly less likely to be a Multiple Investor.

The final columns in Table 8.6 show a different pattern for the start-up plants compared with that for all New Plants. In particular, a start-up has a greater re-investment probability if in chemicals or communications, if it originates from the Far East or it receives RSA at start-up. The probability is smaller if the plant is in the urban areas or outside of manufacturing. There is a weak effect related to the initial scale (significant at just outside the 10 per cent level), with re-investment increasing up to an initial plant size of around 400 jobs and then decreasing. The model was estimated separately for the acquisition plants.[14] For these plants, the probability of re-investment increases if the plant is in the urban areas, and if it is in manufacturing, younger in age or originates from the Far East. Further, the re-investment probability increases the larger is the scale of the acquired plant.

The Re-investment Duration

Having examined the re-investment probability, the time duration to re-investment is now examined, and, in particular, the characteristics that lead a plant to re-invest sooner rather than later. While in principle the results may differ to that of the re-investment probability, as a plant that re-invests sooner may be more or less likely to re-invest, in general it is found that a plant that has a higher probability of re-investment will tend to do so sooner. An advantage of the duration analysis is that the time period between the Initial investment and the first Subsequent investment is modelled explicitly, and allowance can be made for data censoring. This avoids the problem encountered in the previous section, whereby a plant that is observed for a longer time duration has more opportunity to re-invest.

The examination is carried out for New Plants, with a separate analysis for start-up plants. The time origin is the date when the plant commenced in foreign ownership over 1985-98, i.e. the Initial investment, and the re-investment duration is the period in years from the time origin until the first Subsequent investment

---

[14] These results are reported in Jones and Wren (2004d). The predicted probability of re-investment varies between start-up and acquisition plants with baseline characteristics. For a start-up plant it is 0.42, but for an acquisition it is only 0.05, because very few of the acquisition plants in Northumberland re-invest, which is the baseline case.

when the plant becomes a Multiple Investor. The hazard rate is the probability that a plant becomes a Multiple Investor given that it has not already done so, while the survival rate is the probability that a plant gets to 1998 as a Single Investor. The data are right-censored as a Single Investor may become a Multiple Investor at some time after 1998. The Single Investors are included in the analysis, and data censoring is handled through the specification of the likelihood function. Using the same notation as for the survival analysis, the likelihood function is:

$$L = \prod_i f(t_i)^{\delta i} S(t_i)^{1 - \delta i} \qquad (8.11)$$

Taking the log of (8.11) and noting that the hazard function $h(t_i)$ is equal to $f(t_i)$ / $S(t_i)$, the log-likelihood function (dropping i subscripts from here on) is:

$$\log L = \Sigma \{\delta \log h(t) + \log S(t)\} \qquad (8.12)$$

It can be estimated using maximum likelihood techniques, but it requires that a functional form is given to $h(t)$ and $S(t)$. The same functional forms are considered as before, i.e. the Weibull, lognormal and log-logistic distributions.

Empirical Hazard and Survivor Functions

Initially, the raw data are used to evaluate the empirical hazard function $h(t)$. This is the probability that a plant becomes a Multiple Investor in each year given that it has not already done so. For each duration, measured in years, it is calculated as the proportion of remaining Single Investor plants that become a Multiple Investor in that year. The plants are observed over 1985 to 1998, so there are thirteen durations (i.e. t takes a value of 13 for plants observed over 1985-98, 12 for plants observed over either 1985-97 or 1986-98, and so on). The empirical hazard and survival rates for the New Plants, start-ups and acquisition plants are reported in Table 8.7, which also shows the number of observations on which each calculation is based. The re-investment time durations cannot be calculated from the table due to the data censoring, which is more likely to affect the shorter observed durations.

For the New Plants, Table 8.7 shows that the hazard rates are generally in the range 7 to 10 per cent for durations up to 7 years after the Initial investment, but that they are much lower for observed durations of 8 or more years. Indeed, there are only four plants with an observed duration to the first re-investment of 8 years or more, so that the plants carry out their re-investment within seven years or not at all. The hazard rate for the one-year duration is about 8 per cent, which suggests that the plants have a high re-investment probability even one year after the Initial investment. There is an almost identical pattern for the start-ups, but there is a very different pattern for the acquisition plants. The acquisitions have hazard rates that are initially much higher, at between 10 and 13 per cent in the first two years,

Table 8.7 Empirical Hazard and Survivor Functions for Multiple Investment

Duration	New Plants			Start-ups			Acquisitions		
(years)	$h(t)$	$S(t)$	no.	$h(t)$	$S(t)$	no.	$h(t)$	$S(t)$	no.
1	7.9	92.2	(191)	6.2	93.8	(113)	13.1	86.9	(61)
2	9.8	83.2	(164)	10.0	84.4	(100)	10.6	77.6	(47)
3	9.6	75.2	(125)	8.9	77.0	(79)	6.1	72.9	(33)
4	7.8	69.3	(103)	9.2	69.9	(65)	3.5	70.4	(29)
5	7.3	64.3	(82)	7.7	64.5	(52)	4.6	67.2	(22)
6	7.6	59.4	(66)	9.3	58.5	(43)	0	67.2	(17)
7	8.9	54.1	(56)	8.1	53.7	(37)	7.1	62.4	(14)
8	2.4	52.8	(41)	3.3	52.0	(30)	0	62.4	(7)
9	0	52.8	(33)	0	52.0	(26)	0	62.4	(4)
10	9.5	47.8	(21)	5.9	48.9	(17)	50.0	31.2	(2)
11	7.7	44.1	(13)	9.1	44.5	(11)	-	-	(0)
12	0	44.1	(7)	0	44.5	(5)	-	-	(0)
13	0	44.1	(6)	0	44.5	(4)	0	31.2	(1)

Notes: Empirical hazard $h(t)$ and survivor rates $S(t)$ for Multiple Investment, expressed as percentages. Hazard rate is the probability that a plant becomes a Multiple Investor given it has not already done so. Figures in parentheses are number of observations.

but which then fall away sharply and are generally zero after five years.[15] An interpretation of this is that plants are taken over for the purpose of gaining market access, i.e. an ownership advantage, and the inward investor either puts its specific technology into place soon afterwards or not at all.

The empirical survival function $S(t)$ can be found from the empirical hazard rates, as follows: $S(t) = \{1 - h(t)\} \{1 - h(t - 1)\} \ldots \{1 - h(1)\}$, and these are shown in Table 8.7. These are the Kaplan-Meier survival functions (Kaplan and Meier, 1958; Lawless, 1982, pp. 53-71).[16] Three-quarters of New Plants are Single Investors after 3 years, so that a quarter have carried out their first re-investment. After 8 years around a half of the plants are still Single Investors, while from then on the gradient flattens out, suggesting that the plants that are going to re-invest have done so by this time. Again, there is a similar pattern for the start-up plants, but a different pattern is exhibited by the acquisitions. While three-quarters of the

---

[15] There is a very high hazard rate for the observed duration of 10 years, but it is based on only two observations, so can be discounted.

[16] Given the manner in which the empirical survival function is arrived at, the Kaplan-Meier technique is also known as the product-limit method. Often it is graphed by plotting the observed duration against the proportion of plants that are Single Investors at the end of each duration (i.e. 'survivors'). The plots are available from the authors on request.

acquisition plants are Single Investors after 2 years, the proportion of Single Investors levels out at about two-thirds after 5 years. For an observed duration of 10 years there is a sudden increase in the proportion of plants that are Multiple Investors, but again this is of no real importance.

Appropriate Functional Form

One way to examine the appropriateness of the Weibull distribution is to consider what is known as a 'log-log plot'. The Weibull survival function in conditional form is $S(t \mid x) = \exp[-(t / \beta x)^{\alpha}]$ by (8.3) and (8.4), so that:

$$\ln [-\ln S(t \mid x)] = \alpha \ln t - \alpha \ln \beta x \qquad (8.13)$$

For plants with similar covariates x, the plot of $\ln [-\ln S(t \mid x)]$ against $\ln t$ should be linear, where the second right-hand side of (8.13) is treated as a constant term if the plants have similar covariates (or a shift factor if the covariates differ). The 'log-log plot' for all New Plants is shown in Figure 8.1. The plot does not refute the Weibull distribution, as it is broadly linear. The exceptions are longer observed durations ($t = 12$ and 13), but for which there is a relatively small number of observations. The issue can be further investigated by OLS estimation of (8.13). Of course, there are only thirteen observations, but a good fit is obtained:

$$\ln [-\ln S(t)] = 0.865 \ln t - 2.301 \qquad (8.14)$$
$$\quad (21.6) \qquad (29.5)$$

$R^2 = 0.97$, n = 13, t-statistics in parentheses.

The regression gives an estimate for the shape parameter α of 0.865, which is significantly less than unity. It implies negative duration dependence, so that the re-investment probability decreases with time. It suggests a plant is less likely to re-invest the longer is the time period from the Initial investment, which is not surprising given the pattern exhibited in Table 8.7. However, when re-estimated with a quadratic term in $\ln t$ the following result is obtained:

$$\ln [-\ln S(t)] = 1.336 \ln t - 0.165 [\ln t]^2 - 2.522 \qquad (8.15)$$
$$\quad (25.1) \qquad (9.2) \qquad (68.7)$$

$R^2 = 0.99$, n = 13, t-statistics in parentheses.

The quadratic term is strongly significant, which refutes a monotonic hazard rate, and hence the Weibull distribution.

To decide on the appropriate functional form, a comparison was made of the shape parameters obtained from maximum likelihood regression of (8.12) for each of the Weibull, lognormal and log-logistic distributions, including the covariates as

ln[-lnS(*t*)]

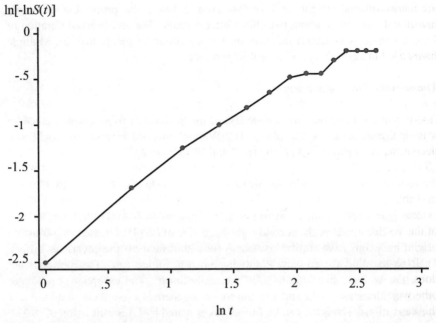

Figure 8.1 The 'Log-Log Plot'

before.[17] For the Weibull distribution the shape parameter was significantly greater than unity for each of the New Plant, start-up and acquisition regressions, implying positive duration dependence, so that the re-investment probability increases with the time period over which a plant is observed, i.e. longer time durations imply an increased re-investment probability. The log-logistic function allows for negative duration dependence, but this was rejected in favour of an increasing and then decreasing failure rate. The lognormal distribution imposes an increasing and decreasing failure rate on the data, but it did not provide a good fit, as the ancillary parameter σ for the variance in (8.5) was insignificant.

These regressions suggest that the choice is between the Weibull and log-logistic distributions, but these are non-nested, while it is difficult to prefer one of these models on the basis of the Akaike information criterion alone.[18] However,

---

[17] Only those for the latter are presented below. The results for the Weibull model are in an accelerated failure-time form, which means that the coefficients are directly comparable with the other two models. The three models gave similar estimates of the covariates.

[18] The Akaike information criterion essentially involves comparing the log-likelihoods. It is given by - 2 (log likelihood) + 2 ($c + p + 1$), where c is the number of model covariates and p is the number of model-specific ancillary parameters. The parameters c and p are the same for the respective models, so in effect it involves choosing the model with the highest log likelihood, but in this respect there is little difference between the models.

the log-logistic distribution is favoured for a number of reasons.[19] It means the hazard rate is increasing and then decreasing with the observed time duration.

Estimation Results

The results from maximising (8.12) with the log-logistic model are given in Table 8.8. These are for New Plants, start-ups and for Small and Large start-up plants (more than 50 jobs in the Initial investment). The estimate of the shape parameter κ is significantly greater than unity in each case, implying an increasing and then decreasing hazard rate. The median re-investment duration is given by $1 / \lambda = \exp (\beta x)$, and the results give an estimate for this that is similar to the period at which the re-investment duration is at a maximum.[20] The estimates of the constant terms in Table 8.8 suggest median re-investment durations for baseline plants that are extremely large. However, it is because the baseline country of origin is the Rest of the World, from which the plants are all Single Investors. For other countries of origin, Table 8.8 shows that the re-investment duration is much shorter.

In terms of a baseline plant, Table 8.8 suggests that the re-investment duration does not vary significantly between the start-up and acquisition plants, but that otherwise there are strong differences in the median re-investment duration.[21] In the case of the start-ups the estimates suggest that Far Eastern plants re-invest sooner than those from North America or Western Europe (15 years against 26 and 18 years respectively), although these are not significantly different from one another ($\chi^2 (2) = 2.45$). There is a shorter re-investment duration for plants in the transport activity, no doubt related to developments surrounding the Nissan car

---

[19] There are three reasons. First, the significant coefficient on the quadratic ln t term in (8.15) does not support the Weibull. Second, the generalised gamma model nests the Weibull model, but this distribution is rejected at the 1 per cent level (the generalised gamma model also nests the lognormal distribution, but is rejected at the 5 per cent level). Third, positive duration dependence found for the Weibull model contradicts the estimate of α in (8.14), which is significantly less than unity. Positive duration dependence is implausible, as it implies the probability of re-investment increases the longer is the time period after the Initial investment. Further, it confounds the evidence for the empirical hazard rates given in Table 8.7. When the longer time durations are excluded from the data, an estimate of α in excess of 2 is obtained, which implies that the hazard rate increases at an increasing rate, and is even less plausible.

[20] Differentiating the hazard function in (8.6), and setting it equal to zero for a maximum, gives $t^{max} = (\kappa - 1)^{1/\kappa} \exp (\beta x)$, so that t^{max} is equal to the median re-investment duration multiplied by $(\kappa - 1)^{1/\kappa}$. In the case of the New Plants $(\kappa - 1)^{1/\kappa}$ is equal to 0.89, and for the start-up plants it is 1.09, so that these results are almost identical to those for the median re-investment duration.

[21] When maximising (8.12) separately for the acquisitions, the median re-investment durations are 1, 3 and 2 years respectively for plants from the Far East, North America and Western Europe. However, for the start-ups the respective figures are 15, 26 and 18 years. It corresponds to the differences reported in Table 8.7.

Table 8.8 Results for the Re-investment Duration

		New Plants	Start-ups		
			All	Small	Large
TYPE	Start-ups	-0.16	-	-	-
TYPE	Acquisitions	-0.62	-	-	-
URBAN		0.32	0.16	-0.16	0.68
SECTOR		0.25	0.05	1.04	-0.99
MANUF	Chemicals	-0.33	-0.54	-0.44	-0.62
MANUF	Machinery	0.18	-0.06	0.21	0.12
MANUF	Communications	0.33	0.25	1.10	-0.19
MANUF	Transport	-0.63**	-0.68*	0.30	-0.98*
ORIGIN	North America	-8.84**	-7.57**	-6.47**	-0.01
ORIGIN	Western Europe	-9.06**	-7.97**	-6.97**	-
ORIGIN	Far East	-9.56**	-8.11**	-6.83**	-0.82
AGE		0.02	-	-	-
SIZE (x 10^3)		-5.81**	-5.90**	-23.12**	1.10
RSA		-0.12	-0.25	0.88*	-0.33
REG		-0.16	-0.26	-0.09	0.37
NAT		7.53**	7.32**	5.54**	5.22**
GDP		-0.10	-0.06	-0.08	-0.16
Constant		12.06**	10.83**	9.31**	2.41**
Shape parameter (κ)		1.81**	2.20**	3.07**	2.42**
N		191	113	64	49
LogL		-136.9	-75.2	-25.67	-39.94
Pseudo R^2		0.22	0.29	0.44	0.23

Note: ML estimation of (8.12) with log-logistic distribution. *AGE* is zero for the start-ups and omitted, and *OTH* terms are included but not reported. Small = plants with less than 50 jobs in the Initial investment and Large = all other plants. Robust standard errors. ** = significant at 5 and * = 10% level.

plant, while plants involved with the national agency are not observed to re-invest. The scale term, *SIZE*, suggests the re-investment duration decreases with plant size.[22] Equation (8.12) was re-estimated for the start-ups with a constant term and shape parameter only. For a plant promising 10 jobs at start-up the median re-investment duration was 14 years, but for a plant with 100 jobs it is 11 years, for a plant with 250 jobs it is 7 years and for 500 jobs it is only 4 years. These suggest that the re-investment duration diminishes sharply with size.

---

[22] There was weak evidence of a non-linear effect, although the quadratic *SIZE* term was insignificant at the 10% level and excluded. This was the case for other functional forms.

The last two columns of Table 8.8 undertake sensitivity analysis for the start-ups. For a Large plant the median re-investment duration is about 11 years, but otherwise many of the covariates are insignificant.[23] For a Small start-up plant, the results show that the re-investment duration increases for plants outside of the manufacturing sector and in communications. There is a large negative coefficient on the *SIZE* term, indicating that the re-investment duration decreases sharply for this plant-size range. Some other regressions were run to examine the robustness of the result.[24] It included an estimation for both surviving and exiting New Plants, to maximise the observations, and an estimation that defined the first Subsequent investment as that in involving at least some new jobs. In both cases qualitatively similar results were obtained.

Plant Embeddedness

The introduction to this chapter mentioned that re-investment is potentially a source of plant 'embeddedness', leading to longer survival time durations. This is important as foreign-owned plants have high exit rates, and re-investment offers a potentially useful handle for policymakers to root these plants in the economy. An incumbent plant has the option to re-invest or not, while a potential entrant has the opportunity to initially invest or not. Only if there are differences in these, is there scope for the policymaker to 'embed' the plants through re-investment. Previous empirical testing of 'embeddedness' has tended to concentrate on supply linkages, but this evidence is not convincing (see Chapter 4).

It seems trivially obvious that a re-investing plant is likely to have a longer survival time duration, so that there is an endogeneity problem. However, the issue that is addressed is not whether re-investing plants survive for longer. Rather the issue is whether re-investing plants (i.e. Multiple Investors) have longer survival durations from the time of the first re-investment relative to plants with similar characteristics that do not re-invest (the Single Investors), but which invest for the first time at the same time as the re-investment. In effect, the Single Investors are used to establish the counter-factual position for the Multiple Investors, which is advantageous for several reasons. First, Single Investors are also foreign-owned, whereas domestic plants are likely to have lower failure rates. Second, the data for

---

[23] The countries of origin for Large plants are: North America: 12 plants; Western Europe: 21; Far East: 16; and the Rest of the World: 0, so that the baseline-case for a Large plant is Western Europe, but otherwise the baseline characteristics are the same as before. For the Small plants the respective number of plants are 35, 18, 24 and 3.

[24] One of these involved regressing (8.12) separately for the acquisition plants. The re-investment durations were four-times longer for plants in the metropolitan counties of Tyne and Wear and Cleveland, suggesting different motivations between these areas. Acquired plants outside of the manufacturing sector and older plants also had much longer re-investment durations.

these were collected on an identical basis, while it is difficult to identify Single Investors using other sources. Finally, it can be argued that it does not address the endogeneity issue, as the *prospect* of longer survival durations can affect re-investment, but this argument applies equally to the plants carrying an Initial investment. The focus throughout is on the start-up plants, which in terms of exit have the greatest policy interest.

Estimation Results

First, it is examined if the Multiple Investors have longer survival durations than the Single Investors from the time of the Initial investment.[25] This is not a test of embeddedness, as it is reasonable that a re-investing plant survives for longer from the time of the Initial investment. It is examined by re-estimating (8.2) for the start-ups, but with the Multiple Investor term *MULT* included as an extra covariate (see Appendix Table 2). The results (not shown) give an estimated coefficient on *MULT* of 0.508 (z-value = 3.58), indicating that the median survival duration for a Multiple Investor is 1.66 times greater than for a Single Investor (i.e. exp 0.508).[26] Table 8.4 shows that the median survival duration for a start-up plant is 14.1 years, but for the Multiple and Single Investors these are 19.4 and 11.7 years respectively (i.e. a ratio of 1.66), so that the difference is 7 to 8 years.

These results suggest that a Multiple Investor start-up plant survives for about 7 to 8 years longer than a Single Investor. It would seem to provide support for re-investment as a source of plant embeddedness, but if comparison is made with the estimated re-investment durations in the previous section it is much less certain. While a Multiple Investor survives for 7 to 8 years longer than a Single Investor, the results found earlier suggest a plant can take this long to re-invest for the first time.[27] A comparison really needs to be made at the project level rather than at the plant level. As a more direct test, (8.2) was re-estimated for the start-up plants, but with the time origin taken to be the year of the first Subsequent investment for the Multiple Investors and the year of the Initial investment for the Single Investors. The results are given in Table 8.9. It explicitly models the survival time duration from the date of the first Subsequent investment for the Multiple Investors. To test

---

[25] 37 per cent of the plants are Multiple Investors (98 out of 265 plants), but the proportion of surviving plants that re-invest is 41 per cent (87 of 215). There is a similar pattern for start-up plants, where the respective figures are 39 and 43 per cent, and for the Small (32 and 51 per cent) and Large start-up plants (38 and 53 per cent).

[26] These estimates, and those that follow, are derived by re-estimating (8.2) with all the covariates excluded, except for the *SIZE* and constant terms. It means that they give an average effect across all plants in each size group. As indicated above, this is better than using the baseline plant, which is not representative of the typical inward investor. It means the estimates are directly comparable with those derived for the re-investment duration in the previous section.

[27] It was found that while a plant promising 50 employees at start-up takes 12 years to re-invest, the respective figures for plants with 100, 250 and 500 jobs are 11, 7 and 4 years.

Table 8.9 Survival Results with Differing Time Origins

| | | Start-ups | | |
		All	**Small**	**Large**
URBAN		-0.028	-0.133	-0.248**
SECTOR		-0.248	-0.392	0.406**
MANUF	Chemicals	-0.045	2.903**	-0.370**
MANUF	Machinery	0.177	2.559**	0.748**
MANUF	Communications	-0.366*	2.873**	-0.573**
MANUF	Transport	0.109	-0.129	0.604**
ORIGIN	North America	-0.068	-0.276	0.582**
ORIGIN	Western Europe	0.080	-0.066	-
ORIGIN	Far East	0.001	0.064	0.217
SIZE (x 10^{-3})		-0.018	-0.664	-0.007
RSA		-0.008	0.245	0.256**
RDA		-0.495**	-0.331*	-0.773**
IUK			3.168**	2.964**
GDP		0.009	-0.043	0.011**
MULT		0.035	0.171	-0.116
Constant		2.606**	2.846**	1.973**
Shape parameter (κ)		4.933**	5.339**	14.16**
N		147	86	61
Pseudo R^2		0.31	0.43	0.33
LogL		-37.9	-21.0	2.579

Notes: ML estimation of (8.12) with log-logistic distribution. Small = plants with less than 50 jobs in the Initial investment and Large = all other plants. *TYPE* and *AGE* omitted, while there are no Large start-ups from the Rest of the World. *OTH* terms are included but not reported. Duration is from the time of first Subsequent investment for Multiple Investors. Shape parameter is significantly greater then unity in each case. Robust standard errors. ** = significant at 5 and * = 10 per cent level.

for a difference in the survival time duration between the Multiple and Single Investors the *MULT* term was again included, and the results for the start-up plants are reported in the first column of Table 8.9. A comparison with Table 8.3 shows the result is actually similar to that found previously. Stripping out the covariates and re-estimating the equation for all start-ups in Table 8.9, but with a constant term only, gives a survival duration of 12 years. As expected, it is shorter than the 14 years found previously, but of interest is that the coefficient on *MULT* is now heavily insignificant, with a z-value of 0.22.[28]   It suggests that re-investments do not lead to significantly longer survival durations compared to Initial investments.

Tests of Robustness

A potential reason why a difference cannot be found between the Multiple and Single Investors is because the pattern of survival durations is restricted to be the same, i.e. κ in the log-logistic distribution, whereas in fact these differ. To address this, non-parametric and semi-parametric methods were used, although neither of these over-turned the result. In the first case, a Wilcoxon test showed a significant difference in the empirical survivor function between the Multiple and Single Investors when the time origin of the Multiple Investors was the Initial investment (χ^2 (1) = 21.04), but when it was the first Subsequent investment there was no difference (χ^2 (1) = 1.22). For the semi-parametric case, a Cox proportional hazards model was used, but stratified to allow the baseline survivor function to differ between Multiple and Single Investors. A Chi-square test again showed that there is no statistical difference in the baseline function between the two kinds of plant (χ^2 (13) = 2.30).

As a further test, the sample was divided into two roughly equal groups to examine if there were any differences by size of plant, i.e. the Small and Large start-up plants, where the latter have more than 50 prospective jobs on entry.[29] The exit rates for these are similar (26 and 20 per cent respectively over the study period), although the Large plants account for 90 per cent of the job losses (Table 8.1). The re-investment behaviour also differs. When re-estimating (8.2) with the *MULT* term included as an extra covariate, the ratio of median survival durations for the Multiple and Single Investors for Small plants is 1.95 (z-value = 2.29) but for Large plants it is only 1.24 (z-value = 1.64). Thus, both Small and Large start-ups survive for longer, but smaller plants much more so. However, again, there is no evidence that re-investment is associated with a longer survival duration. A Small start-up takes about 13 years to carry out its first re-investment, but has an extra survival duration of about this length of time, while a Large plant carries out its first re-investment much sooner, but its extra survival time is much shorter.[30] Allowing the time origins to vary between Multiple and Single Investors, the results are given in Table 8.9 for Small and Large plants. Again, the coefficients on the *MULT* term are heavily insignificant, with z-values in the Small and Large plant equations of 0.77 and 0.91 respectively.

---

[28] Another potential criticism is that the plant characteristics of the Multiple Investors are measured for the Initial investment. Instead, these were measured for the first Subsequent investment, but in the stripped-down regressions of the equations in Table 8.9 (with *SIZE* and constant terms only) the *MULT* term was insignificant (z-value =1.08).

[29] 31 of the 61 Large start-up plants are Multiple Investors, but 20 of the 86 Small plants.

[30] The differences by size class could reflect different strategic motivations.

One further possibility is that the 'better' plants carry out re-investment, but their projects perform poorly, so that there is no net effect on plant survival. As a test, Inverse Mills ratio terms were formed from probit estimations for selection as a Multiple Investor, and included as additional terms in Table 8.9 for both Multiple and Single Investors. However, they were insignificant (z-values of 0.59 and 1.24), which indicates that better plants do not select themselves as Multiple Investors. Finally, the plant survival term, *SURV*, was included as an additional regressor in the re-investment regressors for a potential endogeneity, but it lacked significance in each case.[31]

Conclusions

The chapter focuses on the survival of foreign-owned plants. Plant survival is seen as a critical issue for the regional development, as exit rates that are much higher than for domestic plants. In the case of foreign-owned start-up plants arriving in the North-East region since the mid-1980s, a fifth exited by the year 2000, taking with them 7,500 jobs. Overall, the chapter finds that a start-up plant has a lifetime of about 14 years. Unlike many other studies, but mainly of domestic plants, it is significantly shorter for larger plants on entry, indicating the 'footloose' nature of these plants, although only by about a year or so. A feature of the analysis is the very high hazard rate that sets in around the time of the median survival duration. For the smaller plants two-thirds exist after 10 years, but only one-third after 15 years, while for large plants the figures are three-quarters and one-quarter. Not only is the life of these plants relatively short, but there is little variation.

An issue that is explored at length in the chapter is plant re-investment. It is of interest as about 60 per cent of the investment by start-up plants is in re-investment projects, while the average Multiple Investor start-up plant is three-times the size of a Single Investor by the end of the study period. Further, re-investment may be a source of plant 'embeddedness', leading to longer survival time durations, and a handle for policymakers to root these foreign investments in the regional economy. The annual hazard rates reveal that the probability of plant re-investment (given it has not already occurred) is in the range 7 to 10 per cent up to 7 years after the Initial investment, but then generally zero, so that a plant re-invests within seven years or not at all. Only half the plants re-invest. For acquisitions the hazard rates are initially much higher, but generally zero after five years, so that the investors either put their specific technology into place much sooner or not at all. In terms of 'embeddedness', the chapter finds that a Multiple Investor start-up plant has a survival time duration that at the median is 7 to 8 years longer than that of a Single Investor. However, on average, it takes about this long for the plant to carry out its

---

[31] Of course, the Multiple Investors may go on to implement many Subsequent investment, but this adds further weight to our finding that a re-investment project is not associated with a significantly longer survival duration.

first re-investment, so that a Subsequent investment is appears to be qualitatively the same to that of an Initial investment.

Overall, the results of the detailed analysis in this chapter suggest that may be little role for policymakers. The plants have high failure rates that set in after a period of time, but there is little variation in these across plants. Further, plant re-investment does not appear to be a source of 'embeddedness', which accords with the results of other studies reported in Chapter 4. An implication is that greater weight to re-investment compared to plants that are investing for the first time. As an explanation for the result, one possibility is that the plants are subject to random shocks, and that a second investment makes a plant no more able to withstand these shocks. Another possibility is that re-investment is a product of a mixture of motives, and for some plants re-investment shows a lack of commitment, whereby it stages its investment. It suggests that the timing of the re-investment decision is important, i.e. is it taken on entry or at some time down the line?, but it is beyond the scope of the kind of data analysed in this book.

Conclusions

Foreign direct investment (FDI) is the process whereby a firm in one country provides capital to an existing or newly-created firm in another country. Over recent decades FDI has increased spectacularly, so that world flows have increased from an estimated $13 billion in 1970 to nearly $1,500 billion by the year 2000. While FDI has fallen-back recently, there is no doubt about the central role played by FDI in 'globalisation' and its importance to modern economic activity. Indeed, the channel for FDI is the multinational enterprise (MNE), and it is believed that there are 60,000 MNEs in the world economy, with production occurring in nearly one million foreign affiliates. Much of this is associated with the developed world, which accounts for over 90 per cent of FDI outflows – and most of the inflows – so that over 80 of the top 100 MNEs have headquarters in either the United States or the European Union. It is perhaps surprising that FDI is a modern phenomenon, as it is generally accepted that the appearance of the modern MNE, with control over foreign production units, did not occur until the Nineteenth Century. However, it was not until the latter half of the Twentieth Century that world FDI flows began to increase substantially, and when academics and policymakers became interested.

FDI Location

Early interest in foreign direct investment regarded it as like any other capital flow, and it was analysed using standard neoclassical theories, which lacked either a spatial or a truly international dimension. It was only in the 1960s that the role of control in FDI was recognised, and that independent theory was developed with its own unique characteristics. Since then, numerous theories have been propounded on the motivations for FDI, leading to different schools of thought. In broad terms, they range from the 'ownership' school, which emphasises the specific advantages of the MNE that are necessary to overcome the barriers to international operation; the 'internalisation' school, which stresses the lack of a market in knowledge, as an essential ingredient to overseas production; and to the explanations based on the strategic actions of firms that operate on an international stage. Finally, Dunning's eclectic paradigm encompasses the ownership and internalisation advantages of MNEs in the decision to invest abroad, as well as location. While representing the main theory of FDI, it is criticised as being purely taxonomic, and is modified to incorporate new ideas and trends, suggesting an elastic theory. These include the increased importance of knowledge, greater liberalisation of cross-border markets, the emergence of non-equity strategic alliances and the dramatic rise in mergers and acquisitions activity in the late 1990s. Knowledge and technology are seen as the most significant resources of the firm, and the driving force of FDI.

FDI occurs across national boundaries, but, rather strangely, empirical studies on the location pattern of MNE plants tend to be at the national level, using regional or firm-level data for a single country. Of interest to these studies are two potential reasons for location – the classical and the agglomeration factors – which have important implications. The classical determinants are traditionally believed to influence the location decision, and include such things as the size of the market that the enterprise is entering and labour costs. The agglomeration factors are the external effects and externalities, perhaps in the form of a 'spillover', which gives rise to agglomeration economies, and may encourage a foreign-owned plant to set-up where firms in a similar activity are already present. Clearly, if agglomeration factors are important, then not only may FDI be self-perpetuating, i.e. the arrival of FDI may attract further FDI, but they may work against the classical determinants, so that these have little or no effect. The econometrics evidence seems clear-cut. The classical factors, particularly the market size and labour market conditions, are significant, but become insignificant when agglomeration factors are included. It suggests that public policy is largely ineffective, except perhaps early-stage FDI, in order to establish the conditions for agglomeration economies.

Despite the almost overwhelming econometrics-based evidence that has built-up on FDI location, there are many reasons to be sceptical of this literature. First, there is a problem of distinguishing empirically between the agglomeration and classical factors. Agglomeration may be measured by the infrastructure of an area, but which directly affects the firm's costs and is a classical factor. It may also be measured by the stock of FDI, e.g. foreign-owned plants, but the importance of this could just reflect existing supplier or buyer relationships, which strictly are not an agglomeration economy. Second, a sizeable proportion of FDI is through merger and acquisition, and it is not surprising that this will reflect the existing industrial structure and conditions. Third, it may be that the econometric studies are biased against the classical explanation, as these studies tend to be for a single country, where there is relatively little variation in the classical variables. A good example is the grants for FDI in the UK Assisted Areas, which are determined centrally for large projects and used to compete internationally for projects. Finally, very recent work examines the plant location decision as a two-stage or hierarchical process, i.e. a particular country is chosen before a decision is made to locate at a particular site or region in that country. It finds that the significance of classical variables depends on whether the analysis is across-countries or at the regional level.

Regional Development

Perhaps some of the most persuasive evidence for the effect of the classical factors, and for the effect of policy, is provided by the operation of policy itself. These are the Government grants for job creation under regional policy that have been available in designated Assisted Areas since the 1960s. Since the late-1980s about half the total grant amount has been gone to foreign direct investment. Most of the early post-war FDI originated from the United States of America and went to the

South East and East Anglia, which together had more than two-thirds of the UK manufacturing employment in foreign ownership. While Scotland did receive substantial inward investment, it is noticeable that the South East has experienced an attrition in its share of UK manufacturing employment in foreign ownership, which has fallen steadily over time from 51 per cent in 1963 to just 13 per cent by 1997. It may just be the process by which FDI arrives in a country over time, going form the 'core' to the 'periphery', but the regions with substantial Assisted Areas (Scotland, Wales, Northern Ireland and northern England) have consistently outperformed all other regions in terms of the share of new FDI projects and jobs relative to their size. Further, the West Midlands experienced the steepest rise in FDI after 1984 when it was designated for grants, and by 1997 it is reckoned to have the greatest share of UK manufacturing employment in foreign ownership.

While the regions have received a proportionately greater share of FDI there are signs that this is on the wane, perhaps occasioned by the gradual weakening of regional policy (in Assisted Area coverage and in expenditure), and by the increase in foreign presence in the service sector, which seems to be locating in the 'core'. Indeed, since 1998 the number of non-manufacturing FDI projects recorded by *UK Trade and Investment* has for the first time exceeded those in manufacturing. It is such that, relative to total employment, the South East now has a similar proportion of its employment in foreign ownership compared to each of Scotland, Wales and the North East of England. It is a trend established in the 1990s, which was fuelled by the mergers and acquisitions boom towards the end of the decade – that mainly affected the service sector in the South-East region – but it appears to have been maintained since that time. Indeed, relative to their size, the Assisted Area regions have experienced a decline in the number of FDI projects over the 1990s. What is striking from the analysis of the dataset for the North-East region is how few of the projects are in the service sector. Thus, the 1990s were a period of transition in the regional location pattern of FDI, and it remains to be seen if the service-based FDI will fan-out to the regions in the same way as the FDI in manufacturing.[1]

While FDI is highly prized by the economic development agencies for its job creation, with the Government financially assisting the location of this investment in the Assisted Areas with relatively high unemployment, much of the economics literature on the potential benefits of FDI focuses on its efficiency effects. These are in the form of beneficial 'spillovers' to domestic plants through externalities and other external effects (e.g. market linkages). Underlying this is the 'ownership' motivation for FDI, which views foreign-owned plants as possessing advantages, such as superior production techniques and knowledge. However, while research was initially supportive of the foreign investment increasing the productivity of domestic firms, as the methodology has improved, the evidence has become much weaker. At best, the results are mixed, and, indeed, recent research has focused on 'reverse spillovers', which flow from domestic plants to foreign-owned firms, so

---

[1] There are already signs that the more-mature FDI, from the US, is more broadly based in the regions in terms of activity.

that the motive for FDI is 'technology sourcing'. Further, other literatures, such as the 'new regionalism', have drawn a blank. This argues that it is the nature of relations or networks within a region that 'embed' FDI, serving both to attract and retain this investment. The evidence for this, and for plant 'embeddedness' more broadly, including supply linkages, suggests that these relations are weak, and as such it points to the 'footloose' nature of FDI.

The exit of foreign-owned plants has been a concern in both the regional and industrial organisation literatures. A natural focus for this is the multi-plant nature of MNEs, and the potentially lower-order functions undertaken by these plants, leading to the so-called 'branch plant economy', which has a large proportion of its employment in low-skill, low-wage jobs. This view was popularised in the 1970s, but reappraised in the 1990s, following the fresh wave of investment from the Far East and western Europe. It has re-emerged in recent years, being given weight by the outward investment to take advantage of the cheaper labour markets in the new accession countries of the European Union and Asia. The industrial organisation literature finds that plants belonging to a multi-plant firm are more prone to exit compared to single-plant firms, but that the foreign-owned plants are more liable to closure even when firm structure is held constant. While it is almost a stylised fact that smaller plants have higher exit rates, some studies find that, for a multi-plant enterprise, larger plants have higher exit rates compared to smaller plants, perhaps related to the foreign plants. One possibility is that foreign plants are remote from the parent plant, making them prone to closure due to issues of communication and control. However, it may just be that MNE plants serve international markets, and that location across national boundaries means they possess the specific assets and know-how to shift production between countries. The classical location factors are likely to show greatest variation between countries, and since they are likely to be pro-cyclical then it suggests instability, working against the regional economy.

The implications of all this for regional development seem poor. The regions primarily receive FDI in the manufacturing sector, there is an absence of spillovers to domestic firms and the nature of relations with private and public agents does not appear to 'embed' these plants, reducing the 'footloose' of large FDI plants. The major benefit of FDI to the regions therefore seems to be the employment that the plants generate. This leads naturally to the second part of the book, where the employment and investment pattern is explored at the individual project level. It is the first time that such a detailed study of FDI has been undertaken for a single UK Assisted Area region over a long period. This is the North East of England for the period 1985-98, covering the fresh wave of FDI that has arrived since the mid-1980s and up to the end of the FDI 'boom' at the turn of the century (although the boom was largely about mergers and acquisitions in the service sector of the South East of England). It offers new insights on the nature of FDI.

FDI in an English Assisted Region

Perhaps one of the most striking aspects of the investment undertaken by foreign-owned companies is its concentration in a small number of projects. Since the mid-1980s, 28 projects in the North-East region (8 per cent of projects), each in excess of £50 million, together account for 80 per cent of investment. While this may be an over-estimate – as the investment data are known for only about two-thirds of projects – at a minimum it is at least half of the investment.[2] It means a relatively small number of projects largely accounts for the regional pattern of FDI. Based on the known investment, projects in excess of £150m account for three-quarters of investment by start-up and over half by re-investment. The investment is spatially concentrated, as it tends to locate towards eastern-seaboard, close to the centres of population, and reflects the operation of public policy in the laying-out of estates. It is also concentrated by activity, with three-quarters of the investment in just four 2-digit manufacturing activities. These four activities account for more than 95 per cent of investment coming from each of Germany, Japan and Korea. FDI has tended to occur in a narrow range of activities since World War Two, which seems to be a feature of all UK regions.[3] However, the concentration of investment is probably much greater than has previously been appreciated, as earlier studies tend to measure this using employment. This is because the larger projects tend to be heavily capital intensive, so that the elasticity between the number of jobs and the investment scale is only about one half.[4]

As a result, the pattern of jobs is much less concentrated than is investment, although there is still a concentration. However, it is not so much that the jobs are concentrated in projects, so much as the projects tend to be associated with certain characteristics (i.e. it is the projects rather than the jobs that are concentrated). In total, the 550 FDI projects in the region over 1985-98 promised a total of 80,300 jobs, of which about 45,700 are 'new' jobs, and the remainder are 'safeguarded' or pre-existing, e.g. as part of a re-investment or an acquisition project. Of the new jobs, half originate from the Far East, half are located in the metropolitan county of Tyne and Wear and half are in three 2-digit industries (communications, transport and machinery and equipment). It suggests a vulnerability of employment to events that adversely affect particular countries, localities or industries. Further, while

---

[2] Based on project job data, which is known in virtually all cases, the investment data are believed to be representative of total investment, except that the very large investments are slightly more likely to be known. The 28 projects account for £6,860 million in investment, which is 80 per cent of the known investment of £8,714 million. Based on a *pro rata* apportionment by project type, total investment is believed to be £14,267 million, of which the 28 projects represent fifty per cent. The figure of £14,267 million may also be an over-estimate, due to fact that the large investments are more likely to be known.

[3] See Chapters 2 and 4, and Hennart (2001).

[4] On average, a £500m project has 1,000 jobs, whereas a £50m project has 300 jobs and a £5m project is associated with 90 jobs (ratios of 2, 6 and 18 respectively).

there is a preponderance of projects with new jobs arising from the Far East and locating at the 'core' of the region, the analysis finds that neither of these factors affects the size of a project. In particular, there are systematic differences in the job size of projects – associated with the type of project (e.g. start-up, acquisition or re-investment), activity at the 1- and 2-digit levels and involvement of the public agencies – but once these have been controlled for, then other factors do not influence the project job size. Thus, the project job scale neither reflects where the project came from, nor where it goes to and nor when it arrives, so that what are important are the intrinsic project characteristics.

The analysis at the plant level permits a distinction between the plants that commencing in foreign ownership since 1985 ('new' plants) and those that set up prior to this time ('mature' plants). The new plants capture the new wave of FDI since the mid-1980s, for which there is a complete set of data on projects, while the data for the mature plants are truncated (only the re-investing plants are observed). Nevertheless, they show the earlier investment was more likely to manufacturing (but in different activities), to be from the US and more likely to locate to the north of the region. Of the new investment, most employment at the turn of the century is in plants that arrived in the late 1980s, although an analysis at the project level reveals that most jobs are provided by projects implemented in the mid-1990s. It indicates the importance of the re-investment projects and the plants that multiply invest over time. At the turn of the century, a multiply-investing new plant is two-times the size of a single investor, and in the case of start-ups plants it is larger by a factor of three.[5] An analysis of the re-investment duration for start-ups shows that the probability of plant re-investment (given that it has not occurred) is in the range 7 to 10 per cent up to 7 years after the Initial investment, but then generally zero, so that a plant re-invests within seven years or not at all. Only half the plants re-invest. For plants acquired by foreign investors, the re-investment hazard rates are initially much higher, but generally zero after five years, so that the investors either put their specific technology into place much sooner or not at all.

Finally, the book analyses the survival of the plants, which as we have seen is a crucial issue in the regional development literature. Indeed, of the foreign-owned start-up plants arriving in the North-East region since the mid-1980s, a fifth exited by the year 2000, taking with them a prospective 7,500 jobs. A start-up plant is found to have a lifetime of about 14 years, but there is relatively little variation in this about the median survival duration. Allowing for data censoring (i.e. lifetimes can be observed only for exiting plants), the estimates suggest that three-quarters of plants exist after 10 years, but only one-quarter after 15 years. Like some other studies, the larger plants on entry have significantly shorter survival durations than the smaller plants, but it is only by a year or so. Another feature is that the pattern

---

[5] The mean investment scale of a subsequent investment is about the same as that of an initial investment, so that the larger scale of the muliple-investor plants is because they carry out more projects. Sixty per cent of investment by start-ups is in re-investment projects, but plants that enter small in investment terms tend to stay small.

of job loss in exiting plants seems just to reflect the pattern of entry, so that there do not seem to be special factors affecting particular activities or locations.[6] As an exercise the issue of whether re-investment leads to substantially longer survival durations was examined. However, as with other studies of plant 'embeddedness' of various forms, the evidence is disappointing. While re-investing plants survive for an extra 7 years on average, at the median it takes about this long for a plant to carry out its first re-investment. Thus, there seems to be no qualitative difference between re-investment projects and that by which a plant commences in foreign ownership. One possibility is that a plant that stages its investment over time may indicate a lack of commitment to the region, rather than increased commitment.

Concluding Remarks

There is no doubt about the importance of FDI to the regional economy over recent decades. In the North East region it is reckoned that foreign direct investment was up to £1 billion per annum over the period 1985-98, which is about 4 to 5 per cent of regional GDP at 1995 and 15 per cent of its manufacturing output. Further, the study identifies about 62,400 jobs in 282 foreign-owned plants at 1999, of which the vast majority are in manufacturing. This represents 35 per cent of the region's manufacturing employment of 176,000, and in addition there could be a substantial number of other foreign-owned plants that set up prior to 1985, but which did not subsequently undertake a 'significant' investment by 1999.[7] However, as we have seen, research on the effects and nature of FDI tends to be negative, so that the jobs and income generated are likely to be the principal benefit to a region's economy. Indeed, neither does the FDI benefit domestic industry through positive 'spillover' effects, but it agglomerates, suggesting that there is no role for policy. Further, the investment is heavily concentrated in large plants, but these are poor performing. Not only are the large plants heavily capital-intensive, offering relatively few jobs, but they are less able to deliver on their job promises and have exit rates that are no better than for smaller plants. Moreover, the jobs arrive in projects demonstrating similar characteristics, such as by activity, so that while FDI has made a substantial contribution to the region it indicates the limitations of this investment. Finally, FDI is changing in nature, and most projects are now outside of manufacturing, but the North East, like similar regions, has been unable to capture these projects. It all adds to this investment reinforcing the existing industrial structure, and to the fragility of this employment when and if economic conditions change.

---

[6] Of the 7,500 prospective job losses in start-ups, 58 per cent are in Tyne and Wear, 93 per cent are in manufacturing, of which 69 per cent are in the Communications activity, and 54 per cent are in plants originating from the Far East.

[7] The regional inward investment agency reckons that there were 475 foreign-owned plants in the region at 1999. This employment is substantially more than the 39,400 jobs in the region at 1997 reported by the *Business Monitor*, possibly because it based on the location of the enterprise headquarters within the UK.

Data Appendix

The Inward Investment Dataset

This Appendix outlines the two databases that were used to construct the Inward Investment Dataset used in the second part of this book, and sets out the nature of the variables. It describes the work undertaken to check, refine and add to these data in order to form the Inward Investment Dataset. It is believed that this dataset provides a comprehensive account of 'significant' investments undertaken by foreign-owned plants in the North-East of England over the period 1985-98. It includes new foreign-owned plants entering over this period, as well as investment undertaken by plants entering prior to this time. In the next section, the databases from which the Inward Investment Dataset is constructed are set out. Definitional issues are then considered, including that of 'plant', 'entry' and 'exit'. The work undertaken to check and add to these data is described, and the representativeness of the Inward Investment Dataset and the nature of variables are also considered.

The *One NorthEast* Databases

A number of sources were contacted to inquire about the availability of data on individual inward investment projects in the North-East of England. These were *UK Trade and Investment* (which prior to the end of 2003 was known as *Invest UK*, and prior to July 2000 was known as the *Invest in Britain Bureau*), the Department of Trade and Industry (DTI) and the Regional Development Agency (RDA) for the North-East region, *One NorthEast*. Of these, the RDA proved the most fruitful source for data.[1] The RDA is the main agent for promoting economic development in the North-East region. It is core-funded by central government, and its brief concerns a number of regional and industrial issues to do with raising the competitiveness of the regional economy (DTI, 1998; *One NorthEast*, 1999).

---

[1] *UK Trade and Investment* had consistent data for Japanese inward investment, and similar data were kept by the Japanese Desk of the Inward Investment Bureau of the DTI. *UK Trade and Investment* suggested the Regional Development Agency as the best source. A second lead was a DTI study carried out by PA Cambridge Economic Consultants (PACEC, 1995). This involved a compilation of data on major UK inward investments, from which a questionnaire survey of projects was undertaken. With DTI permission the list of companies for North-East England was released by Barry Moore of PACEC. However, it consisted of around 125 overseas investors, so that the data supplied by *One NorthEast* were relied upon.

A meeting was arranged with the Director of Business Development of *One NorthEast*, who agreed to make available information on foreign direct investment. This included the agency's datasets on foreign-owned firms and inward investment projects.[2] In return, assurances were given about the confidentiality of these data, and it was agreed to let the agency have first sight of any findings from the study. A further meeting was arranged with the Investor Development Manager, who had the responsibility for maintaining the agency's overseas company directories. This determined the nature of the data to be supplied, which consisted of two databases: the 'Success' database and the Investor Development Programme database.

The 'Success' Database

All Regional Development Agencies are required to make quarterly returns on FDI projects to the main UK inward investment agency, *UK Trade and Investment*, on its foreign-owned investment successes. In the case of the North-East region this is the 'Success' database, which comprises the returns made by *One NorthEast* and its predecessors on 'significant' project-based investments undertaken by foreign-owned companies in the region since the mid-1980s. The projects are 'significant' in the sense that they consist of all new foreign-owned start-up investments, and include acquisitions, joint ventures and 'expansions'. The last of these is perhaps the most contentious and it is referred to as re-investments. The 'Success' database takes a comprehensive definition of FDI, as not only does it include start-ups, but the acquisition of UK-based plants by foreign-owned firms and joint ventures by these firms, for which standard definitions apply.[3] An 'acquisition' could include a merger and a joint venture may occur between two foreign plants or between a foreign-owned plant and a UK-based plant.

The 'Success' database includes all those projects with which the RDA (and its predecessors) were directly involved, and also those that are notified to it by the DTI and by *UK Trade and Investment* itself. It is supplemented by information collected from other sources, including local knowledge, business contacts and the scrutiny of national, local and other media. The RDA's Investment Development Manager believes it is a good account of all 'significant' inward investments taking

---

[2] Potentially, it included individual company files, which contained newspaper cuttings and other details of the firms, but in the event the RDA decided against this in the interest of maintaining the confidentiality of on-going discussions with firms.

[3] Start-up projects are referred to as 'greenfield' investments, although this is misleading as a new plant could establish itself at an existing industrial site. Acquisitions are defined as projects where a foreign firm takes more than a 50 per cent stake in a UK company, which also includes mergers. A joint venture is where a foreign-owned firm has at least a 50 per cent stake, possibly with another foreign-owned firm. The RDA and its predecessors adhere to these definitions, but there could be some variation at the margin where a project not strictly fulfilling these criteria is regarded as 'significant' for economic development.

place in the region. It contains all the major investments, and it is the source from which *UK Trade and Investment* and the government base their statistics on the nature of inward investment undertaken in the UK. At the individual project level it is the most accurate and comprehensive account of inward investment taking place in the North East of England since the mid-1980s.

The 'Success' data are recorded from the first quarter of 1985, shortly after the Nissan car factory set-up just outside Sunderland. To protect current investments the data were not made available for the recent period, so that they run from 1985 to 1998. In total, they give information for 569 projects (i.e. about 40 projects per annum), recording details at the time that the inward investor makes a commitment to the project. It is not necessarily the same as the time of announcement, and the gestation period between the commitment/announcement and the implementation is likely to be shorter for merger and acquisition projects compared with start-ups. The data give information on the firm's name, the calendar quarter of commitment, the town location of the plant, a description and coding of the activity at the 2-digit level, the country of origin and the type of investment, e.g. start-up, or acquisition. The prospective scale of the investment and the number of jobs that are projected to be 'created' or 'safeguarded' by the project are also given. Both the investment scale and project jobs are expected to be realised within two years of the decision to commit. The records indicate whether the RDA or *UK Trade and Investment* had 'significant' involvement with each project, although they do not indicate the nature of this involvement. More is said on these issues below.

The data are both historical and prospective, which have several implications. First, where construction work is involved, such as for a start-up or re-investment, it will typically commence within 12 to 18 months of the commitment date, whereas an acquisition may occur immediately or even be notified retrospectively. Second, a project is a discrete, identifiable investment that the investor plans to have in place over the short run (Maylor, 2003). If the investment is staged over many years then it is considered to be more than one project. Third, the database gives figures for gross inward investment, so that it does not record the subsequent performance of the plants, including possible divestment or closure. Finally, and related to this, it is possible that the project scale may not be realised, or may not even be implemented, and this is examined below and in the body of the text.

The 'Investor Development Programme' Database

The second dataset that was supplied by the RDA gives information on all foreign-owned establishments believed to be located and trading in the Northern region as at November 1999. It is compiled by the RDA from many sources, including local knowledge, personal contacts, the media and occasional company surveys carried out by the agency. It is plant based, giving details of major UK-owned companies with which *One NorthEast* has dealings, including Cumbria. After excluding these and making other adjustments it gives a total count of 475 foreign-owned plants in the North-East region at around the turn of the century.[4] It records information on the name, address (including postcode) and telephone number of each plant. It also gives a description of the plant's activity, the name of the parent company, the country of origin and details of the date when the plant started in the region and the nature of the plant opening, although these details can be patchy in their coverage.

The 'Success' database forms the basis for this study. However, many projects are in respect of the same plants, e.g. one project involved the plant start-up and another involved its subsequent expansion, so that it is necessary to organise the data on a plant basis. For this, a definition of a 'plant' is required. This needs to be straightforward in order to operationalise across a large number of plants, and it also defines what is meant by plant entry into foreign ownership and exit.

The Definitions of Plant, Entry and Exit

A 'plant' is defined simply as an individual production unit at which broadly the same economic activity is carried out more or less continuously over time and in the North-east region.[5] It reflects the interest in the economic use to which the assets provided by the inward investor are being put to in the region over time.[6] It means a production unit is treated as the same plant and on-going even though it may have changed its name, ownership or location within the region. It gives a consistent method for dealing with the large number of changes that occur in the status of firms, and it is easy to operationalise, being well suited for the purpose of examining issues surrounding the nature and performance of plants. The definition of a plant differs from what is a 'firm' or 'enterprise', which can involve more than one production unit. It also differs from an 'establishment', which is usually taken to imply production at a particular site, whereas a production unit that relocates within the region is regarded as the same plant in this book, as the assets provided by the investor continue to contribute to the region's economic development.

The definition of a plant frames the definitions of plant entry and exit. A plant that commences in foreign-ownership over the study period 1985-98 is regarded as an entrant plant, whether by start-up, acquisition or otherwise, while a plant that is

---

[4] In total, there were 690 plants in the 'Investor Development Programme' database, but of which 49 were located outside the North East, 147 are UK-owned plants and 5 are foreign-owned plants which established themselves in the region after the end of the study period, giving 489 plants. After adjustments (e.g. excluding certain activities, sales offices, holding companies and so on) it gives a final count of 475 plants.

[5] As an example, the Siemens plant on Tyneside ceased trading in 1998 about 18 months after it opened, but according to this definition it is an exit, even though it was later acquired by Atmel of the US in September 2000 to carry on basically the same activity, i.e. microchip production. Likewise for the Fujitsu plant at Newton Aycliffe in County Durham.

[6] Disney *et al* (2003) find that the number of plants changing industry (i.e activity) in any year is extremely small.

no longer regarded as the same plant by the middle of the year 2000 is an exit or closure. According to this view, a foreign-owned plant that is later taken over by a UK plant is not regarded as an exit provided the assets remain in broadly the same use within the region. The definitions of entry and exit are similar to that adopted by Dunne *et al* (1988), although there are some differences, reflecting the different purposes of these studies. Dunne *et al* regard a plant that changes its name or location as on-going, but here a plant that relocates outside the region is treated as an exit. The plant definition is now considered in greater detail, according to the name, ownership and location characteristics. It helps give flesh to the definition, but as we see, like other plant definitions (see Haltiwanger and Schuh, 1999), it is not free of ambiguities, although these are of minor practical significance.

Name A plant is defined independent of name changes, reflecting the focus on the assets provided by the investors. It is like Dunne *et al* (1988), and while it can cause difficulties, the converse is just as problematic. If neither of these two polar views is adopted, then it is necessary to identify and investigate the nature of every name change to see if it constitutes a plant closure or not, which is a substantial task. For example, if a change in legal status or management is used to define exit, then it is necessary to determine this in every case. In fact, foreign-owned plants often anglicise their names after start-up, while a change of name can be made for marketing purposes, but neither of these are regarded as exits.

Location A relocation is not treated as an exit provided the activity is broadly unchanged and the plant remains within the North-East region. For many firms a change of address is straightforward, so that, for example, several biotechnology firms relocated to the Newcastle *Centre for Life*, and supplier firms relocated near to the Nissan car plant. However, relocation can be more complicated than this, and be associated with a change in economic function or legal status, of which the former is an exit. A difficulty is that there are instances where two plants under the same ownership merged, but the approach is to treat these as a single plant and to code the relocation resulting from merger as a re-investment. A further difficulty arises when a foreign-owned firm relocates to the North-East from elsewhere in the UK. This is viewed as an inward investment, although there are few such cases.

Ownership The most problematic aspect of the plant definition is ownership. Once a plant has entered into foreign ownership (e.g. through acquisition) then a subsequent takeover or some other change in ownership is not treated as an exit provided the activity is unchanged and it is carried on more or less continuously within the region. This could include a foreign-owned plant becoming or returning to UK ownership, although again there are a small number of these cases. Dunne *et al* suppose that ownership is relatively unimportant, except that a plant that is taken over by another firm in the same industry is regarded as an exit, reflecting their interest in market structure. However, in this book we do not regard a change of ownership as an exit, and indeed a re-investment project could include a case where an inward investor is acquired by another plant.

Refinements to the 'Success' Database

The 'Success' database is project-based and a major task of the study was to assign these projects to individual plants. Initially, information on each project was matched according to the plant name, town location, country of origin, activity and project type (e.g. start-up). However, this left a large number of unresolved cases, where the name, location, ownership or activity had changed. Further, it needed to be determined if the plant came to the region in the first place (i.e. an entry), and if so whether it survived to the end of the period (i.e. an exit), according to our above definitions. Other information on the plants was sought, including employment and public-sector support. These tasks were carried out in a systematic way, which involved an extensive series of investigations that spanned a period of nine months. The nature of the exercises is now outlined.

Sources of Information

To check, refine and improve on the data, a number of directories were consulted. Two of these were the BT computerised telephone directory at December 1999 and the Royal Mail postcode computerised directory at about the same time. Company directories were also consulted, including the 'Investor Development Programme' database referred to above and the Dun and Bradstreet Business Directories for the North East for the years 1999 and 2000. For plants not in any of the directories (or where contradictions arose) there are a number of possibilities: a plant had avoided capture, its details had changed, it had not set up or it had closed. It was necessary to check each of these possibilities.

To determine which of the possibilities applied, interviews were conducted with numerous individuals and agencies. These included the Investor Development Manager at *One NorthEast*, who had responsibility for maintaining the agency's directories, and various county-level agencies concerned with inward investment.[7] In addition, the Companies House web-based search facility was consulted, which was useful for locating those companies that while giving a commitment to set up in the North-East had actually established themselves elsewhere, of which there were a number. Access was also obtained to historical company directories held by the local authorities and other agencies, and old Dun and Bradstreet Business Directories to determine if some of the plants had located in the region in the past.

---

[7] These comprised the Business Development Manager of Northumberland County Council; the Chief Executive of the Tyne and Wear Development Company; the Business Development Executive of the County Durham Development Company; and the Inward Investment Manager of the Tees Valley Development Company. Sub-regional agencies were contacted to tap local knowledge on outstanding problem cases. These were the Tyne and Wear Research and Information Unit at Newcastle, the district council in Darlington, which is a unitary local authority, and local councils at Hartlepool, Middlesbrough, Redcar and Stockton on Teesside.

These were especially useful for projects in the 1980s, which were more likely to be outside the recall of local agencies. For very difficult cases, companies in broadly the same activity in the same locality were telephoned to find out if the plant was known to the firm or not. During the course of these investigations, the data were checked and necessary amendments were made.

Other Data Collection

As well as determining the linkage between projects and the existence and survival of the plants, the sources were used to gather other information. This included the current actual employment of the plants, details of financial assistance received by the projects and changes in the plant status after 1998. In the case of employment, ideally we would have liked data for each year, but it proved impossible to obtain this on a consistent basis. Often the agencies collected the information in a non-systematic way, and overwrote it when updating their company record files. As such, we focused on the employment level towards the end of the study period, at around 1999. The data were generally available, but the coverage was improved by telephoning some plants to request the information directly. At the same time, other deficiencies in the coverage of the data were made good.

The main source of financial assistance received by these plants is Regional Selective Assistance (RSA), which in England has since been renamed as Selective Finance for Investment. This is the Government grant scheme provided to projects in the Assisted Areas, mainly for job-creation purposes, of which about half goes to inward investors. It forms a part of UK regional policy, but in the case of FDI it is used to compete internationally for these projects (see Wren, 2005a). From 1974 details of RSA cases of £5000 or more were published in *British Business*, but the threshold was raised to £75,000 in 1990, when publication was taken over by *Labour Market Trends* (formerly the *Employment Gazette*). Details are published quarterly on the basis of the total offer amount, related to the quarter in which the first payment on the offer was made. It gives the name (which is usually the plant rather than the parent company), location (Employment Office Area), activity, total offer amount and the project category, i.e. whether the purpose was job creation or much more unusually to safeguard employment.

The RSA details were matched to projects undertaken by the plants, using the plant name and supplementary information on the location and activity. Given the gestation lag between the location decision and project construction, details of the RSA offer were generally published between one and two years after the firm gave its formal commitment to the project. One problem with the published RSA data is that it omits smaller cases. However, the Department of Trade and Industry made good this deficiency by supplying details of all RSA offers below £75,000 over 1985-98 from their Selective Assistance Management Information System database (SAMIS).[8] In fact, there were only 32 of these cases and they virtually all related

---

[8] Thanks for this goes to Mark Lea at the Department of Trade and Industry in London.

to the late-1980s, so that they were already published in *British Business*. It shows that foreign-based plants are almost always made larger offers of RSA of at least £75,000 at current prices (see Wren, 2005a), so that the details of grant offers to foreign-owned plants are more or less all in the public domain.

Generally, a good match was obtained between the RSA offers and projects. It was no doubt helped by the fact that the project details in the 'Success' database, such as the name and location, were recorded at the same time as the RSA offer. However, there are difficulties. First, firms may not have taken up the offer in full, although it is known that at least some of the payment on the grant offer was made. Second, in some cases there were problems in linking the RSA data to individual projects, so that it was necessary to exercise judgement. Indeed, some RSA offers could not be tied to any project in respect of a particular plant, but these cases were small in number, amounting to less than 2 per cent of the value of RSA offers.[9]

Some other recent studies have matched RSA details to individual plant-level data, and our matching compares well with these. Devereux *et al* (2003) match published RSA offers to plant-level data in the Annual Respondents Database (ARD).[10] The ARD is the former Annual Census of Production, supplemented by recent surveys by the Office of National Statistics (ONS) (see Barnes *et al*, 2001). Since enterprise names are confidential to the ARD, Devereux *et al* matched these by postcode location and the firm's 4-digit industry. Over the period 1982-96, Devereux *et al* match 2,320 RSA offers for Great Britain as a whole, but which is about 45 per cent of offers by number and value. They find that only 3 per cent of foreign-owned start-ups in the Assisted Areas received an offer of RSA, but this compares with 30 per cent found here. Harris and Robinson (2001) match RSA with ARD plant-level data, but use the RSA data in the DTI's SAMIS database. The SAMIS gives information on the plant name, postcode, industrial classification and employment. The matching process has two stages; first a match between the plants in the SAMIS database to a local unit reference number in the ONS Inter-Departmental Business Register (IDBR); and second the RSA data were matched to the ARD data using the local unit reference number. Around 62 per cent of the relevant cases in the SAMIS were matched to plant-level data in the ARD data.[11] Overall, it indicates the difficulties in attempting to construct these databases, and the trade-off between the size of the database and accuracy of matching.

---

[9] In total, they numbered thirteen cases, amounting to £4.2 million in RSA offers.

[10] The ARD is incorporated into the Annual Business Inquiry, which draws its sample from the Inter-Departmental Business Register of the Office of National Statistics.

[11] In the case of manufacturing, SAMIS contains 12,580 records on RSA for the period 1990-2000 (and another 2,078 records on non-manufacturing). A local unit reference number could be found for 10,780 cases (86 per cent), and of these 7,737 cases (72 per cent) could be matched to plant-level information in the ARD covering the period up to 1998. A further 979 cases were linked at the company level, but a plant match could not be found in terms of postcode, activity and employment.

The Inward Investment Dataset

The result from the above exercises led to the creation of the Inward Investment Dataset. Originally, the data had 569 projects, but to these were added 13 projects, while 32 projects were deleted, so that it consists of 550 projects carried out by 337 plants. The projects were added as 13 plants known to have commenced in foreign ownership since 1985 had no initial project. These plants were contacted, and it was found that eleven were start-ups and the other two were acquisitions. One of the principal reasons for the deletion of projects was that they were not thought to constitute inward investment. This comprised 12 sales offices, which involved no investment in productive assets, and three projects on the basis of activity.[12] For another eleven projects reasonably good information was obtained that they never actually went ahead in the region, two projects were duplicated and one project originated from the Isle of Man. Only three projects could not be traced at all, and these were assumed not to have gone ahead at all.[13]

Representativeness of the Data

Having conducted these investigations it is believed that the Inward Investment Dataset gives a comprehensive and representative account of 'significant' project-based foreign direct investment in North-East England over 1985-98. There is still the possibility of missing data on projects, but this is not thought to be problematic for two reasons. First, in the case of re-investments the analysis in Chapter 9 does not lead us to believe that there are missing data. In general, plants are unable to reach their job targets, which is the opposite of what is to be expected if there are missing data. Second, for initial investments, i.e. start-ups, acquisitions and joint ventures, there is still the possibility of missing plants, and while this would affect the representativeness of the data, little came to light in the course of our extensive investigations to make us believe that this is problematic.

The Inward Investment Dataset comprises 550 projects, implemented by 337 plants. It includes all foreign-owned plants that are known to have carried out 'significant' investment in the region over the period 1985-98, including plants that set up prior to 1985. It records the flow of foreign-owned capital over this period, but comparison can be made with the stock of foreign-owned plants in the region. This comparison is made with the 'Investor Development Programme' database, which is a record of foreign-owned plants believed to be in the North-East region at November 1999 (see above). The 'Investor Development Programme' database

---

[12] These were a clothing store, an insurance office and the takeover of a utilities company. Utilities are not the main focus of the activities of *One NorthEast* and the coverage of these in their databases is not good, so that these are generally excluded. The insurance office was later closed down and merged with an existing regional office.

[13] They were a window-frame manufacturer, a takeover of a plumbing-equipment plant and an engineering firm, which proposed to set up in the late 1980s promising 400 jobs.

has 475 foreign-owned plants in the region at the turn of the century, whereas the Inward Investment Dataset has details of 282 plants at this time (i.e. 337 plants less 55 closed plants).[14] Thus, there is information on about 60 per cent of the foreign-owned plants in the region, suggesting that the other 40 per cent of plants existing at 1985 failed to make a 'significant' investment after this time.

The Inward Investment Dataset can also be compared with the stock of plants in the 'Investor Development Programme' by the country of origin of the plant's ultimate parent. Since the latter is based on the most recent ownership status of the plants, it includes some UK-owned plants that were previously foreign-owned. The comparison is made in Appendix Table 1. It shows that there is an above average coverage of plants in the Inward Investment Dataset from the Far East, although it is not surprising given the recent nature of investment from this source. Otherwise, the coverage of the plants is reasonably even across the different countries, which suggests that the Inward Investment Dataset is representative by nationality of all foreign-owned plants currently in the region.[15]

The Variables

The Inward Investment Dataset is organised on a plant basis, where a plant record can hold multiple project records. Project details relate to the time of commitment, while the plant details generally relate to date of the initial investment during the study period. Descriptive statistics on the variables are given in Appendix Table 2, both for the plant and project variables. It shows the number of cases, the minimum and maximum values, the mean and the coefficient of variation.

A description of each variable is now given. It can be seen that there are different kinds of variable, including qualitative variables (e.g. *NAME*), continuous variables (e.g. *INV*) and discrete variables that are treated as continuous (e.g. *EMP*). Discrete variables are categorical (e.g. *COUNTY*) or dummy variables (e.g. *RSA*). Generally, there is good coverage of the data, except that the investment scale (*INV*) is not known for about a third of projects, the number of jobs (*JOB*) is not known for thirty-nine projects and the date of the initial establishment of the production unit (*ESTDATE*) is not known for nine plants. For some categories there are no

---

[14] Nine firms had closed but were still in the 'Investor Development Programme' database, while there we had details of a further nine firms which were not in this database.

[15] It would also be of interest to examine the representativeness of the Inward Investment Dataset against the total stock of foreign-owned investment by other characteristics such as activity, sector and size of the plants, but data limitations prevent this.

Appendix Table 1 Coverage of Inward Investment Dataset by Country of Ultimate Owner

Country of Ultimate Parent	Number of Plants in IDP	Proportion of IDP Plants in IID (%)
United States	177	57.6
Japan	53	79.2
Rest of Far East	22	68.2
Scandinavia	63	54.0
Germany	51	56.9
France	20	65.0
Benelux	27	40.7
Rest of Europe	36	47.2
Rest of World	21	52.3
UK	11	81.8
Total	**481**	**58.8**

Notes: Number of plants in the Investor Development Programme (IDP) and proportion in the Inward Investment Dataset (IID). Because of joint ventures the number of plants in the IDP sum to more than 475. The plants that have an ultimate UK parent include UK partners in joint ventures and foreign-owned plants that were later taken over by UK firms or through management buy-out.

observations.[16] It would have been desirable to have details of other characteristics, like the company structure, employment for each year and all forms of public support, but these were not available, although the *OTH* terms go some way towards making up for these deficiencies.

Plant Variables

The plant variables, by label, for which we have information, are as follows:

> *NAME*: Plant name. Where the plant name changes, it is also recorded. Sometimes the name of the parent company is known.
>
> *COUNTY*: County in which plant is located: Northumberland, Tyne and Wear, County Durham and Cleveland.
>
> *TOWN*: District local authority in which the plant is located, of which there are twenty-three in the region.
>
> *PCODE*: Full postcode location of the plant.

---

[16] There are 23 local authority districts in the North-East region, but one of these had no inward investment over 1985-98, so that *TOWN* takes 22 different values. Similarly, there are 99 NACE activities, but *IND* takes 92 values.

Appendix Table 2 Description of the Variables

	No.	Min.	Max.	Mean	CV
Plant variables	337				
NAME	337	-	-	-	-
COUNTY	337	1	4	-	-
TOWN	337	1	22	-	-
PCODE	315	-	-	-	-
IND	337	1	92	-	-
SECTOR	337	1	11	-	-
MANUF	337	0	18	-	-
ORIGIN	337	1	29	-	-
ESTDATE	328	1873	1998	1980	0.01
AGE	328	0	136	11.7	1.89
EMP	337	0	4,912	185.3	1.84
MULT	337	0	1	0.39	-
SURV	337	0	1	0.84	-
OTH1	337	0	1	0.15	-
OTH2	337	0	1	0.02	-
OTH3	337	0	1	0.04	-
OTH4	337	0	1	0.06	-
OTH5	337	0	1	0.02	-
OTH6	337	0	1	0.01	-
Project variables	550				
YEAR	550	1985	1998	1992	0.002
QTR	537	1	4	2.5	0.47
DATE = YEAR + QTR	537	85.1	98.3	92.2	0.002
TYPE	550	1	4	-	-
INV	364	0.06	1,100	23.94	3.91
JOBNEW	511	0	3,000	111.4	2.30
JOBSAFE	511	0	1,400	199.1	1.10
JOB = JOBNEW + JOBSAFE	511	0	3,000	157.2	1.72
RSAAMT	550	0	53.6	1.6	3.50
RSA	550	0	1	0.33	-
REG	550	0	1	0.25	-
NAT	550	0	1	0.11	-

Notes: The number of cases for which each variable is known includes zero values, but the mean and the CV are calculated for non-zero cases only. *OTH1* to *OTH6* are known with certainly only for those cases that are coded as unity. *MANUF* takes a zero value for firms outside the manufacturing sector. *EMP* takes a zero value for the 55 closed plants.

IND: Plant activity, according to the Nomenclature generale des Activities economiques dans les Communautes Europeennes (NACE). It is the industrial classification used by the European Union. It is recorded at the 2-digit level, according to 17 sections (or sectors) and 99 activities.

SECTOR: 2-digit sector of the plant according to the NACE.

MANUF: Manufacturing activity of the plant.

ORIGIN: Country of origin of ultimate owner of plant.

ESTDATE: Original date of commencement of production unit.

EMP: Total number of employees at plant, including full and part-time, for latest available employment figure, generally 1999 but 1996 in some cases. Closed plants have zero employment.

MULT: Dummy variable for plants undertaking more than one project over the period 1985-98.

SURV: Survival to the year 2000.

OTH: Dummy variables that code other information on plant where known. Some details relate to events occurring after the end of the sample period around the middle of the year 2000. The information were not collected on a systematic basis:

OTH1: Other plants in the region with the same owner.

OTH2: Other plants at the same site. Mainly holding companies.

OTH3: The plant is known to have relocated since 1985.

OTH4: Plant taken over by a foreign-owned firm since 1998.

OTH5: Plant taken over by a UK-owned firm or subject to management buy-out since 1998.

OTH6: Plant re-opened after closure at 1998.

Project Variables

For projects associated with the plants the following information is held:

YEAR: Calendar year in which the firm gave its commitment to project.

QTR: Calendar quarter in which firm commits to project.

DATE: Project date, equal to $DATE = YEAR + QTR$.

TYPE: Type of project, according to whether it is a start-up, an acquisition, joint venture or re-investment.

INV: Prospective project investment scale that firm expects to realise within two years of project date (£' millions, 1995 prices).

JOBNEW: Number of new jobs not pre-existing project but which the firm expects to have in place within two years of project date.

JOBSAFE: Number of safeguarded jobs that pre-exist the project.

JOB: Total jobs, equal to $JOB = JOBNEW + JOBSAFE$.

RSAAMT: Amount of RSA grant offered to the project on which the first payment is made (£' millions, 1995 prices).

RSA: Grant offer, that is coded to unity if *RSAAMT* non-zero, otherwise zero.

REG: Dummy variable coded to unity if *One NorthEast* or predecessor had a 'significant' involvement with project.

NAT: Dummy variable coded one if *UK Trade and Investment* or predecessors had a 'significant' involvement with project.

Plants and Project Characteristics

The plant and project characteristics are now considered, making reference to the variables outlined above and in Appendix Table 2.

Plant Characteristics

The characteristics of the 337 plants are now considered in turn.

Plant Type The plant type (*TYPE*) is defined by the nature of the first investment project undertaken by a plant over the period 1985-98, i.e. the Initial investment. It gives a two-fold classification of plants by New Plants, i.e. commencing in foreign ownership over 1985-98, and Mature Plants, i.e. commencing in foreign ownership prior to 1985. For New Plants the Initial investment is observed, and a further classification is possible by start-ups, acquisitions and joint ventures. For Mature Plants, not only is it not known how these commenced in foreign ownership, but it is not known how many Subsequent investments were carried out prior to 1985. Further, the data for the Mature Plants are truncated, as only plants carrying out a Subsequent investment over 1985-98 are observed.

In the case of the New Plants, a start-up is often referred to as 'greenfield' investment, although this can be misleading, as it may involve a plant locating to a 'brownfield' site or taking on a redundant facility that is mothballed, such as a dry-dock or fixed-crane facility. According to our definition a start-up can include the relocation to the region of an existing UK-based foreign-owned plant, or a new investment by a foreign-owned firm that already has a presence in the region but at a different site. An acquisition is where a foreign-owned plant acquires a majority stake in a North East plant that was previously in UK ownership. In general, these are takeovers, but there are a small number of mergers. A joint venture involves two partner companies, of which a foreign partner has at least a 50 per cent stake in the venture. The other partner may be UK or foreign-owned. Where these are of interest the data can include joint ventures in which a foreign-owned company has only a minority stake, but overall joint ventures are small in number.

The number of plants of each type is shown in Appendix Table 3, along with the number of projects undertaken by these. In total, there are 265 New Plants, of which 164 plants (49 per cent of the total plants) are start-ups, 79 plants (23%) are acquisitions, but only 22 (7%) are joint ventures. The other 72 plants (21%) are Mature Plants. The table shows the number of projects implemented by each plant type over 1985-98, but there is a complete record for the New Plants only. The

Appendix Table 3 Plant Types and the Number of Projects

	All Plants		New Plants			Mature Plants
			SU	AC	JV	
Total plants	265	(100%)	164	79	22	72
1 project only	167	(63%)	100	53	14	38
2 projects only	62	(23%)	43	16	3	19
3 projects only	25	(10%)	14	6	5	10
4 projects only	8	(3%)	5	3	0	3
5 projects only	0	(0%)	0	0	0	1
6 projects only	3	(1%)	2	1	0	0
7 + projects	0	(0%)	0	0	0	1
Projects per plant	1.57		1.58	1.53	1.59	1.86
Total Projects	**550**		**260**	**121**	**35**	**134**
(% total)	**(100)**		**(48)**	**(22)**	**(6)**	**(24)**

Notes: Plants are categorised according to the nature of the first project (*TYPE*) implemented over 1985-98. SU = start-ups, AC = acquisitions and JV = joint ventures.

New Plants implemented 416 projects (76 per cent of all projects), with around half of all projects carried out by the start-up plants. The mean projects per plant for New Plants is 1.57, which is remarkably similar across the plant types, although higher for Mature Plants (of which one plant carried out as many as 11 projects). Two-thirds of the New Plants undertook a single project over 1985-98, and 23 per cent of plants carried out two projects, so that only 14 per cent implemented more than two projects. There is a similar pattern across the plant types.

Plant Location The location of the plants is shown in Appendix Table 4 by county (*COUNTY*). The plants tend to be located in Tyne and Wear and County Durham, with only 33 foreign-owned plants investing in Northumberland over the study period. There are differences in the type of investment in the different parts of the region, reflecting the industrial structure, but also the operation of policy. Start-ups and joint ventures are more-heavily represented in Tyne and Wear, while the acquisitions favour Cleveland, which has a predominance of heavy engineering and chemicals. Plants outside the built-up areas, i.e. Northumberland and County Durham, are more likely to be Mature Plants, but these areas include the former New Towns of Cramlington, Peterlee and Newton Aycliffe, which received large amounts of inward investment in the 1960s and 1970s. An analysis was undertaken at the sub-county level (*TOWN*). While the results are not re-produced here, a heavy concentration of FDI was found in particular parts of the study area, with a strong focus on the area to the East of Newcastle, both north and south of the Tyne

Tunnel. In Tyne and Wear FDI is more likely to occur in Sunderland, in County Durham in the Sedgefield and Easington districts and in Cleveland at Stockton-on-Tees. Together with Newcastle, Gateshead and Blyth Valley in Northumberland, these seven districts account for two-thirds of all the new start-up plants over 1985-98, i.e. 110 of the 164 start-up plants.

Plant Activity The plant activity (*IND*) is given in Appendix Table 5. This uses the 17 sections of the Nomenclature generale des Activities economiques dans les Communautes Europeennes (NACE). It shows that the majority of plants are in manufacturing (72 per cent), even though it accounts for only around 28 per cent of output of the North-East economy. In the services, FDI is mainly in Real Estate, Renting and Business Activities (10 per cent of plants), and Wholesale and Retail Trade (8 per cent). The first of these includes computer-related activities, such as software development and consultancy, and business activities like engineering consultancy, training and Call Centres. The distribution of plants in manufacturing is shown in Appendix Figure 1, which gives a breakdown by plant type. Overall, plants are concentrated in six activities: Chemicals and Chemical Products, Rubber and Plastic Products, Fabricated Metal Products, Machinery and Equipment, Communications (including cable television and mobile telephones) and Transport Equipment (including motor cars). These account for 173 of the 243 plants in manufacturing, or about half the total number of plants. Start-ups are concentrated in a few activities, most notably Rubber and Plastic Products, Communications and Transport Equipment.

Plant Country of Origin The supranational of origin of plants (*ORIGIN*) is given in Appendix Table 6. 40 per cent of plants originate from Western Europe and a similar number come from North America. The other plants come mainly from the Far East, so that there is hardly any other FDI from elsewhere. In Western Europe investment mainly originates from Scandinavia, Germany and France, and in North America it comes almost exclusively from the USA. Japan is the main source of FDI from the Far East, with a similar but much smaller number of plants from each of Korea, Hong Kong and Taiwan. The start-up plants are over-represented in the plants coming from the Far East, although over the study period more start-ups originated from each of Western Europe and North America.

Plant Age The initial establishment dates of the production units (*ESTDATE*) are given by Appendix Table 7. These trace the origin of each unit back to its original establishment, even though there may have been changes in the name, ownership or location within the North-East region. For the start-up plants it is just the date of entry, but for plants commencing in foreign ownership by other means it pre-dates entry, which is from the time a plant commences in foreign ownership. The table shows that 189 plants established themselves after 1985, which includes the 164 start-up plants, but also the plants that may have been acquired over this period

Appendix Table 4 Plant Location

| | New Plants | | | | | | Mature Plants | |
	SU		AC		JV			
Northumberland	9	(6)	6	(8)	1	(5)	17	(20)
Tyne and Wear	70	(43)	29	(37)	14	(63)	19	(26)
County Durham	52	(31)	20	(25)	4	(18)	24	(33)
Cleveland	33	(20)	24	(30)	3	(14)	12	(17)
Total	**164**	**(100)**	**79**	**(100)**	**22**	**(100)**	**72**	**(100)**

Notes: The table shows the number of plants in each county (*COUNTY*). SU = start-up, AC = acquisition and JV = joint venture. Percentages in parentheses.

Appendix Table 5 Activity of Plants

Section and Activity		No. of Plants	%
A	Agriculture, Hunting and Forestry	0	0.0
B	Fishing	0	0.0
C	Mining and Quarrying	1	0.3
D	Manufacturing	242	71.8
E	Electricity, Gas and Water Supply	3	0.8
F	Construction	11	3.3
G	Wholesale and Retail Trade	28	8.3
H	Hotel and Restaurants	4	1.2
I	Transport, Storage and Communication	7	2.1
J	Financial Intermediation	3	0.9
K	Real Estate, Renting and Business Activities	32	9.5
L	Public Administration, Defence and Social Security	0	0.0
M	Education	1	0.3
N	Health and Social Work	0	0.0
O	Community, Social and Personal Service Activities	5	1.5
P	Private Households with Employed Persons	0	0.0
Q	Extra-Territorial Organisations and Bodies	0	0.0
Total		**337**	**100.0**

Note: The number of plants by the industrial activity (*IND*) according to the NACE code.

Appendix Figure 1 Distribution of Plants by Manufacturing Activity

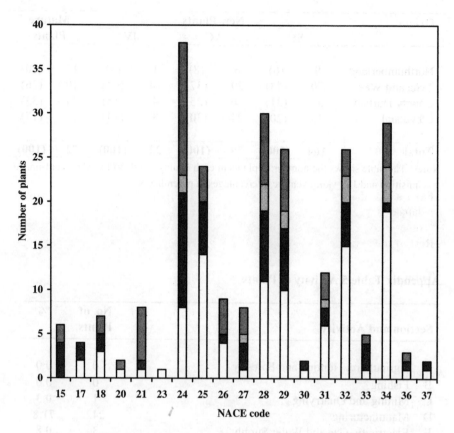

□ Start-up plants ■ Acquisition plants ▨ Joint venture plants ▨ Mature plants

Notes: NACE classification, as follows: 15 = Food Products and Beverages; 17 = Textiles; 18 = Wearing Apparel; 20 = Wood and Wood Products; 21 = Pulp, Paper and Paper Products; 23 = Coke, Refined Petroleum Products and Nuclear Fuel; 24 = Chemicals and Chemical Products; 25 = Rubber and Plastic Products; 26 = Other Non-Metallic Products; 27 = Basic Metals; 28 = Fabricated Metal Products, except Machinery and Equipment; 29 = Machinery and Equipment not elsewhere classified; 30 = Office Machinery and Computers; 31 = Electrical Machinery and Apparatus not elsewhere classified; 32 = Radio, Television and Communication Equipment and Apparatus; 33 = Medical, Precision and Optical Instruments, Watches and Clocks; 34 = Transport Equipment; 36 = Furniture; Manufacturing not elsewhere classified; and 37 = Recycling.

Appendix Table 6 Supranational Origin of Plants

Origin	No. of Plants	(%)	No. of Start-ups	(%)
Western Europe	**133**	**(40)**	**59**	**(36)**
Scandinavia	47		24	
Germany	37		12	
France	17		10	
other	32		13	
North America	**128**	**(38)**	**52**	**(32)**
USA	124		51	
Canada	4		1	
Far East	**67**	**(20)**	**49**	**(30)**
Japan	45		33	
other	22		16	
Rest of the World	**9**	**(2)**	**4**	**(2)**
Total	**337**	**(100)**	**164**	**(100)**

Appendix Table 7 Age of Establishment of Production Unit

Period	No. of Plants	Cum. %
Pre-1900	6	1.8
1900 – 45	15	6.4
1946 – 60	11	9.8
1961 – 70	39	21.6
1971 – 80	32	31.4
1981 – 85	36	42.4
1986 – 90	96	71.6
1991 – 95	58	89.3
1996 – 98	35	100.0
Missing	9	-
Total	**337**	-

Notes: Establishment date of production unit (*ESTDATE*). In the case of acquisitions and joint ventures this pre-dates year when plant commenced in foreign ownership.

but entered in production after 1985. Overall, most production units are relatively recent, with more than two-thirds of plants (69 per cent) establishing themselves after 1980, and a further 22 per cent of plants setting-up in the 1960s and 1970s. Only 21 plants (6 per cent) set up before 1945.

Plant Employment Size The distribution of plant employment levels (*EMP*) is given in Appendix Table 8. This records the size at around the middle of the year 1999. It shows that 55 of the plants exited with an employment level of zero. The surviving plants have an employment level of around 62,400. This is about 7 per cent of employment in the North-East region, but relative to employment in the manufacturing sector it is much higher at 32 per cent, indicating the importance of the foreign-owned sector to the regional economy.[17] The vast majority of plants are small and medium-sized enterprises. Indeed, a third of plants have fewer than 50 employees, and a further third have between 51 and 200 employees. While only 27 plants have more than 500 employees, these represent a half of all employment in the foreign-owned plants in the Inward Investment Dataset.

Other Characteristics The Inward Investment Dataset includes other information (*OTH*) on plants, which was collected on a non-systematic basis. This is shown in Appendix Table 9. These essentially act as controls. It can be seen that 52 plants are known to have a related plant in the region under the same ownership, 6 share a common site and 13 plants have relocated. Twenty-eight plants are known to have been taken over or subject to a management buyout since 1998, and 4 of the 55 exits have subsequently re-opened since 1998, possibly under a new owner.

Project Characteristics

In total the 337 plants in the Inward Investment Dataset implemented 550 projects over the period 1985-98. Of these, 164 projects (30 per cent) are start-ups, 93 are acquisitions (17 per cent), 24 are joint ventures (4 per cent) and 269 projects are re-investments (49 per cent).[18] The project variables are now described.

Project Date The distribution of the projects by the year of the formal commitment (*YEAR*) is shown in Appendix Figure 2. Overall, the pattern that emerges is that of a steady increase in the total number of projects over the study period, but with a dip in the early 1990s, perhaps related to a widespread recession. The decline in the year 1998 is because there is not complete data. Given the relatively small number

---

[17] It expresses employment relative to the manufacturing sector, even though 28 per cent of the foreign-owned plants are known to be outside the manufacturing sector.

[18] The number of start-up projects is the same as the number of start-up plants (Appendix Table 3), but there are more acquisition projects than plants (93 projects, but only 79 plants). It is because 14 plants were subsequently acquired by another foreign-owned plant. The same reasoning applies to the joint ventures (24 projects, but only 22 plants).

Appendix Table 8 Distribution of Plant Employment

	No. of Plants	Cum. %	Employment	Cum. %
1 – 5	10	3.5	40	0.06
6 – 10	21	10.9	166	0.3
11 – 25	33	22.6	549	1.2
26 – 50	34	34.7	1,309	3.3
51 – 200	92	67.3	11,251	21.3
201 – 500	65	90.4	21,476	55.7
501 – 1000	20	97.5	13,155	76.8
1001 – 2500	5	99.3	7,036	88.1
2501 +	2	100.0	7,449	100.0
Survivors	282	-	62,431	-
Exits	55	-	0	-
Total	**337**	-	**62,431**	-

Note: The employment level (*EMP*) is generally measured in the year 1999.

Appendix Table 9 Other Information on Plants

	No. of Plants	%
Other Plants in Region (*OTH 1*)	52	15.2
Other Plants at Same Site (*OTH2*)	6	1.8
Relocation Of Plant (*OTH3*)	13	3.8
Plant Taken Over by Foreign Firm Since 1998 (*OTH4*)	20	5.9
Plant Taken Over by UK Firm Since 1998 (*OTH5*)	8	2.3
Plant Closed and then Reopened Since 1998 (*OTH6*)	4	1.2
None of the Above Known	238	69.8
Total	**341**	**100.0**

Note: Plants may occur in more than one category.

Appendix Figure 2 Type of Projects by Year

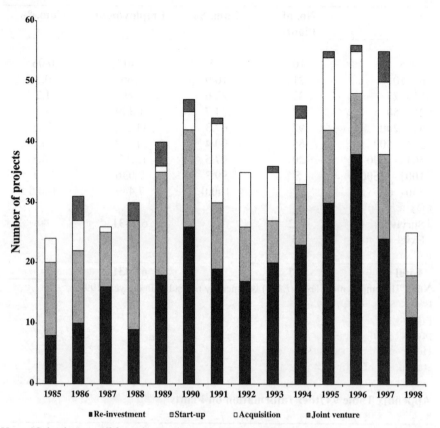

Note: Calendar year of formal commitment to project (*YEAR*).

of plant exits shown in Appendix Table 8, an increase in the number of projects over time is perhaps expected, as the stock of plants builds-up and they undertake re-investment. Indeed, Appendix Figure 2 shows the increase in the total number of projects is closely related to the number of re-investments. There is an increase in the number of acquisitions projects in the late-1980s, which is maintained in the subsequent decade, and at a similar level to that of start-up projects. Joint ventures occur reasonably evenly across the study period.

Project Investment Details of the proposed investment scale are known for 364 of the 550 projects, and as Appendix Table 10 shows it is more likely to be known for the start-up and re-investment projects. This is the investment that is expected to be realised within two years of the formal commitment to the project (i.e. *DATE*), although in the case of acquisitions it is usually the actual investment. A total of £8.7 billion (1995 prices) in investment is identified in the dataset. The start-ups and acquisitions account for half this investment (33 and 16 per cent respectively), and the re-investments for much of the remainder (43 per cent), while the joint ventures represent only 8 per cent of total investment. The mean investment scale is £23.9 million but the median investment is much smaller at £3.5 million because of a few extremely large investments (1995 prices). The distribution of proposed project investment scales (*INV*) is shown in Appendix Figure 3. Most projects are in the range £2m to £10m, although there are fourteen very large projects, in excess of £150m, involving both start-ups and re-investments. However, at the mean the re-investments are relatively smaller, at £17.6m, compared with £28.2m for start-ups and £39.2m for acquisition projects.

Project Jobs The proposed number of project jobs (*JOB*) are shown in Appendix Table 11. These are the jobs that are expected to be either created or safeguarded within two years of the date of commitment, although in the case of acquisitions it may refer to the date of takeover. The jobs are known for 511 of the 550 projects. The Inward Investment Dataset identifies 80,318 proposed jobs, of which about 45,684 are new jobs and 34,634 are safeguarded jobs. Of the 80,318 jobs, nearly half are in re-investment projects (45 per cent). A further 24 per cent of jobs are in start-ups and 28% are in acquisitions. The joint ventures are of minor significance. Virtually all the jobs in start-ups are new but it is the case for about half the jobs in re-investment projects, while the acquisitions are about 'safeguarding' jobs.[19] The project job scales are different between the types. The mean size of an acquisition project is nearly twice that of either a start-up or a re-investment, at 250 jobs. However, the distributions are heavily skewed, so that while the mean size of a start-up is 131 jobs, the median job size is only 45 jobs, so that most start-ups are very small. Overall, there are only 29 projects associated with more than 500 jobs, and it was noted previously that there are 27 plants with more than 500 employees at 1999. Finally, the number of jobs per £1 million (1995 prices) of investment is 9.2 jobs. This is much higher for acquisitions, but smaller for start-ups (6.7 jobs) and re-investments (9.6 jobs). However, the re-investments are more likely to involve safeguarded jobs.

Regional Selective Assistance About a third of the projects received a central Government grant in the form of Regional Selective Assistance (RSA), i.e. 182 of 550 projects (see Appendix Table 12). This is much higher for the re-investment projects (41 per cent) than for start-ups (30 per cent) and acquisitions (16 per cent). In total, the 182 projects involved around one quarter of a billion pounds of grant (£283 million at 1995 prices) over the study period (*RSAAMT*). These are grant offers on which a first payment is made. In fact, virtually all of it was offered to start-up and re-investments (87 per cent). The distribution of grants is skewed (not shown), as while the mean grant amount is £1.6 million, the median grant is £0.4m.

---

[19] A few jobs are safeguarded where a foreign-owned entrant took over an existing facility that was previously mothballed, e.g. crane or dry-dock facilities.

Appendix Table 10 Project Investment Scales

Investment Scale	Total	SU	AC	JV	RE
Known Cases	364	103	36	12	213
Missing Cases	186	61	57	12	56
% Missing	34	37	61	50	21
Total Investment (£'m)	8,714	2,868	14,010	659	3,778
% of Total Investment	100	33	16	8	43
Mean Investment (£'m)	23.9	28.4	39.2	54.9	17.6
Median Investment (£'m)	3.5	2.9	7.8	5.3	3.6
Coefficient of Variation	3.9	4.5	1.5	2.9	4.1

Notes: Proposed investment scales of projects (*INV*) at 1995 prices. SU = start-up; AC = acquisition; JV = joint venture; and RE = re-investment.

Appendix Figure 3 Distribution of Project Investment Scales

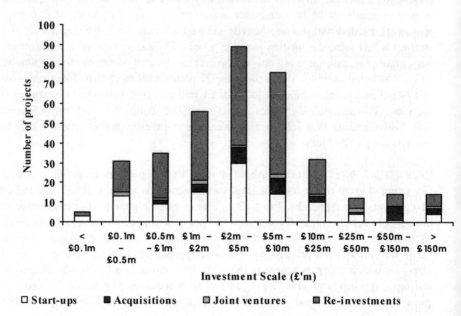

Notes: The number of projects by the proposed investment scale (INV).   Figures in the table are in £'millions at 1995 prices.

Appendix Table 11 Project Job Scales

Job Size	Total	SU	AC	JV	RE
Total Known Cases	511	147	88	22	254
Missing Cases	39	17	5	2	15
% Missing	7	10	5	8	6
Total Jobs	80,318	19,276	22,002	2,687	36,353
(% Total Jobs)	(100)	(24)	(28)	(3)	(45)
New Jobs	45,684	18,930	3,716	1,957	21,081
Safeguarded Jobs	34,634	346	18,286	730	15,272
(% New to Total Jobs)	(57)	(98)	(17)	(73)	(58)
Mean Jobs	157.2	131.1	250.0	122.1	143.1
Median Jobs	61.0	45.0	155.0	55.0	62.0
Coefficient of Variation	1.7	2.5	1.1	1.2	1.6
Jobs / £1m Investment*	9.2	6.7	15.6	4.0	9.6

Notes: Number of proposed jobs projects (*JOB*), and by new (*JOBNEW*) and safeguarded jobs (*JOBSAFE*). SU = start-up; AC = acquisition; JV = joint venture; and RE = re-investment. * Projects where investment scale known only.

Appendix Table 12 Regional Selective Assistance Offers to Projects

Amount of Assistance	Total	SU	AC	JV	RE
Total RSA cases	182	49	16	6	111
% Receiving RSA	33	30	16	25	41
Total RSA (£'m)	283.2	117.0	23.5	11.5	131.1
% of Total RSA	100	41	9	4	46
Mean RSA (£'m)	1.6	2.4	1.5	1.9	1.2
Median RSA (£'m)	0.4	0.5	0.5	0.8	0.4
Coefficient of Variation	3.2	2.9	1.9	1.7	4.3
Grant Rate (%)*:					
Mean	17.3	17.2	12.0	14.7	18.2
Coefficient of Variation	1.6	0.9	0.7	0.8	1.8

Notes: SU = start-up; AC = acquisition; JV = joint venture; and RE = re-investment. * Grant rate is calculated as the Regional Selective Assistance amount (*RSAAMT*) offered relative to the proposed investment scale of project, i.e. 100 x *RSAAMT* / *INV*, for known investments only.

Appendix Table 13 Agency Involvement with Projects

	Total	SU	AC	JV	RE
Regional agency	**138**	**51**	**10**	**6**	**71**
(% Projects)	(25.1)	(31.1)	(10.8)	(25.0)	(26.4)
(% Known Investment)	(39.3)	(59.4)	(8.2)	(5.4)	(41.5)
National agency	**56**	**15**	**16**	**4**	**21**
(% Projects)	(10.4)	(9.1)	(17.2)	(16.7)	(7.8)
(% Known Investment)	(7.6)	(1.0)	(38.2)	(0.04)	(2.6)

Note: Involvement of regional (*REG*) and national (*NAT*) inward investment agencies with projects, both relative to the number of projects and total known investment (*INV*).

For the start-up projects the respective figures are £2.4m and £0.5m. Eight RSA grant offers are in excess of £5m, of which four are start-up projects. An attempt is made to calculate the grant rates in Appendix Table 12. These are based on the total investment scale, not all of which may be eligible for RSA. It shows that the average grant rate is around 17 per cent, although slightly higher for re-investment projects. The coefficients of variation suggest there is not a great variation in this grant rate across projects, except for the re-investments.

Inward Investment Agencies Finally, Appendix Table 13 shows the involvement of the public agencies in the inward investment projects in the North-East region. The data for these agencies is not comprehensive, and it probably has a bias towards later projects in both cases. Nevertheless, it shows that the Regional Development Agency and its predecessors are involved in some way with a quarter of the 550 projects, comprising around 40 per cent of investment. These are mainly start-ups, representing about 60 per cent of investment by these, but also the re-investments. By contrast, *UK Trade and Investment* and its predecessors has a much lower level of contact, and it is more involved with the acquisitions, as well as start-up and re-investment projects, although as indicated the data are not comprehensive for this.

Bibliography

Acocella, N, 'Trade and Direct Investment within the EC: The Impact of Strategic Considerations', in J. Cantwell, *Multinational Investment in Modern Europe: Strategic Interaction in the Integrated Community* (Aldershot: Edward Elgar, 1992a), pp. 192-213.

---, 'The Multinational Firm and the Theory of Industrial Organisation', in A. Del Monte, *Recent Developments in the Theory of Industrial Organisation* (London: Macmillan, 1992b), pp. 232-51.

Aitken, B. J. and Harrison, A.E., 'Do Domestic Firms Benefit from Foreign Direct Investment? Evidence from Venezuala', *American Economic Review*, 89 (1999): 605-18.

Alden, J., *The Impact of Foreign Direct Investment on Job Creation: Who Gains? The Experience of Wales* (Frankfurt: Conference on European Regional Frontiers, 1997).

Amin, A., Bradley, D., Howells, J. and Gentle, C., 'Regional Incentives and the Quality of Mobile Investment in the Less Favoured Regions of the EC', *Progress in Planning*, 41, 1 (1994): 1-112.

Amin, A. and Thrift, N., 'Living in the Global', in A. Amin, and N. Thrift, *Globalisation, Institutions, and Regional Development in Europe* (Oxford: Oxford University Press, 1994), pp. 1-22.

Anand, B. and Kogut, J., 'Technological Capabilities of Countries, Firm Rivalry and Foreign Direct Investment', *Journal of International Business Studies*, 28, 3 (1987): 445-66.

Aoyama, Y., 'Integrating Business and Location: An Overview of Two Theoretical Frameworks on Multinational Firms', *Berkeley Planning Journal*, 11 (1996): 49-70.

Armstrong, H. and Taylor, J., *Regional Economics and Policy* (Oxford: Blackwell, 2000).

Arrow, K. J., 'The Economic Implications of Learning by Doing', *Review of Economic Studies*, 29, 3 (1962): 155-73.

Arthur, W. B., 'Industry Location Patterns and the Importance of History', *Center for Economic Policy Research Paper 84, Stanford University* (1986).

---, 'Positive Feedbacks in the Economy', *Scientific American*, 262 (1990): 92-9.

Attack, J. and Passell, P., *A New View of Economic History* (New York: W. W. Norton & Company, 1994).

Audretsch, D. and Mahmood, M., 'The Rate of Hazard Confronting New Firms and Plants in US Manufacturing', *Review of Industrial Organisation*, 9 (1994): 41-56.

Audretsch, D. B. and Mahmood, T., 'New-firm Survival: New Results using a

Hazard Function', *Review of Economics and Statistics*, 77 (1995): 97-103.

Baden-Fuller, C., 'Exit from Declining Industries and the Case of Steel Castings', *Economic Journal*, 99 (1989): 949-69.

Bain, J., *Barriers to New Competition* (Cambridge: Harvard University Press, 1956).

Banerjee, A. V., 'A Simple Model of Herd Behavior', *The Quarterly Journal of Economics*, 107, 3 (1992): 797-817.

Barnes, M., Haskel, J. and Ross, A., *Understanding Productivity: New Insights from the ONS Business Data Bank* (University of Durham: Royal Economic Society Conference, 2001).

Barrell, R. and Pain, N., 'The Growth of Foreign Direct Investment in Europe', *National Institute Economic Review*, 60 (1997): 63-75.

---, 'Domestic Institutions, Agglomerations and Foreign Direct Investment in Europe', *European Economic Review*, 43 (1999a): 925-34.

---, 'Foreign Direct Investment, Innovation and Economic Growth within Europe', in C. Driver, and P. Temple, *Investment Growth and Employment: Perspectives for Policy* (London: Routledge, 1999b), pp. 199-220.

Belderbos, R. and Sleuwaegen, L., 'Foreign Investment and International Plant Configuration: Whither the Product Life Cycle?' *NIBOR Research Memorandum RM/00/03* (Maastricht: Netherlands Institute of Business Organisation and Strategy Research, 2001).

Billington, N., 'The Location Of Foreign Direct Investment: An Empirical Analysis', *Applied Economics*, 31 (1999): 65-76.

Blomstrom, M., 'Foreign Investment and Productive Efficiency: The Case of Mexico', *Journal of Industrial Economics*, 35 (1986): 97-110.

Blomstrom, M. and Persson, H., 'Foreign Investment and Spillover Efficiency in an Underdeveloped Economy: Evidence from the Mexican Manufacturing Industry', *World Development*, 11, 6 (1983): 493-501.

Blomstrom, M. and Kokko, A., 'Multinational Corporations and Spillovers', *Journal of Economic Surveys*, 12 (1998): 247-77.

Blomstrom, M. and Wolff, E.N., 'Multinational Corporations and Productivity Convergence in Mexico', *NBER Working Paper*, No. W3141 (1989).

Blonigen, B. A., 'Firm Specific Assets and the Link Between Exchange Rates and Foreign Direct Investment', *American Economic Review*, 87 (1997): 447-65.

Bourguignon, F., Coyle, D., Fernandez, R., Giavazzi, F., Marin, D., O'Rourke, K., Portes, R., Seabright, P., Venables, A., Verdier, T. and Winters, L., *CEPR Policy Paper No.8: Making Sense of Globalisation: A Guide to the Economic Issues* (London: Centre for Economic Policy Research, 2002).

Brahmbhatt, M., *Measuring Global Economic Integration: A Review of the Literature and Recent Evidence* (Washington: The World Bank, 1998).

Brand, S., Hill, S. and Munday, M., 'Assessing the Impacts of Foreign Manufacturing on Regional Economies: The Cases of Wales, Scotland and the West Midlands', *Regional Studies*, 34, 4 (2000): 343-55.

Braunerhjelm, P. and Svensson, R., 'Host Country Characteristics and

Agglomeration in Foreign Direct Investment', *Applied Economics*, 28 (1996): 833-40.

Bresman, H., Birkinshaw, J. and Nobel, R., 'Knowledge Transfer in International Acquisitions', *Journal of International Business Studies*, 30, 3 (1999): 439-62.

Buckley, P. and Casson, M.C., *The Future of the Multinational Enterprise* (London: Macmillan, 1976).

Cantwell, J. and Randaccio, F. S., *Intra-Industry Direct Investment in the European Community: Oligopolistic Rivalry and Technological Competition* (Aldershot: Edward Elgar, 1992).

Cantwell, J. and Iammarino, S., 'Multinational Corporations and the Location of Technological Innovation in the UK Regions', *Regional Studies*, 34, 4 (2000): 317-32.

Cantwell, J. and Narula, J. R., *International Business and the Eclectic Paradigm - Developing the OLI Framework* (London: Routledge, 2003).

Carlos, A. and Nicholas, S., '"Giants of an Earlier Capitalism": The Chartered Trading Companies as Modern Multinationals', *Business History Review*, 62, 3 (1988): 398-419.

Casson, M., *The Firm and the Market* (Cambridge: MIT Press, 1987).

Cassou, S. P., 'The Link Between Tax Rates and Foreign Direct Investment', *Applied Economics*, 29 (1997): 1295-301.

Castellani, D. and Zanfei A., 'Multinational Companies and Productivity Spillovers: Is There a Specification Error?' *SSRN working paper 303392* (2002).

Caves, R. E., 'Industrial Corporations: The Industrial Economics of Foreign Investment', *Economica*, 38 (1971): 1-27.

---, 'Causes of Direct Investment: Foreign Firms' Shares in Canadian and United Kingdom Manufacturing Industries', *The Review of Economics and Statistics*, 56 (1974a): 279-93.

---, 'Multinational Firms, Competition, and Productivity in Host-Country Markets', *Economica* (1974b): 176-93.

---, *Multinational Enterprise and Economic Analysis* (Cambridge: Cambridge University Press, 1982).

---, *Multinational Enterprise and Economic Analysis* (New York: Cambridge University Press, 1996).

Chan, S., *Foreign Direct Investment in a Changing Global Political Economy* (Basingstoke: Macmillan, 1995).

Chandler, A. D., 'A Framework for Analysing the Modern Multinational Enterprise and Its Comeptitive Advantage', *Business and Economic History*, 16 (1987): 3-17.

Coase, R. H., 'The Nature of the Firm', *Economica*, 4 (1937): 386-405.

Collis, C., 'Overseas Inward Investment in the UK Regions', in P. Townroe and R. Martin, *Regional Development in the 1990s: The British Isles in Transition* (London: Jessica Kingsley, 1992), pp. 142-9.

Collis, C., Noon, D. and Edwards, T., 'Overseas Inward Investment and Regional

Development: The Case of the West Midlands', in S. Hill, B. Morgan, and D. Rowe-Beddoe, *Inward Investment, Business Finance and Regional Development* (Basingstoke: Macmillan, 1998), pp. 134-49.

Colombo, M. G. and Delamstro, M., 'A Note on the Relation between Size, Ownership Status and Plant Closure: Sunk Cost versus Strategic Size Liability', *Economics Letters*, 69 (2000): 421-27.

Conyon, M., Girma, S., Thompson, S. and Wright, P., 'The Productivity and Wage Effects of Foreign Acquisition in the United Kingdom', *Journal of Industrial Economics*, 50 (2002): 85-102.

Cooke, P., *Knowledge Economies* (London: Routledge, 2002).

Coughlin, C., Terza, J. and Arromdee, V., 'State Characteristics and the Location of FDI within the United States', *Review of Economics and Statistics*, 73 (1991): 675-83.

Cressy, R., 'Are Business Start-ups Debt-Rationed?' *Economic Journal*, 106 (1996): 153-70.

Crone, M., 'Multinationals and the Branch Plant Economy: An Investigation into Plant Quality in Yorkshire and Humberside and Northern Ireland', *Northern Ireland Economic Research Centre, Working Paper Series, No. 51* (2000).

Crone, M. and Watts, H. D., 'MNE Supply Linkages and the Local SME Sector: Evidence from Yorkshire and Humberside', *Local Economy*, 15, 4 (2000): 325 - 37.

Crozet, M., Mayer, T. and Mucchielli, J-L., 'How Do Firms Agglomerate? A Study of FDI in France', *Regional Science and Urban Economics*, 34 (2004): 27-54.

Culem, C. G., 'The Locational Determinants of Direct Investments Among Industrialised Countries', *European Economic Review*, 32 (1988): 885-904.

Darnell, A. and Evans, L., 'The Economic Record Since 1975', in L. Evans, P. Johnson, and B. Thomas, *The Northern Region Economy: Progress and Prospects in the North of England* (London: Mansell, 1995), pp. 1-28.

Das, D. K., *The Economic Dimensions of Globalisation* (Basingstoke: Palgrave Macmillan, 2004).

David, P. A., 'Path Dependence, Its Critics and the Quest for "Historical Economics", in P. Garrouste, and S. Ionnides, *Evolution and Path Dependence in Economic Ideas: Past and Present* (Cheltenham: Edward Elgar Publishing, 2001), pp. 15-40.

David, P. A. and Rosenbloom, J. L., 'Marshallian Factor Market Externalities and the Dynamics of Industrial Location', *Journal of Urban Economics*, 28 (1990): 349-70.

Davis, S. J., Haltiwanger, J. and Schuh, S., *Job Creation and Destruction* (Massachusetts: Cambridge, 1996).

Delacroix, J., 'The European Subsidiaries of American Multinationals: An Exercise in Ecological Analysis', in S. Ghosal and E. Westney, *Organisational Theory and the Multinational Enterprise* (New York: St Martin's Press, 1993).

Department of Trade and Industry, *The Government's Proposals for New Assisted Areas* (London: HMSO, 1999).

---, 'Supplementary Guidance for the Regional Development Agencies in Relation to the Regional Economic Strategies', *August* (London: HMSO, 2002).

Devereux, M. P., Griffith, R. and Simpson, H., 'Agglomeration, Regional Grants and Firm Location', *The Institute for Fiscal Studies Working Paper WP04/06* (London: The Institute of Fiscal Studies, 2003).

Dewit, G., Gorg, H. and Montagna, C., 'Employment Protection and Globalisation in Dynamic Oligopoly', *CEPR Discussion Paper No. 3871* (London: Centre for Economic Policy Research, 2003).

---, 'Should I Stay or Should I Go? Foreign Direct Investment, Employment Protection and Domestic Anchorage', *Dundee Discussion Papers in Economics, Working Paper No. 145, July* (2004).

Dicken, P., 'Seducing Foreign Investors: The Competitive Bidding Strategies of Local and Regional Agencies in the UK', in M. Hebbert, and J-C. Hansen, *Unfamiliar Territory: The Reshaping of European Geography* (Aldershot: Gower, 1990), pp. 162-86.

Dicken, P. and Lloyd, P., 'Geographical Perspectives on United States Investment in the United Kingdom', *Environment and Planning A*, 8 (1976): 685-705.

Dicken, P., Forsgren, M. and Malmberg, A., 'The Local Embeddedness of Transnational Corporations', in A. Amin, and N. Thrift, *Globalisation, Institutions, and Regional Development in Europe* (Oxford: Oxford University Press, 1994), pp. 23-45.

Dietzenbacher, E., 'Interregional Multipliers: Looking Backward, Looking Forward', *Regional Studies*, 36, 2 (2002): 125-36.

Disney, R., Haskel, J. and Heden, Y., 'Entry, Exit and Establishment Survival in UK Manufacturing', *Journal of Industrial Economics*, 51 (2003): 91-112.

Dixit, A. K. and Pindyck, R. S., *Investment under Uncertainty* (Princeton: Princeton University Press, 1994).

Driffield. N., 'Indirect Employment Effects of Foreign Direct Investment into the UK', *Bulletin of Economic Research*, 51, 3 (1999): 207-21.

---, 'The Impact on Domestic Productivity of Inward Investment in the UK', *The Manchester School*, 69, 1 (2001): 103-19.

Driffield, N. and Girma, S., 'Regional Foreign Direct Investment and Wage Spillovers: Plant Level Evidence from the UK Electronics Industry', *Oxford Bulletin of Economics and Statistics*, 65, 4 (2003): 453-74.

Driffield, N. and Love, J. H., 'Foreign Direct Investment, Technology Sourcing and Reverse Spillovers', *Manchester School*, 71, 6 (2003): 659-72.

Driffield, N. and Munday, M., 'The Impact of Foreign Direct Investment on UK Manufacturing: Is there a Profit Squeeze in Domestic Firms?' *Applied Economics*, 30, 5 (1998): 705-9.

---, 'Industrial Performance, Agglomeration and Foreign Manufacturing Investment in the UK', *Journal of International Business Studies*, 39 (2000): 21-38.

Driffield, N., Munday, M. and Roberts, A., 'Inward Investment, Transaction Linkages and Productivity Spillovers', *Papers in Regional Science*, 83, 4

(2004): 699-722.

Driver, C. and Wood, A., 'Hysteresis of Plant Closures and Re-openings in the UK Brick Industry: Real Options and/or Strategy', *Working Paper No. 04/05* (Department of Accounting, Finance and Management: University of Essex, 2005).

Dunne, T., Roberts, M. and Samuelson, L., 'Patterns of Firm Entry and Exit in US Manufacturing Industries', *RAND Journal of Economics*, 19 (1988): 495-515.

---, 'The Growth and Failure of US Manufacturing Plants', *Quarterly Journal of Economics*, 104 (1989): 671-98.

Dunning, J. H., 'Trade, Location of Economic Activity and the MNE: A Search for an Eclectic Approach', in B. Ohlin, P. Hesselborn, and P. Wijkman., *The International Allocation of Economic Activity: Proceedings of a Nobel Symposium* (London: Macmillan Press, 1977), pp. 395-418.

---, *International Production and the Multinational Enterprise* (London: George Allen & Unwin, 1981).

---, 'Changes in the Level and Structure of International Production: The Last One Hundred Years', in M. Casson, *The Growth of International Business* (London: George Allen and Unwin, 1983), pp. 84-139.

---, 'The Globalisation of Firms and the Competitiveness of Countries: Some Implications for the Theory of International Production', in J. H. Dunning, B. Kogut, and M. Blomstrom, *Globalisation of Firms and the Competitiveness of Nations* (Lund: Lund University Press, 1989), pp. 9-57.

---, 'Reappraising the Eclectic Paradigm in an Age of Alliance Capitalism', *Journal of International Business Studies*, 26, 3 (1995): 461-91.

---, 'The Nature of Transnational Corporations and Their Activities', in J. H. Dunning, *Transnational Corporations and World Development* (London, England: International Thomson Business Press, 1996), pp. 27-43.

---, 'The Eclectic Paradigm as an Envelope for Economic and Business Theories of MNE Activity', *International Business Review*, 9, 2 (2000): 163-90.

---, 'The Key Literature on IB Activities: 1960-2000', in A. R. Rugman, and Brewer, T. L., *The Oxford Handbook of International Business* (Oxford: Oxford University Press, 2001a), pp. 36-68.

---, 'The Eclectic (OLI) Paradigm of International Production: Past, Present and Future', *International Journal of the Economics of Business*, 8, 2 (2001b): 173-90.

---, *Theories and Paradigms of International Business Activity: The Selected Essays of John H. Dunning, Volume 1* (Cheltenham: Edward Elgar, 2002a).

---, *Global Capitalism, FDI and Competitiveness: The Selected Essays of John H. Dunning, Volume 2* (Cheltenham: Edward Elgar, 2002b).

Dunning, J. H. and Rugman, A.M., 'The Influence of Hymer's Dissertation on the Theory of Foreign Direct Investment', *American Economic Review*, 75 (1985): 228-32.

Dunning, J. H. and Pearce, R.D., *The World's Largest Industrial Enterprises, 1962-1983* (New York: St. Martin's Press, 1995).

Dussage, P. and Garrette, B., 'Determinants of Success in International Strategic Alliances: Evidence from the Global Aerospace Industry', *Journal of International Business Studies*, 26, 3 (1995): 505-30.

Economists Advisory Group, *Invest in Britain Bureau,* Evaluation Report, (Department of Trade and Industry: London, 2000).

Ernst and Young, *Ernst and Young's European Investment Monitor 1999 Results* (Ernst and Young, 1999).

Evans, D. S., 'The Relationship between Firm Growth, Size and Age: Estimates for 100 Manufacturing Industries', *Journal of Industrial Economics*, XXXV (1987): 567-81.

Findlay, R., 'Relative Backwardness, Direct Foreign Investment, and the Transfer of Technology: A Simple Dynamic Model', *The Quarterly Journal of Economics*, 92, 1 (1978): 1-16.

Firn, J. R., 'External Control and Regional Development: The Case of Scotland', *Environment and Planning A*, 7 (1975): 393-414.

Flamm, K., 'The Volatility of Offshore Investment', *Journal of Development Economics*, 16 (1984): 231-48.

Flowers, E. B., 'Oligopolistic Reactions in European and Canadian Direct Investment in the United States', *Journal of International Business Studies*, 7, 2 (1976): 43-55.

Fosfuri, A. and Motta, M., 'Multinationals Without Advantages', *Scandinavian Journal of Economics*, 101 (1999): 617-30.

Fosfuri, A., Motta, M. and Ronde, T., 'Foreign Direct Investment and Spillovers through Workers Mobility', *Journal of International Economics*, 53 (2001): 205-22.

Fothergill, S. and Guy, N., 'Retreat from the Regions: Corporate Change and the Closure of Factories', *Regional Policy and Development Series 1* (London: Regional Studies Association, 1990).

Fraser, A., *Case Study: Inward Investment in the UK* (Hawaii: Conference on Industrial Globalisation in the 21st Century, Impact and Consequences for Asia and Korea, 1999).

Friedman, J., Gerlowski, D. and Silberman, J., 'What Attracts Foreign Mulinational Corporations? Evidence from Branch Plant Location in the United States', *Journal of Regional Science*, 32, 4 (1992): 403-18.

Gabel, M. and Bruner, H., *Global Inc.: An Atlas of the Multinational Corporation* (New York: New Press, 2003).

Ghemawat, P. and Nalebuff, B., 'The Devolution of Declining Industries', *Quarterly Journal of Economics*, 105 (1990): 167-86.

Ghertman, M., and Allen, M., *An Introduction to the Multinationals* (London: Macmillan Press, 1984).

Giddy, I. H., 'The Demise of the Product Cycle in International Business Theory', *Columbia Journal of World Business*, 13, 1 (1978): 90-97.

Girma, S., Greenaway, D. and Wakelin, K., 'Who Benefits from Foreign Direct Investment in the UK?' *Scottish Journal of Political Economy*, 48, 2 (2001):

119-33.

Glass, A. J. and Saggi, K., 'International Technology Transfer and the Technology Gap', *Journal of Development Economics*, 55 (1998): 369-98.

Glickman, N. J. and Woodward, D. P., *The New Competitors: How Foreign Investors are Changing the US Economy* (New York: Basic Books, 1989).

Globerman, S., 'Foreign Direct Investment and 'Spillover' Efficiency Benefits in Canadian Manufacturing Industries', *Canadian Journal of Economics* (1979): 42-56.

Glyn, A., 'The Assessment: How Far Has Globalisation Gone?', *Oxford Review of Economic Policy*, 20, 1 (2004): 1-14.

Gorg, H., '"Fancy a Stay at the Hotel California?" Foreign Direct Investment, Taxation and Exit Costs', *Leverhulme Centre for Research on Globalisation and Economic Policy, Research Paper No. 2002/30* (2002).

Gorg, H. and Greenaway, D., 'Much Ado About Nothing? Do Domestic Firms Really Benefit from Foreign Direct Investment', *World Bank Research Observer* (Washington: World Bank, 2004).

Gorg, H. and Strobl, E., 'Multinational Companies and Productivity Spillovers: A Meta-Analysis', *The Economic Journal*, 111, 475 (2001): 723-39.

---, 'Multinational Companies and Indigenous Development: An Empirical Analysis', *European Economic Review*, 46 (2002): 1305-22.

Gorg, H. and Wakelin, K., *The Impact of Exchange Rate Variability on US Direct Investment* (Leverhulme Centre for Research on Globalisation and Economic Policy: University of Nottingham, 2001).

Graham, E. M., 'Transatlantic Investment by Multinational Firms: A Rivalistic Phenomenon', *Journal of Post-Keynesian Economics*, 1 (1978): 82-99.

---, 'Market Structure and the Multinational Enterprise: A Game-Theoretic Approach', *Journal of International Business Studies*, 29, 1 (1998): 67-83.

Granovetter, M., 'Economic Action and Social Structure: The Problem of Embeddedness', *American Journal of Sociology*, 91 (1985): 481-510.

Greenaway, D., 'Policy Forum: Foreign Direct Investment In OECD Countries', *The Economic Journal*, 107 (1997): 1768-69.

Greene, W. H., *Econometric Analysis*, 5th edition (New Jersey: Prentice Hall, 2003).

Griffith, R., 'Using the ARD Establishment Level Data to Look at Foreign Ownership and Productivity in the United Kingdom', *The Economic Journal*, 109 (1999): 416-42.

Guimaraes, P., Figueiredo, O. and Woodward, D., 'Agglomeration and the Location of Foreign Direct Investment in Portugal', *Journal of Urban Economics*, 47, 1 (2000): 115-35.

Haaland, J. I. and Wooton, I., 'Multinational Investment, Industry Risk and Policy Competition', *CEPR Discussion Paper No. 3152* (London: Centre for Economic Policy Research, 2002).

---, 'Domestic Labour Markets and Foreign Direct Investment', *CEPR Discussion Paper No. 3989* (London: Centre for Economic Policy Research, 2003).

Haddad, M. and Harrison, A., 'Are There Positive Spillovers From Direct Foreign Investment?: Evidence From Panel Data For Morocco', *Journal of Development Economics*, 42 (1993): 51-74.

Hagedoorn, J., 'Trends and Patterns in Strategic Technology Partnering since the Early Seventies', *Review of Industrial Organisation*, 11, 5 (1996): 601-16.

Haltwinger, J. C. and Schuh, S., 'Gross Job Flows between Plants and Industries', *New England Economic Review, Federal Reserve Bank of Boston* (1999): 41-64.

Hansen, R. E., 'Industrial Location Choice in Sao Paulo, Brazil: A Nested Logit Model', *Regional Science and Urban Economics*, 17, 1 (1987): 89-108.

Hanson, G. H., *Countries Promote Foreign Direct Investment* (Geneva: United Nations Conference on Trade and Development, 2001).

Harrigan, K., 'Strategic Alliances: Their New Role in Global Competition', *Columbia Journal of World Business*, 22, 2 (1987): 67-9.

Harris, R., 'Market Structure and External Control in the Regional Economies of Great Britain', *Scottish Journal of Political Economy*, 35, 4 (1988): 334-60.

Harris, R. and Robinson, K., *An Analysis of Current DTI Support Patterns, Final Report to the Department of Trade and Industry, April* (London: 2001).

---, *Spillovers from Foreign Ownership in the United Kingdom: Estimates for UK Manufacturing Using the ARD* (Warwick: Royal Economic Society Annual Conference, 2002a).

---, 'Foreign Ownership and Productivity in the United Kingdom - Some Issues When Using the ARD Establishment Level Data', *Scottish Journal of Political Economy*, 49, 3 (2002b): 318-35.

Hart, P. E., 'Theories of Firms' Growth and the Generation of Jobs', *Review of Industrial Organisation*, 17 (2000): 229-48.

Haskel, J. E., Pereira, S.C. and Slaughter, M. J., 'Does Inward Foreign Direct Investment Boost the Productivity of Domestic Firms?' *Queen Mary University Working Paper No. 452* (2002).

Head, K., Ries, J. and Swenson, D., 'Agglomeration Benefits and Location Choice: Evidence from Japanese Manufacturing Investments in the United States', *Journal of International Economics*, 38 (1995): 223-47.

Head, K., Mayer, T. and Ries, J., 'Revisiting Oligopolistic Reaction: Are FDI Decisions Strategic Complements?', *Journal of Economics, Management and Strategy*, 11, 3 (2002): 452-71.

Heckman, J. J., 'The Common Structure of Statistical Models of Truncation, Sample Selection and Limited Dependent Variables and a Simple Estimator for such Models', *Annals of Economic and Social Measurement*, 5 (1976): 475-92.

Hennart, J.-F., *A Theory of Foreign Direct Investment* (University of Maryland: Ph. D. Dissertation, 1977).

---, 'International Financial Capital Transfers: A Transaction Cost Framework', *Business History*, 36, 1 (1994): 51-70.

---, 'Theories of the Multinational Enterprise', in A. R. Rugman, and T. L. Brewer, *The Oxford Handbook of International Business* (Oxford: Oxford University

Press, 2001), pp. 127-49.

Hill, S. and Munday, M., 'The UK Regional Distribution of Foreign Direct Investment: Analysis and Determinants', *Regional Studies*, 26, 6 (1992): 535-44.

---, *The Regional Distribution of Foreign Manufacturing Investment in the UK* (Basingstoke: Macmillan, 1994).

---, 'The Determinants of Inward Investment: A Welsh Analysis', *Applied Economics*, 23 (1991): 1761-69.

Hines, J. R., 'Altered States: Taxes and the Location of Foreign Direct Investment in America', *American Economic Review*, 86, 5 (1996): 1076-94.

Hirschman, A. O., *The Strategy of Economic Development* (New Haven: Yale University Press, 1958).

HM Treasury, 'Productivity in the UK: The Evidence and the Government's Approach' (London: HM Treasury, 2000).

Holmes, P., Stone, I. and Braidford, P., 'An Analysis of New Firm Survival using a Hazard Function', *Research Paper 3, University of Durham, Barclays Centre for Entrepreneurship* (2003).

Hood, N., 'Inward Investment and the Scottish Economy: *Quo Vadis?*', *Royal Bank of Scotland Review*, October (1991): 17-32.

Hood, N. and Taggart, J. H., 'German Foreign Direct Investment in the UK and Ireland: Survey Evidence', *Regional Studies*, 31, 2 (1997): 139-50.

Hood, N. and Young, S., *The Globalisation of Multinational Enterprise Activity and Economic Development* (Basingstoke: Macmillan, 1999).

Horn, H. and Persson, L., 'The Equilibrium Ownership of an International Oligopoly', *Journal of International Economics*, 53 (2001): 307-33.

Horst, T., 'Firm and Industry Determinants of the Decision to Invest Abroad: An Empirical Study', *The Review of Economics and Statistics*, 54, 3 (1972): 258-66.

Hsiao, C., *Analysis of Panel Data* (Cambridge: Cambridge University Press, 2003).

Hudson, R., 'The Role of Foreign Investment', in L. Evans, P. Johnson, and B. Thomas, *The Northern Region Economy: Progress and Prospects in the North of England* (London: Mansell, 1995), pp. 79-96.

---, 'Restructuring Region and State: The Case of North East England', *Tijdschrift voor Economische en Sociale Geografie*, 89, 1 (1998): 15-30.

Hughes, K. and Oughton, C., 'Foreign and Domestic Multinational Presence in the UK', *Applied Economics*, 24, 7 (1992): 745-50.

Hymer, S. H., *International Operations Of National Firms* (Cambridge: The MIT Press, 1976).

Ietto-Gillies, G., *International Production: Trends, Theories, Effects* (Cambridge: Polity Press, 1992).

Inkpen, A. C., 'Strategic Alliances', in A. R. Rugman, and T. L. Brewer, *The Oxford Handbook of International Business* (Oxford: Oxford University Press, 1991), pp. 402-27.

Invest UK, *Invest UK: Operations Review 2003* (London: Invest UK, 2003).

Iranzo, S., *FDI Mode of Entry and Acquisition of Firm Specific Assets* (Chicago: International Industrial Organisation Conference, 2004).

Itaki, M., 'A Critical Assessment of the Eclectic Theory of the Multinational Enterprise', *Journal of International Business Studies*, 22, 3 (1991): 445-60.

Jacobs, J., *The Economy of Cities* (New York: Vintage, 1969).

John, R., Cox, H., Ietto-Gillies, G. and Grimwade, N., *Global Business Strategy* (London: International Thompson Publishing, 1997).

Jones, G., *British Multinationals: Origins, Management and Performance* (Aldershot: Gower, 1986).

---, *The Evolution of International Business: An Introduction* (London: Routledge, 1995).

---, *Merchants to Multinationals. British Trading Companies in the 19th and 20th Centuries* (Oxford: Oxford University Press, 2000).

Jones, J., *The Nature and Performance of Inward Investment in North-East England: 1985-98* (University of Newcastle: Ph.D. Thesis, 2004).

Jones, J. and Wren, C., 'Inward Foreign Direct Investment and Employment: A Project-Based Analysis in North-East England', *Journal of Economic Geography*, 4, 5 (2004a): 517-44.

---, 'Do Inward Investors Achieve their Job Targets?' *Oxford Bulletin of Economics and Statistics*, 66, 4 (2004b): 483-513.

---, 'FDI Acquisition and Plant Re-investment, *unpublished mimeo* (2004c).

---, 'Re-Investment and the Survival of Foreign-Owned Entrants', *unpublished mimeo* (2004d).

Kaplan, E. L. and Meier, P., 'Nonparametric Estimation from Incomplete Observations', *Journal of the American Statistical Association*, 53 (1958): 457-81.

Kirchner, P., 'The German-owned manufacturing sector in the North-East of England', *European Planning Studies*, 8 (2000): 601-17.

Knickerbocker, F. T., *Oligopolistic Reaction and the Multinational Enterprise* (Cambridge: Harvard University Press, 1973).

Kogut, B., 'International Business: The New Bottom Line', *Foreign Policy*, 110 (1998): 152-65.

Kogut, B. and Znder, U., 'Knowledge of the Firm and the Evolutionary Theory of the Multinational Corporation', *Journal of International Business Studies*, 24, 4 (1993): 625-45.

Kokko, A., 'Technology, Market Characteristics, and Spillovers', *Journal of Development Economics*, 43 (1994): 279-93.

---, 'Productivity Spillovers from Competition Between Local Firms and Foreign Affiliates', *Journal of International Development*, 8 (1996): 517-30.

Kravis, I. and Lipsey, R. E., 'The Location of Overseas Production and Production for Export by US Multinational Firms', *Journal of International Economics*, 12 (1982): 201-23.

Krugman, P., 'Increasing Returns and Economic Geography', *Journal of Political*

Economy, 99, 3 (1991): 483-99.

---, *Geography and Trade* (Cambridge: MIT Press, 1993).

Lawless, J. F., *Statistical Models and Models for Lifetime Data* (Toronto: Wiley, 1982).

Leahy, D. and Montagna, C., 'Union Bargaining Power, Labour Standards and Foreign Direct Investment', *University of Nottingham Research Paper Series*, No. 2004/19 (2004).

Li, J., 'Foreign Entry and Survival: Effects of Strategic Choices on Performance in International Markets', *Strategic Management Journal*, 16 (1995): 333-51.

Liu, X., Siler, P., Wang, C. and Wei, Y., 'Productivity Spillovers from Foreign Direct Investment: Evidence from UK Industry Level Panel Data', *Journal of International Business Studies*, 31, 3 (2000): 407-25.

Lovering, J., 'Theory Led By Policy: The Inadequacies Of 'The New Regionalism' (Illustrated From The Case Of Wales)', *International Journal of Urban and Regional Research*, 23 (1999): 379-95.

---, 'MNCs and Wannabes - Inward Investment, Discourses of Regional Development, and the Regional Service Class', in N. Phelps, and P. Raines, *The New Competition for Inward Investment: Companies, Institutions and Territorial Development* (Cheltenham: Edward Elgar, 2003), pp. 39-60.

Lundan, S. and Hagedoorn, J., 'Alliances, Acquisitions and Multinational Advantage', *International Journal of the Economics of Business*, 8, 2 (2001): 229-42.

MacKinnon, D., Cumbers, A. and Chapman, K., 'Learning, Innovation, and Regional Development: A Critical Appraisal of Recent Debates', *Progress in Human Geography*, 26, 3 (2002): 293-311.

Mariotti, S. and Piscitello, L., 'Information Costs and Location of FDIs within the Host Country: Empirical Evidence from Italy', *Journal of International Business Studies*, 26 (1995): 815-39.

Markusen, A., 'Fuzzy Concepts, Scanty Evidence, Policy Distance: The Case for Rigour and Policy Relevance in Critical Regional Studies', *Regional Studies*, 33, 9 (1999): 869-84.

Markusen, J. R., 'The Boundaries of Multinational Enterprises and the Theory of International Trade', *The Journal of Economic Perspectives*, 9 (1995): 169-89.

---, 'Multinational Firms, Location and Trade', *World Economy*, 21 (1998): 733-56.

Markusen, J. R. and Venables, A., 'Foreign Direct Investment as a Catalyst for Industrial Development', *European Economic Review*, 43 (1999): 335-56.

Marshall, A., *Principles of Economics* (London: Macmillan, 1890).

Mata, J. and Portugal, P., 'Life Duration of New Plants', *Journal of Industrial Economics*, 42, 3 (1994): 227-45.

---, 'Closure and Divesture by Foreign Entrants: The Impact of Entry and Post-Entry Strategies', *Strategic Management Journal*, 21 (2000): 549-62.

Mata, J., Portugal, P. and Guimaraes, P., 'The Survival of New Plants: Start-up Conditions and Post-entry Evolution', *International Journal of Industrial*

Organisation, 13 (1995): 459-81.

Maylor, H., *Project Management,* 3rd edn (London: Prentice Hall, 2003).

McCann, P., 'How Deeply Embedded is Silicon Glen? A Cautionary Note', *Regional Studies,* 31, 7 (1997): 695-03.

---, *Urban and Regional Economics* (Oxford: Oxford University Press, 2001).

McCann, P. and Sheppard, S., 'The Rise and Fall Again of Industrial Location Theory', *Regional Studies,* 37, 6&7 (2003): 649-63.

McCloughan, P. and Stone, I., 'Life Duration of Foreign MNE Plants: Evidence from UK Northern Manufacturing, 1970-93', *unpublished mimeo* (1996).

---, 'Life Duration of Foreign Multinational Subsidiaries: Evidence from UK Northern Manufacturing Industry, 1970-93', *International Journal of Industrial Organisation,* 16 (1998): 719-47.

McManus, J.C., 'The Theory of the Multinational Firm', in G. Paquet, *The Multinational Firm and the Nation State* (Houndmills: Macmillan, 1972), pp. 66-93.

Micklethwait, J. and Wooldridge, A., *The Company: A Short History of a Modern Idea* (Westminster: Modern Library, 2003).

Miyake, M. and Sass, M., 'Recent Trends in Foreign Direct Investment', *Organisation for Economic Co-operation and Development Financial Market Trends,* 76 (2000): 23-41.

Moosa, I. A., *Foreign Direct Investment: Theory, Evidence and Practice* (Basingstoke: Palgrave, 2002).

Morgam, K., 'The Learning Region: Institutions, Innovation and Regional Renewal', *Regional Studies,* 31, 5 (1997): 491-503.

Mucchielli, J.-L. and Puech, F., 'Globalisation, Agglomeration and FDI Location: The Case of French Firms in Europe', in J-L. Mucchielli, and T. Mayer, *Multinational Firms' Location and the New Economic Geography* (Cheltenham: Edward Elgar, 2004), pp. 35-58.

Mudambi, R., 'The Multinational Investment Location Decision: Some Empirical Evidence', *Managerial and Decision Economics,* 16 (1995): 249-57.

National Audit Office, 'The Department of Trade and Industry: Regional Grants in England', *Report by the Comptroller and Auditor General, HC702 Session 2002-03* (2003).

Neary, P. J., 'Cross-Border Mergers As Instruments of Comparative Advantage', *Discussion Papers 34* (Goettingen: Center for Globalisation and Europeanisation of the Economy, 2004).

Neven, D. and Siotis, G., 'Foreign Direct Investment in the European Community: Some Policy Issues', *Oxford Review of Economic Policy,* 9 (1993): 72-93.

Nilsen, O. A. and Schiantarelli, F., 'Zeros and Lumps in Investment: Empirical Evidence on Irreversibilities and Nonconvexities', *Review of Economics and Statistics,* 85 (2003): 1021-37.

Office for National Statistics, *Regional Trends* (London: HMSO, 1994).

---, *Business Monitor MA4: Overseas Direct Investment* (London: HMSO, 1996).

---, *Regional Trends* (London: HMSO, 1996).

---, *Business Monitor PA 1002: Report on the Census of Production Summary Volume* (London: HMSO, 1997).

Ohmae, K., *The Borderless World* (London: William Collins, 1990).

Organisation for Economic Cooperation and Development, *OECD Benchmark Definition of Foreign Direct Investment,* 3rd edn (Paris: OECD, 1996).

Organisation for Economic Cooperation and Development, *The OECD Guidelines for Multinational Enterprises* (Paris: OECD, 2000).

Oulton, N., 'The ABI Respondents Database: A New Resource for Industrial Economics Research', *Economic Trends,* 528 (1997): 46-57.

PACEC, *Assessment of the Wider Effects of Foreign Direct Investment in Manufacturing in the UK* (London: HMSO, 1995).

Pain, N., 'Continental Drift: European Integration and the Location of UK Foreign Direct Investment', *The Manchester School Supplement,* 65 (1997): 94-117.

Parkhe, A., 'Interfirm Diversity, Organisational Learning, and Longevity in Global Strategic Alliances', *Journal of International Business Studies,* 22 (1991): 579-602.

---, 'Strategic Alliance Structuring: A Game Theoretic and Transaction Cost Examination of Interfirm Cooperation', *Academy of Management Journal,* 36 (1993): 794-829.

Pauly, L. W. and Reich, S., 'National Structures and Multinational Corporate Behavior: Enduring Differences in the Age of Globalisation', *International Organisation,* 51, 1 (1997): 1-30.

Phelps, N. A. and Fuller, C., 'Multinationals, Intracorporate Competition, and Regional Development', *Economic Geography,* 76, 3 (2000): 224-43.

Phelps, N. and MacKinnon, D., 'Industrial Enclaves or Embedded Forms of Economic Activity? Overseas Manufacturing Investment in Wales', *Contempory Wales,* 13 (2000): 46-67.

Phelps, N. A., MacKinnon, D., Stone, I. and Braidford, P., 'Embedding the Multinationals? Institutions and the Development of Overseas Manufacturing Affiliates in Wales and North East England', *Regional Studies,* 37, 1 (2003): 27-40.

Porter, M., *The Competitive Advantage of Nations* (London: Macmillan, 1990).

Potter, J., Moore, B. and Spires, R., 'The Wider Effects of Inward Foreign Direct Investment in Manufacturing on UK Industry', *Journal of Economic Geography,* 2 (2002): 311-41.

Proenca, I., Fontoura, M.P. and Crespo, N., 'Productivity Spillovers from Multinational Corporations in the Portugese Case: Evidence from a Short Time Period', *Working Paper Instituto Superior de Economia e Gestao Universidade Tecnica de Lisboa* (2001).

Puhani, P., 'The Heckman Correction for Sample Selection and its Critique', *Journal of Economic Surveys,* 14, 1 (2000): 53-68.

Radulesco, R. and Robson, M.T., 'Does Stricter Employment Protection Legislation Deter FDI?' *University of Newcastle Seminar Series* (2003).

Reynolds, S. S., 'Plant Closings and Exit Behaviour in Declining Industries',

Economica, 55 (1988): 493-503.

Rivera-Batiz, F., 'Increasing Returns, Monopolistic Competition and Agglomeration Economies in Consumption and Production', *Regional Science and Urban Economics*, 18 (1988): 125-53.

Rodriguez-Clare, A., 'Multinationals, Linkages and Economic Development', *American Economic Review*, 86, 4 (1996): 852-73.

Romer, P. M., 'Increasing Returns and Long-Run Growth', *Journal of Political Economy*, 94 (1986): 1002-37.

Rugman, A., *Inside the Multinationals: The Economics of Internal Markets* (New York: Columbia University Press, 1981).

Scaperlanda, A. E. and Mauer, L. J., 'The Determinants of US Direct Investment in the EEC', *American Economic Review*, 59 (1969): 558-68.

Scholte, J., *Globalisation: A Critical Introduction* (New York: Palgrave, 2000).

Schuh, S. and Triest, R. K., 'The Role of Firms in Job Creation and Destruction in U.S. Manufacturing', *New England Economic Review*, March (2000): 29-44.

Sekiguchi, S., *Japanese Direct Foreign Investment* (Montclair: Osmun & Co, 1979).

Simonin, B. L., 'Ambiguity and the Process of Knowledge Transfer in Strategic Alliances', *Strategic Management Journal*, 20 (1999): 595-623.

Stiglitz, J., *Economics of the Public Sector,* 3rd edn (New York: W. W. Norton & Company, 2000).

Stocker, H., 'Growth Effects of Foreign Direct Investment - Myth or Reality?' in J.-R. Chen, *Foreign Direct Investment* (New York: St Martin's Press, 2000), pp. 115-37.

Stone, I. and Peck, F., 'The Foreign-owned Manufacturing Sector in UK Peripheral Regions, 1978-1993: Restructuring and Comparative Performance', *Regional Studies*, 30, 1 (1996): 55-68.

Stopford, J. M., 'Changing Perspective of Investment by British Manufacturing Multinationals', *Journal of International Business Studies*, 7, 2 (1976): 15-28.

Sugden, R. and Williams, A., *The Principles of Practical Cost-Benefit Analysis* (Oxford: Oxford University Press, 1978).

Sugden, R. and Wilson, J. R., 'Globalisation, the New Economy and Regionalisation', *Globalisation and World Cities Study Group and Network 70*, *Loughborough University* (2001).

Taylor, J., 'An Analysis of the Factors Determining the Geographical Distribution of Japanese Manufacturing Investment in the UK, 1948-91', *Urban Studies*, 30, 7 (1993): 1209-24.

Teece, D. J., 'Multinational Enterprise, Internal Governance, and Industrial Organisation', *American Economic Review*, 75, 2 (1985): 233-38.

Teeple, G., 'What Is Globalisation?' in S. McBride, and Wiseman, J., *Globalisation and its Discontents* (Basingstoke: Macmillan, 2000), pp. 9-23.

Thomsen, S., *Investment Patterns in a Longer-Term Perspective, Working Papers on International Development* (Paris: Organisation for Economic Co-operation and Development, 2000).

Thomsen, S. and Nicolaides, P., *The Evolution of Japanese Direct Investment in Europe: Death of a Transistor Salesman* (London: Harvester Wheatsheaf, 1991).

Thomsen, S. and Woolcock, C., *Direct Investment and European Integration: Competition Among Firms and Governments* (London: Royal Institute of International Affairs, Pinter Publishers, 1993).

Tolentino, P. E., 'From a Theory to a Paradigm: Examining the Eclectic Paradigm as a Framework in International Economics', *International Journal of the Economics of Business*, 8, 2 (2001): 191-209.

Townroe, P., 'Branch Plants and Regional Development', *Town Planning Review*, 46 (1975): 47-62.

Tugendhat, C., *The Multinationals* (Middlesex: Penguin Books, 1981).

Turok, I., 'Inward Investment and Local Linkages: How Deeply Embedded is Silicon Glen?' *Regional Studies*, 27 (1993): 487-97.

---, 'Linkages in the Scottish Electronics Industry: Further Evidence', *Regional Studies*, 31, 7 (1997): 705-11.

UNCTAD, *World Investment Report: Cross-border Mergers and Acquisitions and Development* (New York: United Nations, 2000).

---, *World Investment Report: Transnational Corporations and Export Competitiveness* (New York: United Nations, 2002).

---, *World Investment Report 2003: FDI Policies for Development: National and International Perspectives* (New York: United Nations, 2003).

---, *World Investment Report 2004: The Shift Towards Services* (New York: United Nations, 2004).

---, *Foreign Direct Investment Database* (New York: United Nations, 2005).

United Nations, *Prospects for Foreign Direct Investment and the Strategies of Transnational Corporations, 2004-2007* (New York: United Nations, 2004).

Venables, A. J., 'Equilibrium Locations of Vertically Linked Industries', *International Economic Review*, 37, 2 (1996): 341-59.

Vernon, R., 'International Investment and International Trade in the Product Cycle', *Quarterly Journal of Economics*, 80 (1966): 90-207.

---, 'Competition Policy Toward Multinational Corporations', *American Economic Review*, 64, 2 (1974): 276-82.

---, 'The Product Cycle Hypothesis in a New International Environment', *Oxford Bulletin of Economics and Statistics*, 41 (1979): 255-67.

Voutilainen, T., 'Foreign Direct Investment (FDI) Theories Explaining the Emergence of Multinational Enterprises (MNEs)', *YU-91.167 Seminar in Strategy and International Business* (Helsinki: Helsinki University of Technology, 2005).

Walker, J., 'OECD Benchmark Definition of Foreign Direct Investment', *Statistical News* (1983): 61.1-61.4.

Watts, H. and Kirkham, J., 'Plant Closures by Multi-Locational Firms: A Comparative Perspective', *Regional Studies*, 33 (1999): 413-24.

Webb, D. and Collis, C., 'Regional Development Agencies and the 'New

Regionalism' in England', *Regional Studies*, 34, 9 (2000): 857-73.

Wei, Y., Liu, X., Parker, D. and Vaidya, K., 'The Regional Distribution of Foreign Direct Investment in China', *Regional Studies*, 33, 9 (1999): 857-67.

Weiss, J., *Industrialisation and Globalisation Theory: Theory and Evidence from Developing Countries* (London: Routledge, 2002).

Wheeler, D. and Mody, A., 'International Investment Location Decisions: The Case of US Firms', *Journal of International Economics*, 33 (1992): 56-76.

Wilkins, M., 'Modern European Economic History and the Multinationals', *The Journal of European Economic History*, 6 (1977): 575-95.

---, 'The History of European Multinationals: A New Look', *The Journal of European Economic History*, 15 (1986): 483-510.

---, 'European and North American Multinationals', *Business History*, 30 (1988): 8-45.

Wilkins, M., *The Growth of Multinationals* (London: Edward Elgar, 1991).

---, 'The History of Multinational Enterprise', in A. R. Rugman, and Brewer, T. L., *The Oxford Handbook of International Business* (Oxford: Oxford University Press, 2001), pp. 3-35.

Williamson, O. E., 'Transaction-Cost Economics: The Governance of Contractual Relations', *Journal of Law and Economics*, 22 (1979): 233-61.

---, 'The Modern Corporation: Origins, Evolution, Attributes', *Journal of Economic Literature*, 19, 4 (1981): 1537-68.

World Bank, 'Assessing Globalisation', *World Bank Briefing Papers* (2000).

Wren, C., *Industrial Subsidies: The UK Experience* (London: Macmillan Press, 1996).

---, 'Entrepreneurship and Economic Development: A Framework for Policy', *International Journal of Entrepreneurship and Innovation Management*, 4, 1 (2004): 28-40.

---, 'Regional Grants: Are They Worth It?', *Fiscal Studies*, June (2005a).

---, 'Understanding the Metrics Used by International Development Agencies to Assess the Impact of International Development Support', *Report to Scottish Development International, Glasgow* (2005b).

Young, S., Hood, N. and Hamill, J., *Foreign Multinationals and the British Economy* (London: Croom Helm, 1988).

Young, S., Hood, N. and Peters, E., 'Multinational Enterprises and Regional Economic Development', *Regional Studies*, 28 (1994): 657-77.

Index